WEIMAR CULTURE

*the text of this book is printed
on 100% recycled paper*

Peter Gay

WEIMAR CULTURE

THE OUTSIDER AS INSIDER

HARPER TORCHBOOKS
Harper & Row, Publishers
New York, Hagerstown, San Francisco, London

Substantial parts of this book appeared, in somewhat different forms, in
Perspectives in American History, II (1968).

First HARPER TORCHBOOK edition published 1970·

ISBN: 0—06—131482—X

87 88 89 90   20 19

To FELIX GILBERT

Ambassador of the Weimar Spirit

/ CONTENTS

/ *ILLUSTRATIONS*

Der Deutsche ist im fremden Land
Meist als ein Vieh-losoph bekannt.

—OTTO REUTTER,
"Der gewissenhafte Maurer"

/ *PREFACE*

The Weimar Republic died only thirty-five years ago, in 1933, yet it is already a legend. Its tormented brief life with its memorable artifacts, and its tragic death—part murder, part wasting sickness, part suicide—have left their imprint on men's minds, often vague perhaps, but always splendid. When we think of Weimar, we think of modernity in art, literature, and thought; we think of the rebellion of sons against fathers, Dadaists against art, Berliners against beefy philistinism, libertines against old-fashioned moralists; we think of *The Threepenny Opera, The Cabinet of Dr. Caligari, The Magic Mountain,* the *Bauhaus,* Marlene Dietrich. And we think, above all, of the exiles who exported Weimar culture all over the world.

The exile holds an honored place in the history of Western civilization. Dante and Grotius and Bayle, Rousseau and Heine and Marx, did their greatest work in enforced residence on alien soil, looking back with loathing and longing to the country, their own, that had rejected them. The Greek scholars from Byzantium who flooded the Italian city-states early in the fifteenth century and the Huguenot bourgeois who streamed out of France across Western Europe late in the seventeenth century brought with them energy, learning, and scarce, welcome skills; New England was founded by refugees who transformed wilderness into civilization. But these migrations, impressive as they are, cannot compare with the exodus set in motion early in 1933, when the Nazis seized control of Germany; the exiles

Hitler made were the greatest collection of transplanted intellect, talent, and scholarship the world has ever seen.

The dazzling array of these exiles—Albert Einstein, Thomas Mann, Erwin Panofsky, Bertolt Brecht, Walter Gropius, George Grosz, Wassily Kandinsky, Max Reinhardt, Bruno Walter, Max Beckmann, Werner Jaeger, Wolfgang Köhler, Paul Tillich, Ernst Cassirer—tempts us to idealize Weimar as unique, a culture without strains and without debts, a true golden age. The legend of Weimar begins with the legend of "the golden twenties."[1] But to construct this flawless ideal is to trivialize the achievements of the Weimar Renaissance, and to slight the price it had to pay for them. The excitement that characterized Weimar culture stemmed in part from exuberant creativity and experimentation; but much of it was anxiety, fear, a rising sense of doom. With some justice, Karl Mannheim, one of its survivors, boasted not long before its demise that future years would look back on Weimar as a new Periclean age.[2] But it was a precarious glory, a dance on the edge of a volcano. Weimar culture was the creation of outsiders, propelled by history into the inside, for a short, dizzying, fragile moment.

In this essay I have tried to portray Weimar culture as a whole, without sentimentalizing or sensationalizing it. I know that this is an essay; I have said less than could be said about the sequence of political events and economic developments, about popular culture, about institutions like the churches, the family, the universities, the press, and about the structure of German society. I have said nothing about science. In other words, I have not written the complete history of the Weimar Renaissance, though one day I plan to write it. What I have done here is to bring together themes that dominated the hectic life of the Republic, and to juxtapose them in ways that will, I trust,

[1] Among many others, Theodor Heuss would later deplore the rise of the legend "von den 'goldenen zwanziger Jahren.'" *Erinnerungen, 1905–1933* (1963), 348.

[2] In conversation with Hannah Arendt, reported to the author by Hannah Arendt. Bruno Walter attributes the same term to the powerful Berlin drama critic Alfred Kerr. Walter, *Theme and Variations: An Autobiography* (tr. James A. Galston, 1946), 268. From here on, quotations in the text not specifically identified in the footnotes are from conversations with, or letters to, the author.

permit us to define the Weimar spirit more clearly and more comprehensively than it has been done before.

For those who are unfamiliar with modern German history, I have appended a short political history of the Weimar Republic which obviously makes no claim to originality. My bibliography lists all the titles I cite in the footnotes, and other titles I consulted, with short comments; I trust that it will give an accurate picture of my intellectual debts. Among the historians I have read I should like to single out Karl Dietrich Bracher, whose interpretation of Weimar I found most congenial and most instructive.

My writing of this book has been greatly facilitated by the generous cooperation of a number of survivors and students of Weimar. I appreciate their readiness to talk to me and their permission to print their comments and reminiscences, especially since I know that we do not always agree on our interpretation of events. My greatest debt is to Felix Gilbert, whose influence on this essay is pervasive, and to whom I dedicate this book in gratitude. I was privileged to have a brief conversation with the late Erwin Panofsky. I want also to thank Hannah Arendt, Kurt R. Eissler, James Marston Fitch, George F. Kennan, Walter Gropius, Heinz Hartmann, Hajo Holborn, Paul Lazarsfeld, Rudolph M. Loewenstein, Adolf Placzek, Rudolf Wittkower, for their helpful comments. Joseph P. Bauke, Istvan Deak, and Theodore Reff gave me valuable information. David Segal, John A. Garraty, and above all my wife Ruth stood by in some difficult moments; as always, and to my lasting profit, she read every version of this manuscript with sympathetic care. The book originated in a welcome invitation by Bernard Bailyn and Donald Fleming, gratefully accepted, to preface Volume II of their *Perspectives in American History,* published at Harvard University by the Charles Warren Center for American History, with an article on Weimar culture. I thank George L. Mosse for encouraging me to turn the article into a book.

I delivered a much shorter version of this book as four lectures to the Institute of Philosophy and Politics of Education, Teachers College, Columbia University. I am deeply grateful to its director, my friend Lawrence A. Cremin, for providing me with such a stimulating occasion for testing my ideas.

WEIMAR CULTURE

I / THE TRAUMA OF BIRTH:

From Weimar to Weimar

The Weimar Republic was an idea seeking to become reality. The decision to hold the constituent assembly at Weimar was taken primarily for prudential reasons—as Philipp Scheidemann, the first Prime Minister of the Republic, later admitted, Berlin was not safe.[1] But Weimar also came to symbolize a prediction, or at least a hope, for a new start; it was tacit acknowledgment of the charge, widely made in Allied countries during the war and indignantly denied in Germany, that there were really two Germanies: the Germany of military swagger, abject submission to authority, aggressive foreign adventure, and obsessive preoccupation with form, and the Germany of lyrical poetry, Humanist philosophy, and pacific cosmopolitanism. Germany had tried the way of Bismarck and Schlieffen; now it was ready to try the way of Goethe and Humboldt.

It is easy, too easy, to ridicule this solemn search for a usable past. Fifteen years later, in English exile, the distinguished historian Arthur Rosenberg recalled the constitutional assembly with some acerbity. "History," he wrote, "enjoys discrediting arbitrarily chosen symbols."[2] There is some justice in this observation; the choice of Weimar was in part a symptom of wishful thinking. To found a country in the city of Goethe did not guarantee a country in Goethe's

[1] *Memoiren eines Sozialdemokraten,* 2 vols. (1928), II, 352.
[2] *A History of the German Republic* (tr. Ian F. D. Morrow and L. Marie Sieveking, 1936), 101.

image. It did not even guarantee its survival. The Republic was born in defeat, lived in turmoil, and died in disaster, and from the beginning there were many who saw its travail with superb indifference or with that unholy delight in the suffering of others for which the Germans have coined that evocative term *Schadenfreude*. Still, the choice of Weimar was neither quixotic nor arbitrary; for a time the Republic had a real chance. Whatever some derisive historians have said, if the end of the Republic was implied in its beginning, that end was not inevitable. As Toni Stolper, a survivor and perceptive observer of Weimar, has noted, the Republic was marked by creativity in the midst of suffering, hard work in the midst of repeated disappointments, hope in the face of pitiless and powerful adversaries.[3] I might add that it is precisely this easy pessimism, which then saw (and still sees) the Republic as doomed from the start, that helped to fulfill the prophecies it made. The end of Weimar was not inevitable because there were republicans who took the symbol of Weimar seriously and who tried, persistently and courageously, to give the ideal real content.

The Weimar ideal was both old and new. The striking mixture of cynicism and confidence, the search for novelty and for roots—the solemn irreverence—of the twenties, were a child of war, revolution, and democracy, but the elements that made it up came from both the distant and the recent past, recalled and revived by a new generation. Goethe and Schopenhauer, historic dates like 1848 and 1871, were living realities for the new Weimar, while the immediate ancestry of the Weimar style, still passionately debated, went back to the turn of the century and the 1890s. "In German art, the transition from bourgeois to popular"—that is, from Impressionist to Expressionist— "art had long preceded the Revolution." This view, expressed in a conversation of cultivated amateurs held in early 1919, in the midst of revolution, was accurate enough.[4] After all, Frank Wedekind com-

---

[3] *Ein Leben in Brennpunkten unserer Zeit: Gustav Stolper, 1888–1947* (1960), 211–213. This argument, that the end was by no means unavoidable, has recently been persuasively restated by Karl Dietrich Bracher, notably in Bracher, Wolfgang Sauer, Gerhard Schulze, *Die nationalsozialistische Machtergreifung: Studien zur Errichtung des totalitären Herrschaftssystems in Deutschland, 1933–1934* (1960), 17–18.

[4] It is reported by Harry Graf Kessler in his diary for January 4, 1919. *Tagebücher, 1918–1937* (1961), 91.

pleted his first and still most important play, *Frühlings Erwachen*, in 1891, a year after William II had dismissed Bismarck, and long before the Emperor had fully tested his peculiar talent for disaster.

Imperial Germany was studiedly hostile to the modern movement. The Emperor and his Empress, Auguste Victoria, set the tone, and their taste ran to gaudy parades, glittering medals, sentimental heroic portraits: the Siegesallee in Berlin, an ambitious double row of marble statues commemorating the unmemorable, was expression, and symptom, of Wilhelminian taste. The universities, in which Germans took such ostentatious pride, were nurseries of a woolly-minded militarist idealism and centers of resistance to the new in art or the social sciences; Jews, democrats, socialists, in a word, outsiders, were kept from the sacred precincts of higher learning. The Empress interfered with the staging of Strauss's *Salome* and kept Strauss's *Rosenkavalier* from opening in Berlin, taking charming and talented decadence for impermissible immorality; the government harassed Käthe Kollwitz for her proletarian posters, while in 1908 the Emperor dismissed Hugo von Tschudi, director of the National Gallery in Berlin, for his subversive tastes in art. Four years later, when Kandinsky and Marc published their collective volume of essays, pictures, and musical examples, *Der blaue Reiter*, they fittingly dedicated it to Tschudi's memory. The new art made the ruling circles literally sick: in 1893, the Bavarian statesman Prince Chlodwig zu Hohenlohe-Schillingsfürst went to see Gerhart Hauptmann's *Hanneles Himmelfahrt.* "A monstrous wretched piece of work," he noted in his diary, "social-democratic-realistic, at the same time full of sickly, sentimental mysticism, nerve-racking, in general abominable. Afterwards we went to Borchard's, to get ourselves back into a human frame of mind with champagne and caviar."[5]

But Wilhelminian Germany, though philistine and oppressive, was not a dictatorship; and the modern movement fed on opposition. Ex-

[5] The prince's splenetic outburst is really untranslatable, and deserves to be recorded in German: "Heute abend in 'Hannele.' Ein grässliches Machwerk, sozialdemokratisch-realistisch, dabei von krankhafter, sentimentaler Mystik, nervenangreifend, überhaupt scheusslich. Wir gingen nachher zu Borchard, um uns durch Champagner und Kaviar wieder in eine menschliche Stimmung zu versetzen." Diary entry of December 14, 1893, quoted in Paul Kampffmeyer, *Fritz Ebert* (1923), 41.

pressionism, which would dominate Weimar culture during its formative years, was fully matured in the Empire. Expressionist painters and poets made inflammatory statements, exhibited outrageous pictures, published *avant-garde* little magazines, and gathered, for collaboration and comfort, in informal groups like *Die Brücke* and *Der blaue Reiter*. Their ranks were decimated before the Revolution. Franz Marc and August Macke, whose eccentric colors and exotic landscapes haunted the twenties, were killed in the war; others, like Emil Nolde and Ernst Ludwig Kirchner, who survived, had found their final manner—their aggressive color, primitive subject matter, their untamed, urgent subjectivity—in the first decade of the twentieth century. The precise date of Kandinsky's first wholly nonobjective painting remains a matter of controversy, but it is certain that it must be placed before the war. At all events, Kandinsky wrote his revolutionary manifesto, *Über das geistige in der Kunst*, in 1910 and published it in 1912. And it was in 1914 that Walter Hasenclever completed his first Expressionist play, *Der Sohn*, as prophetic of the Weimar style as Marc's blue horses. Everywhere young artists broke away from the pomposity of academic art and sought to rise above the bombast of their surroundings to cultivate their inner life, articulate their religious yearning, and satisfy their dim longing for human and cultural renewal. In comparison with the circulation figures of popular magazines, Herwarth Walden's *Sturm* and Franz Pfemfert's *Aktion* were negligible; in comparison with the big publishing houses, Ernst Rowohlt and Kurt Wolff were mere amateurs—as Kurt Wolff said later, all that he and Rowohlt had was an obsession for books, enthusiasm, and good taste.[6] The Expressionists were a band of outsiders. But they were determined and active. The Republic would add to their lives nothing but success.

What was true of painting, poetry, and experimental short prose was true in other areas of culture: Thomas Mann's *Buddenbrooks, Tonio Kröger,* and *Tod in Venedig,* all published by 1911, already embodied the grave irony, the relentless symbolism, and the strenuous effort

6 *Autoren, Bücher, Abenteuer: Betrachtungen und Erinnerungen eines Verlegers* (1965), 13.

to make ideas dramatically respectable that were to distinguish, and partly to mar, Mann's work of the twenties. The unrestrained political satire that entertained and frightened visitors to the Kabarett der Komiker and readers of the *Weltbühne* during the Republic, traced back its manner and matter to Heinrich Mann's *Der Untertan*, to Walter Mehring's early political chansons, to Frank Wedekind's eccentric dramas—and Wedekind had died in 1918—and to Carl Sternheim's clipped, mannered dissections of what Sternheim icily called "the heroic life of the bourgeoisie—*bürgerliches Heldenleben*," a life, as he saw it, of surpassing vulgarity, crass scramble for status, and suicidal rush into a great war. "After us, collapse!" exclaims one of Sternheim's characters in a play he wrote in the last year of peace. "We are ripe."[7]

In a less ominous sense, the modern movement was ripe as well. Psychoanalysis was introduced into Germany in 1910, with the founding of the Berlin branch of the International Psychoanalytical Association. Friedrich Meinecke and Otto Hintze, who drew the attention of the historical profession in other countries to Berlin in the 1920s, had done significant work before the war: Meinecke's *Weltbürgertum und Nationalstaat*, which some of his pupils would later fondly remember as his best book, was published in 1907. Max Reinhardt, the magician of the Weimar theatre, had practically filled his bag of tricks by 1914. Arnold Schönberg, who completed the twelve-tone system in 1924, had broken through to atonality before 1912. Even Walter Gropius, whose Bauhaus buildings in Dessau appear as the archetypal expression of the Weimar style, had achieved his characteristic idiom before the war, partly as the pupil of Peter Behrens, partly in association with Adolf Meyer, with whom he built the Fagus Shoe Last Factory in 1911, and, in 1914, the celebrated buildings for the Werkbund Exhibition in Cologne. With these buildings, as Gropius later said, he found his "own ground in architecture."[8] There can be no doubt: the Weimar style was born before the Weimar Republic.

---

[7] This much-quoted speech is in *1913*, Act III, Scene 2. Carl Sternheim, *Gesamtwerk*, 8 vols., ed. Wilhelm Emrich (1963–1968), I, 285.
[8] *Scope of Total Architecture* (1962 ed.), 19.

The war gave it a political cast and a strident tone, and saddled it with a deadly quarrel; the revolution gave it unprecedented opportunities. But the Republic created little; it liberated what was already there.

Just as the Weimar style was older than the Weimar Republic, so was it larger than Germany. Both in the Empire and in the Republic, German painters, poets, playwrights, psychologists, philosophers, composers, architects, even humorists were engaged in a free international commerce of ideas; they were part of a Western community on which they drew and which, in turn, they fed; chauvinism was not merely offensive to the Weimar style, it would have been fatal. Kandinsky embodies this cosmopolitanism in one person: he was born in Russia, learned much from the French Fauves, and found his own style in Munich. Lyonel Feininger was cosmopolitan in a different manner: born in the United States of German immigrant parents, he went to Germany in 1887, lived for two years in Paris, and developed a highly personal style that is as individualistic in expression as it is international in inspiration. Other "German" painters—Kirchner, Heckel, Nolde, Pechstein, Marc, and Klee—each in his own way, went to school to the Norwegian Munch, the Frenchman Gauguin, and the Netherlander Van Gogh. Max Ernst, though born and educated in Germany, found his artistic home in Paris, after his brief visit there in the summer of 1913. The Italian Futurist movement received widespread attention in advanced German circles from 1912 on; when its chief ideologist, Marinetti, came to Berlin in 1913, he felt very much at home there. "He was engaged in conversation everywhere," Rudolf Leonhard remembers, "he spoke a great deal, he liked Berlin enormously, and it was as if there were a special Berlin, his Berlin, his domain, as if Berlin were prepared for him, as if it were suddenly filled with him."[9]

Berlin, though, was not yet the inescapable center it would become later. Munich, the capital of painters in the Empire, mounted influ-

[9] In Paul Raabe, ed., *Expressionismus: Aufzeichnungen und Erinnerungen der Zeitgenossen* (1965), 122.

ential exhibitions of French Neo-impressionists, while Marc and Klee went directly to Paris on visits they would later describe as decisive for their artistic development. Dada, the artists' rebellion against art, was born during the war in Zurich, flourished after the war in Paris, and made Berlin its headquarters during the first years of Weimar. The German Expressionist theatre is unthinkable without the experiments of Strindberg, while German social realism drew on the realistic phase of Ibsen, whose plays were naturalized in Germany well before the First World War. A catalogue of Brecht's foreign sources—though Brecht's poetic diction is purely, superbly German—would have to be long to be at all meaningful, and range from Villon and Rimbaud to such improbable influences as Kipling, and from Chinese lyrics to Augustan satire. Spirits as diverse as Franz Werfel and Ernst Ludwig Kirchner acknowledged the inspiration of Walt Whitman. The philosophical irrationalism of Bergson and the brooding poetic irrationalism of Dostoyevsky appealed to sensitive spirits from the extreme left to the extreme right, who could no longer bear the shape of modernity and were sickened by Wilhelminian culture. In architecture the American Frank Lloyd Wright, the Spaniard Antonio Gaudí, and the Belgian Henry van de Velde supplied the German rebels with most of their ammunition. Mallarmé and Debussy had diligent German disciples. And in all areas Austrians—poets, novelists, psychologists, cultural critics—transmitted to their German audience their obsession with decadence and their attempts to come to terms with eros; Sigmund Freud, Hugo von Hofmannsthal, Karl Kraus, and Arthur Schnitzler had as many readers in Berlin, Munich, and Frankfurt as they had in Vienna—perhaps more.

For the outsiders of the Empire as, later, for the insiders of the Republic, the most insistent questions revolved around the need for man's renewal, questions made most urgent and practically insoluble by the disappearance of God, the threat of the machine, the incurable stupidity of the upper classes, and the helpless philistinism of the bourgeoisie. Seeking answers to their questions, the rebels turned to whatever help they could find, wherever they could find it. There was nothing unusual in this; man's articulate misery or articulate delight has never been a respecter of frontiers. But it was precisely this—the commonplace quality of cosmopolitanism in the Empire—that later gave the Weimar style its toughness of fiber; in its unself-conscious internationalism it shared the vitality of other cultural movements in European history.

What the war did was to destroy the ties of German culture, both to the usable past and to the congenial foreign environment, for all but the most determined cosmopolitans. A very few kept communications open; in 1915, in the midst of war, the Fabian Socialist and distinguished psychologist Graham Wallas wrote to his friend, the German revisionist Socialist Eduard Bernstein: "Nowadays one lives from day to day and scarcely dares to think about the future. But sometimes I hope that when peace comes you and I may meet and shake hands, and tell each other that we have never had one thought of each other that was not kind, and then sit down to consider whether we can help in any way to heal the wounds of civilization."[10] It was the cultural task of the Weimar Republic to capitalize on such noble sentiments, to restore the broken ties.

II

It is the tragedy of the Weimar Republic that while it succeeded in this task—the brilliance of the refugees from Hitler is a measure of that success—the trauma of its birth was so severe that it could never enlist the wholehearted loyalty of all, or even many, of its beneficiaries. The revolution had widespread support at the outset. It was "as a result of the First World War," Walter Gropius has written, that the "full consciousness" of his social "responsibility as an architect" first came to him. Late in 1918, on furlough in Germany from the Italian front, Gropius decided to travel to Berlin, and during his trip the

[10] Peter Gay, *The Dilemma of Democratic Socialism: Eduard Bernstein's Challenge to Marx* (1952, 1967 ed.), 280.

revolution broke out. As he witnessed the indignities visited on officers by the crowds, he was seized by a sudden thought: "This is more than just a lost war. A world has come to an end. We must seek a radical solution to our problems."[11]

Gropius was not alone. The progression of his intellectual career—ideas developed in the Empire, given political direction by the war, and finding open expression in the revolution—was characteristic of many representatives of the Weimar spirit. The revolution aroused the enthusiasm of Bertolt Brecht, who like many other young men had been revolted by years of slaughter. Rilke greeted the revolution with impetuous joy, as he put it in his poetic way, with the ardent hope that mankind would for once turn over a new page.[12] Others discovered similar hopes from different perspectives. Conservative ideologists were delighted to see the collapse of a regime that had not been idealistic enough to embody true conservatism. Bourgeois intellectuals like Friedrich Meinecke, though they were filled with rage against the Allied powers, offered their support. Soldiers and their families, democrats, socialists, pacifists, and Utopians looked to the revolution as the promise of a new life.

But events in the winter of 1918–1919, followed by the turmoil of the founding years, dissipated the capital of goodwill that had accumulated in the days of collapse and hope. As the revolution had pleased, so its course and consequences came to disappoint, many for a variety of reasons. The new conservatives grew to despise precisely the innovations that the Republic introduced; the radicals, for their part, objected to the survivals left from the Empire. The Weimar Republic, it seems, was too successful to satisfy its critics, not successful enough to satisfy its well-wishers. As early as December 1918 Rilke had lost all hope. "Under the pretense of a great upheaval, the old want of character persists." As far as he could see, the revolution had been seized by a ruthless minority, and the majority seduced into

[11] *Scope of Total Architecture,* 19. And Gropius to James Marston Fitch.
[12] Rilke to Dorothea, Baroness von Ledebour, December 19, 1918. *Briefe aus den Jahren 1914 bis 1921,* ed. Ruth Sieber-Rilke and Carl Sieber (1937), 213–215.

"political dilettantism."[13] In the same month, the progressive publisher Paul Cassirer characterized the revolution as "nothing but a great swindle—*Schiebung*"; nothing essential had been changed, he told Count Kessler, "only a few cousins" had been shoved into positions of profit and power.[14] Many of the young enthusiasts, like Brecht, turned their back on politics as quickly as they had taken it up; writers and artists like Wieland Herzfelde and George Grosz quickly joined the Spartacist opposition. While the enemies of the young Republic remained steadfast in their enmity, its enthusiasts wavered and withdrew their support. In February 1919 the journalist Simon Guttmann spoke for this group with the savage chagrin of the disappointed lover: at the moment, he told Kessler, the intellectuals almost without exception opposed the government; it was impossible, he added, to exaggerate their bitterness against the present regime, which shied away from responsibility, did nothing, and was active only when it came to shooting down fellow citizens. Nothing, he said sadly, had been changed by the revolution; everything went on as before, in the old way.[15] And on May 1, 1919, a national holiday, Kessler noted that the festivities gave the impression of "national mourning for a revolution that misfired."[16] It soon became common practice to compress disdain into a single phrase: 1918 was the "so-called revolution."[17]

The causes of this widespread disenchantment are many and familiar. There were many old ghosts at the Weimar Assembly, and while some were laid to rest, new ones emerged. The first four years of

[13] Rilke to the same, *loc. cit.*; and Rilke to Anni Mewes, December 19, 1918. *Briefe*, 2 vols., ed. Karl Altheim (1950), II, 113.

[14] Kessler, *Tagebücher*, 78.

[15] *Ibid.*, 123.

[16] *Ibid.*, 182. The phrase is *"verfehlte Revolution."*

[17] For three instances see Lion Feuchtwanger, writing in the *Weltbühne* in 1928 (quoted in Martin Esslin, *Brecht: The Man and his Work* [1961 ed.], 10); Franz Neumann, "The Social Sciences," in Neumann *et al.*, *The Cultural Migration: The European Scholar in America* (1953), 14; and Siegfried Jacobsohn, editor of the *Weltbühne*, writing in his own journal on March 27, 1919: "We need a second revolution. No: we need a revolution." *Ausnahmezustand* (an anthology from *Weltbühne* and *Tagebuch*), ed. Wolfgang Weyrauch (1966), 24.

the Republic were years of almost uninterrupted crisis, a true time of troubles. The bloody civil war, the re-emergence of the military as a factor in politics, the failure to discredit the aristocratic-industrial alliance that had dominated the Empire, the frequency of political assassination and the impunity of political assassins, the imposition of the Versailles Treaty, the Kapp Putsch and other attempts at internal subversion, the French occupation of the Ruhr, the astronomical inflation—all this gave new hope to monarchists, to fanatical militarists, to anti-Semites and xenophobes of all sorts, to industrialists at first frightened by the specter of socialization and then contemptuous of Socialists who would not socialize, and served to make the Republic appear a fraud or a farce. The very birth of the Republic had its farcical elements: it was proclaimed in the early afternoon of November 9, 1918, by the Socialist Philipp Scheidemann, not from pure republican enthusiasm, but from an anxious desire to forestall the proclamation of a Soviet Republic by Karl Liebknecht. When Friedrich Ebert learned of Scheidemann's action a few minutes later, he was furious with the irregularity of the proceedings. No one could fail to notice that the Republic came into the world almost by accident, and covered with apologies.

Beyond all this there was another, subtler inducement to cynicism and detachment. In August 1914 the Western world had experienced a war psychosis: the war seemed a release from boredom, an invitation to heroism, a remedy for decadence. But it was in Germany that this psychosis reached heights of absurdity. The overaged, the adolescent, the unfit, volunteered with pure joy, and went to death filled with their mission. The war offered "purification, liberation, and enormous hope"; it "set the hearts of poets aflame" with a sense of relief that "a peaceful world had collapsed," a world of which "one was so tired, so dreadfully tired." Only "victory at any price" could give life meaning; the Germans had at last united as a *Volk*, Germans alone were "truthful, authentic, manly, objective," a land of heroes facing opponents saddled with "cowardice, mendacity, and baseness"; grand old words like *Volk* and *Reich* and *Geist* were now given new meaning by this great crusade for *Kultur*. These are not, as they might seem to be, imaginary effusions;

they are the words of Thomas Mann and Friedrich Gundolf, and there were thousands of others, young and old, who sounded precisely like them.[18] But their elation turned into depression, often to mental collapse; the orgy of self-indulgent, self-deceptive chauvinism was followed by guilt and shame and, in some cases, a hollow insistence that one had been right all along—a sequence of oscillations scarcely calculated to induce political realism. Many of the enthusiasts lost their enthusiasm, but not their Utopianism. Some—Thomas Mann among them—learned from war and revolution; it was one of their incidental benefits that they acted as political educators to the few willing to be educated. But there were many who remained political innocents, ready to despise what they could not support, and open to vendors of nostrums even more nauseating than the war they had greeted with such joy.

All this was bad enough, but doubtless the greatest, most effective enemy of the Weimar Republic was the civil war fought within the republican left, the struggle, as Eduard Bernstein said, of "Socialists against Socialists,"[19] which broke out as soon as the Republic was proclaimed; its very proclamation, after all, was an act directed not merely against the monarchy but against the Spartacists.

This struggle was inevitable. Socialist unity had been shattered during, and over the issue of, the war; the Russian Revolution, and the manner of the German collapse, which gave Socialists a rather artificial and tenuous prominence, were not calculated to restore it. With the definitive eviction of the Empire in November 1918, the moment for the confrontation of two competing Socialist groups had come; the stakes in the struggle for immediate power were high, for the holders of power would determine the future of Germany—the Spartacists wanted to turn Germany into a Soviet republic; the majority Socialists, into a parliamentary democracy. It is one of the saddest ironies of German history that while in 1918 no other alternatives seemed possible, the internecine struggle for either of the available alternatives

---

[18] See Thomas Mann's essay "Gedanken im Krieg," written in September 1914 and published in 1915; and postcards sent by Gundolf to Stefan George on August 14 and 30, 1914. *Stefan George–Friedrich Gundolf Briefwechsel*, ed. Robert Boehringer (1962), 256–257, 258–259.
[19] *Die deutsche Revolution* (1921), title of chapter 8.

gave room for forces seeking yet another alternative—a military dictatorship. The confrontation of Socialist with Socialist was everywhere; having swept away old institutions, the Revolution offered new, and many, surfaces for friction. Spartacists and moderate Socialists fought in Berlin and in the provinces, in politicians' meetings and in the streets, in workers' councils and at funerals for victims of right-wing thugs. There were many harsh words, words never forgotten or forgiven, and words were not all. Everyone was armed, everyone was irritable and unwilling to accept frustration, many had been trained and remained ready to kill, the widespread disorder encouraged irrational mass action and offered protective cover to political adventurers. For almost two months the regime managed to keep specious unity among the forces of the left: the six-man provisional government instituted on November 10 had three representatives from the majority Socialists and three from the Independents. But this could not last; on December 27 the Independents walked out, and the split widened and deepened. The enemy on the right needed only to wait.

He did, in fact, do more than wait: he killed, with abandon and with impunity. Rosa Luxemburg and Karl Liebknecht, the leaders of the Spartacist movement, were murdered on January 15, 1919; Kurt Eisner, Prime Minister of Bavaria, was murdered by an aristocratic student on February 21, and the Bavarian Soviet Republic which came out of the assassination was brutally put down by regular and *Freikorps* troops toward the end of April and the beginning of May. And these events could only exacerbate fratricidal hostilities: the Spartacists denounced the governing Socialists as pliant, socially ambitious butchers; the government Socialists accused the Spartacists of being Russian agents. It all seemed like a sarcastic commentary on Marx's call to the workers of the world to unite.

III

Historians have made much of the failures of the politicians who governed the young Republic. Had they failed utterly, it would have been understandable; Ebert and his associates faced difficulties that would have daunted the coolest and most experienced statesman. There was endemic disorder, there was desperate hunger, there was demoralization among intellectuals, there was an army to be brought home and demobilized, there were bitter wounds to be healed and no time to heal them, there was a constitution to be written and put into practice. And beyond this there was a factor which holds a special place in Weimar history, for the myths that surrounded it came to hurt the Republic even more than reality: the Peace of Versailles.

Certainly the settlement imposed on Germany at Versailles was in many ways a harsh and vindictive treaty. Some among the leading Allied negotiators wanted not settlement but revenge; it was not defeat alone that produced traumas—victory, too, after years of frustration, bloodshed, and endless misery, seemed to many somehow unbearable. The making of the treaty was a constant and deliberate humiliation of the Germans. Once the Allies had worked out their differences in a series of compromises, they invited the Germans in mid-April 1919 to send a delegation to Versailles to "receive peace conditions." Their task was to sign, not to negotiate. The treatment of the German delegation, widely publicized in the German press, was one long calculated insult: the train that took them to Paris moved with deliberate slowness through the battlefields of northern France until the sight became unbearable; once in Versailles, the Germans found themselves fenced off, ostensibly to be protected from hostile demonstrations, actually to be isolated from Allied negotiators. The Germans, writes M. J. Bonn, a liberal economist who was a member of the German delegation, "were greatly humiliated. The anguish of defeat and the sense of guilt with which some propagandists had tried to impress them had created a kind of inferiority complex from which most members of the delegation suffered."[20] In his formal presentation of the treaty, Clemenceau did not make the Germans feel any better, and the short time they got to compile their comments and objections —first two weeks, and then a week more—threw the delegation into a frenzy of despairing activity. The outcome was quite inescapable: a

[20] *Wandering Scholar* (1949), 227.

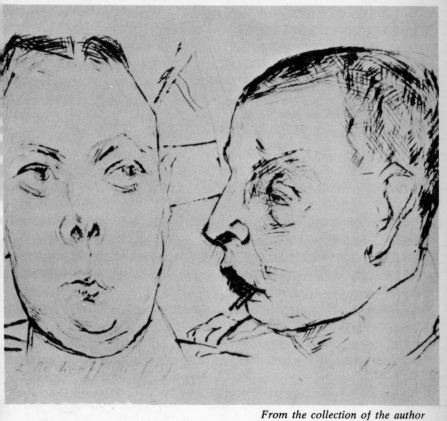

MAX BECKMANN: TWO AUTO OFFICERS   DRYPOINT, 1915

Beckmann, who was in the war, knew that the face of the enemy did not need caricature; realism was quite enough, as long as the realist had Beckmann's graphic talent. In 1919 this drypoint was published in a portfolio of nineteen etchings under the title of *Gesichter*.

Courtesy of the Busch-Reisinger Museum, Harvard University

Friedrich Ebert, first President of the Weimar Republic, 1919 to 1925, wickedly caricatured from the left: the trade unionist as parvenu.

combination of vehement protests, reasoned argument, and second thoughts on the part of Lloyd George and General Smuts produced some marginal modifications, but in its essence the treaty remained unaltered. Germany was to lose Alsace-Lorraine, the Polish Corridor, northern Schleswig-Holstein, and some other smaller areas—about 13 percent of its old territory, six millions in population, valuable resources—and all its colonies. It was to disarm, to pay reparations, and to sign a treaty that contained, as its article No. 231, the acknowledgment that Germany and its allies were "originators" of the war, and "aggressors"—that notorious paragraph that came to be called the "war guilt clause," and caused more debate, perhaps, than all other provisions together.

What could the Germans do? They refused to sign, and they signed. On May 12, Prime Minister Scheidemann had called the treaty unacceptable and asked, rhetorically, "What hand must not wither which puts these fetters on itself and on us?" Scheidemann's hand remained intact; on June 20, after the Catholic Center Party and a majority of his own Social Democratic Party voted to accept the treaty with the exception of article 231 and the article demanding the handing over of war criminals, he resigned. The burden of signing the *Diktat,* the *Schandfrieden*, the *Schmachfrieden*—the shameful, humiliating peace —fell on the shoulders of other Social Democrats, and on Erzberger, the most prominent advocate of peace in the Center Party. They were brave men, accepting as their lot a political liability they would never wholly shake off.

Everyone hated the treaty; those who advocated its acceptance put their argument on grounds of realism—the need for peace, the starvation among the German population, the intransigence of the Allies. The *Frankfurter Zeitung*, the voice of reason at all times, was typical of the best opinion: it protested against the treaty but then urged that it be signed. Thomas Mann, not yet committed to the Republic, thought that Clemenceau, that "poisonous old man," was burying Western culture, or, conversely, that the dominance of Anglo-America would bring "the civilizing, rationalizing, utilitarianizing of the West"

—in either event, the peace was a catastrophe.[21] He was still the unpolitical, cultural aristocrat he had been before and during the war, but Count Kessler, liberal statesman and indefatigable diarist, eminently well informed and remarkably free from caste prejudice, also found Versailles infinitely depressing: from May 7, 1919, the day the Germans were handed the conditions of peace, to June 12, he was so disheartened that he wrote nothing in his diary; on June 22, after the resignation of the Scheidemann cabinet, he reported a general mood of "indescribable dejection; as though all life in the soul had died."[22] The comments of patriots, army officers, conservatives, can be imagined. All states and all nations, Friedrich Meinecke wrote in 1921, must say to themselves, "We are sinners." But "the sins committed by the Allies since 1918 are almost without parallel."[23]

It was this attitude much more than the provisions of the treaty— bad as they were—that saddled the Weimar Republic with one of its many damaging legends. Millions who had no stake in the lost colonies or the lost territories, who were untouched by the enforced disarmament, responded warmly to the demagogues who denounced Versailles as a typical French attack on the very soul of Germany and maligned the signers of the treaty as cowards or traitors, and had little but contempt for the statesmen who worked quietly to revise the treaty article by article. The demand for abrogation of the "dictated peace," and punishment of the "November criminals" who had accepted it, became the staple of right-wing rhetoric, and, with anti-Semitism, the most prominent point in Nazi propaganda. If Versailles was a burden on Weimar, the burden was as much of domestic as of foreign manufacture.

In the light of all this, the revolution and its aftermath accomplished a great deal. It ended the war. It swept away—forever—the Prussian ruling house and the other German monarchies, large and small. It educated at least some Germans in the ways of practical politics. It

[21] Mann to Philipp Witkop, May 12, 1919. *Briefe, 1889–1936,* ed. Erika Mann (1962), 162. Mann to Gustav Blume, July 5, 1919. *Ibid.,* 165.

[22] *Tagebücher,* 183, 184.

[23] Meinecke to A. Friis, May 23, 1921. *Ausgewählter Briefwechsel,* ed. Ludwig Dehio and Peter Classen (1962), 101-102.

established a democratic state. It gave new opportunities to talent ineligible for preferment in the Empire, opening centers of prestige and power to progressive professors, modern playwrights and producers, democratic political thinkers. Hugo Preuss, the architect of the Weimar Constitution, was a symbol of the revolution; as a Jew and a left-wing democrat, he had been kept out of the university establishment for all his merits, and now he, the outsider, gave shape to the new Republic, *his* Republic.

Yet, when all allowances have been made, it remains true that the men of Weimar made grievous mistakes, and recriminations over them poisoned the atmosphere early, preparing the way for further mistakes. The brilliant political journalist Carl von Ossietzky summed it up as early as June 1919: "There were three areas in which we had a right to expect an absolute break with old methods, and reconstruction: in the purely political, the economic, and the spiritual-ethical area." But "what has the revolution accomplished? The answer is sad indeed. In foreign and domestic politics celebrities swagger around who for several decades have of right belonged in a reliquary. Economic reconstruction is steadily being postponed, while anarchy, egotism, profiteering triumph. No resisting hand, only soft persuasion. Poverty of ideas, lack of courage, lack of faith."[24] It is a stern indictment, but not without justice. The republicans' search for order, their fear of Bolshevism, the timidity of leaders themselves the product of the old society and better equipped to oppose than to govern—and, it must be added, the confusion, irresponsibility, bloodthirsty language, and dictatorial pretensions of the Spartacist left—forestalled decisive action in area after area. Preuss, gravely worried by the hegemony of Prussia, wanted to destroy the old federal collection of states, break up Prussia into several *Länder*, and gather a number of small states into larger units. His plan was not adopted, and among its most effective adversaries were Social Democrats, unwilling to yield what they had just acquired, or—as with Eisner in Bavaria—suspicious of the central regime. A compromise kept the old states intact, preserved Prussian

[24] Quoted in Raimund Koplin, *Carl von Ossietzky als politischer Publizist* (1964), 28.

dominance, and left the troublesome relations between the Reich and the *Länder* unappeased. "It remains a historical sin of omission," the Socialist editor and politician Friedrich Stampfer conceded later, his hindsight working at full capacity, "that in that time of stormy progressive development the leap into the unitary state was not taken. Despite all Platonic obeisances to the idea of national unity, some social-democratic holders of power defended particular interests with an eagerness no less intense than that shown earlier by the dynasts."[25] The affair was to provide a painful lesson to Socialists jealous of their office: a short-range parochial gain proved to be a long-range public disaster.

The nationalization of major industries had the same history; ambitious schemes and goodwill were never translated into policy. The economist Rudolph Wissell pointed out the road to socialism through planning, and the road was clear enough. But it was never taken. Big industry proceeded to "nationalize" the economy in its own way—through cartelization. Indeed, "the largest trusts in German history were formed during the Weimar Republic," including the merger in 1926 of four large steel companies, and the formation of the chemical trust, I. G. Farben, the year before, through a merger of "the six largest corporations in this field."[26] The Socialists stood by, either too timid to act or in the doctrinaire and unrealistic conviction that cartelization was an inevitable higher stage of capitalism which must be traversed on the road to socialism. In relying on history, German Socialists became its victim.

These were fateful strategic mistakes, but the men of Weimar made an even more fateful mistake when they failed to tame, or transform, the machinery of the old order—the military, the civil service, and the courts. The military caste had come out of the war demoralized, its prestige shattered, in panic, ready for any compromise. The generals had led Germany into disaster, lying to themselves as much as to the world, wasting uncounted lives. Friedrich Meinecke acknowledged late in 1918 that "the unmeasured claims of the pan-German-militarist-

[25] *Die vierzehn Jahre der ersten deutschen Republik* (3rd ed., 1953), 134.
[26] Franz L. Neumann, *Behemoth: The Structure and Practice of National Socialism, 1933–1944* (2nd ed., 1944), 15–16.

conservative combine" had utterly discredited them.[27] Yet within a few years this combine had regained its charisma for wide circles of the public and burdened the Republic with the legend of an undefeated German Army stabbed in the back at home by Jews and Communists—the notorious *Dolchstosslegende*.

This resurgence was largely the responsibility of the Weimar leaders who made the old army indispensable. On November 10, the day after the proclamation of the Republic, Ebert had concluded a far-reaching agreement with General Groener, accepting the aid of the army in keeping order. Regular troops, aided by hastily formed *Freikorps*, shot down militant Spartacists by the score; the Social Democrat Noske, the "bloodhound" of the Republic, gave the rightwing troops wide latitude for action—that is to say, for organized assassination. There were excesses on all sides—"These were terrible months," Arnold Brecht, a sober observer, later remembered—and the goodwill of Ebert and Noske is beyond question. Their judgment is something else again.[28] On February 2, 1919, more than a month before Noske's notorious edict commanding his troops to shoot on sight anyone found with arms in his hands, and three months before the white terror vented its fury on the conquered Soviet Republic of Bavaria, Count Kessler prophesied that the present regime could not last: "The paradox of a republican-social-democratic government allowing itself and the capitalists' safes to be defended by hired unemployed and by royalist officers, is simply too insane."[29]

The same air of unreality hovers around the continued employment of imperial officials. In the light of the traditional authoritarian structure of German society, which the revolution had done little to shake, the consequences of this policy were predictable. Even without the burden of hostile officials German democracy was fragile enough.

---

[27]Meinecke to L. Aschoff, October 21, 1918. *Briefwechsel*, 97.

[28] Brecht, *Aus nächster Nähe: Lebenserinnerungen, 1884–1927* (1966), 247. The controversy over Noske goes on. I am inclined to agree with Brecht (*ibid.*, 231–247) that Noske had courage and accepted the job of being the "bloodhound" from a sense of responsibility (the epithet, after all, is his own), but that he lacked tact and foresight.

[29] *Tagebücher*, 117.

The German civil service was world-famous for its efficiency and for its neutrality, but during the Republic it used its highly trained capacities mainly for administrative sabotage; their proverbial loyalty to their superiors apparently did not extend to Social Democratic or liberal ministers. But the most astounding instance of this sophistic appeal to independence and objectivity—a fertile breeding ground for cynicism among the beneficiaries on the right as much as among the victims on the left—was the conduct of judges, prosecutors, and juries in the Republic. The surviving judges of the Empire were taken into service after the revolution; they were irremovable and, as their behavior was to show, immovable as well: almost all of them came from the privileged orders; with close connections among aristocrats, officers, conservative politicians, they had little pity for accused Communists but suave forbearance for ex-officers.

The consequences are notorious, but they deserve emphasis: between 1918 and 1922, assassinations traced to left-wing elements numbered twenty-two; of these, seventeen were rigorously punished, ten with the death penalty. Right-wing extremists, on the other hand, found the courts sympathetic: of the 354 murders committed by them, only one was rigorously punished, and not even that by the death penalty. The average prison sentences handed out to these political murderers reflect the same bias: fifteen years for the left, four months for the right. Right-wing putschists like Kapp, who had tried to overthrow the Republic by force and violence—his associates committed several revolting murders—were acquitted, freed on a technicality, or allowed to escape abroad. After the Hitler-Ludendorff Putsch of November 1923 failed, the trial of the putschists was degraded into a political farce; the court permitted the accused and their lawyers to insult the government in the most offensive and incendiary language and finally convicted Hitler to five years of *Festungshaft*, a comfortable form of detention of which, in any event, he served less than a year. The *Feme* murders committed by members of illegal "defense organizations," paramilitary vigilante groups, belong to the most atrocious crimes in a century filled with atrocities: unemployed fanatics and unemployable ex-officers clubbed men to death and strangled women often on the mere suspicion of "unpatriotic activities." Few of the murderers were tried, few of those tried convicted, and none of those convicted long detained or in any way deterred from later criminal activity. Indeed, one of these *Feme* murderers, Edmund Heines, one of Röhm's friends, actually served around a year and a half in jail and was finally disposed of, in an act of poetic justice, in the Nazi purges of June 30, 1934. The two murderers of Erzberger were allowed to escape, the whole network of conspirators against him, though commonly known, was largely unmolested, and the chief conspirator was acquitted. Whenever the judges found it possible to twist the law in behalf of reaction, they twisted it: Hitler, as an Austrian, should have been deported after his putsch, but was allowed to stay in Germany because he *thought* himself a German. Against Spartacists, Communists, or candid journalists, on the other hand, the courts proceeded with the utmost rigor. Whoever was found to have had the slightest connection with the Bavarian Soviet Republic was harshly punished; writers who "insulted" the Reichswehr were convicted even if their exposé was proved to be true.

The soberest of historians must confront these statistics with bafflement and a sense of despair. Socialist and Communist newspapers and politicians orated and warned and exposed; independent and radical journals like the *Weltbühne* or the *Tagebuch* fought the assassins with facts and sarcasm. To no avail. The statistician E. J. Gumbel, who collected and documented all possible details about these crimes with great personal courage and impeccable scholarship, found that none of his reports had any effect. In 1924, in the *Tagebuch,* he compiled another list of crimes and their consequences, and concluded: "One sees that the documents are piling up, mountain high. The courts are working feverishly. One prosecution after another is begun. Each has its own structure. Only the result is always *the same*: the true murderers remain unpunished."[30]

[30] *Ausnahmezustand,* 119. For Gumbel's statistics, see his *Zwei Jahre Mord* (1921), *Vier Jahre politischer Mord* (1922), *Verräter verfallen der Feme* (1929), *Lasst Köpfe rollen* (1932). Historians have accepted his work as authoritative. See Neumann, *Behemoth,* 20–33, 478–479; H. and E. Hannover, *Politische Justiz, 1918–1933* (1966), *passim.*

In 1934, in exile, the Social Democratic Party a little ruefully acknowledged that it had made a tragic mistake: "That the German working class movement, disoriented during the war, should have taken over the old state apparatus practically unchanged, was its grave historical error."[31] True enough. Not content with inviting the Trojan horse into the city, the men of Weimar watched over its construction and solicitously sheltered its designers.

[31] Quoted in Hannover, *Politische Justiz*, 34.

II / THE COMMUNITY OF REASON:

Conciliators and Critics

I

There were thousands in Weimar—professors, industrialists, politicians—who hated the Nazis but did not love the Republic. Well-educated, intelligent, reluctant to exchange the values of the Empire for the dubious dispensations of democracy, many of these men were paralyzed by their conflicts and pursued, through the years of Weimar, public careers of honorable impotence punctuated by fitful activity. They learned to live with the Republic, judged its advent a historical necessity, and respected some of its leaders, but they never learned to love it, and never believed in its future. They came to be called "rational republicans—*Vernunftrepublikaner*," republicans from intellectual choice rather than passionate conviction. On May 7, 1933, after the Nazis had been in power a little more than three months, Friedrich Meinecke confided to a fellow historian, Walter Lenel: "The German people was simply not ripe for parliamentary democracy, especially under the pressure of the Versailles peace. I said that to myself, under my breath, from the beginning."[1] Here is the authentic voice of the *Vernunftrepublikaner*.

Like other rational republicans, Meinecke had prepared for this position even before the Emperor had abdicated. In the fall of 1918 he became convinced that Germany's only chance for survival was to "become democratic," to "throw overboard" the "ballast of con-

[1] *Briefwechsel,* 138.

servative ideas," to fight any attempt at restoration, and to resign itself to progress through a rational, courageous decision. And early in
1919 he was certain: "In the conflict between statesmanlike reason
and inherited ideals, which we are all compelled to experience at this
moment, I believe I must follow, with firm step, the demands of
reason."[2]

What reason demanded, it seemed, was a republic with a strong
President, a cautiously experimental regime ready to preserve the
valuable remnants of a great past, a state, above all, that would reconcile all classes with one another. As these reasonable republicans
reasoned it out, in the old days Bismarck's virulent anti-Socialist
policies had frustrated class reconciliation; now it was threatened by
the radical rhetoric of the Social Democrats. The form of government
was less important that was its effectiveness in producing class collaboration and preventing radical polarization in politics; on this
point Meinecke, who had loved the monarchy, agreed with Robert
Bosch, the liberal engineer and industrialist, who had been indifferent
to it. "In itself," Bosch wrote in 1923, "the Republic is not the decisive
thing." Earlier, Bosch had confessed that he was "not convinced that
a republic is the best thing for us." But, he insisted, "I am of the
opinion that we should stay with the Republic, now that we've got
one."[3] This mood lasted through the twenties; to the *Vernunftrepublikaner* the Republic was, in a sense, the punishment that the Germans,
aristocrats and bourgeois, deserved; it was infinitely preferable to the
barbarism of the right and the irresponsibility of the left; it should
enlist cooperation, even if it could not command enthusiasm.

This cool rationalism had its own characteristic virtues and vices:
it was better equipped to discover defects than excellences; it was more
likely to elicit dispassionate analysis of past errors than passionate
loyalty to new possibilities. It encouraged a curious, rather limited,
Machiavellianism: the *Vernunftrepublikaner* found it conceivable to
collaborate with the military—had it not produced cultivated and

[2] Meinecke to his wife, October 5, 1918. *Ibid.*, 95. Meinecke to Siegfried A.
Kaehler, (end of) January 1919. *Ibid.*, 335.

[3] See Theodor Heuss, *Robert Bosch: Leben und Leistung* (1946), 371.

moderate generals like Groener?[4]—or to see some pedagogic value in the Nazi electoral victory of 1930—might it not compel the Social Democrats to be "statesmanlike" and work with Brüning?[5] The *Vernunftrepublikaner* were reasonable men who had been willing to learn the first lesson of modernity but not the second: they acknowledged that nostalgia for the Empire was ridiculous, but they could not see that the Republic might deserve wholehearted support—or, rather, that it might become deserving if enough deserving persons supported it.

Their very intellectual style kept the rational republicans from forming a party or laying down a program; in fact, some of them markedly changed during the brief life of the Republic. And not all of them were ineffectual; Gustav Stresemann, the politician for whom the name *Vernunftrepublikaner* might have been coined, became an active conciliatory force in German politics.[6] Stresemann's development—from lobbyist to politician, from politician to statesman—was a steady growth, a history of ambitions directed and disciplined, of ideas broadening under the pressure of insistent reality. Stresemann began as a typical, he ended up as an extraordinary German, and it was his tragedy—most of it enacted posthumously—that he could not persuade his own kind to accompany him on his voyage of discovery.

Neither Stresemann's origins nor his early career suggested such potentialities. Born into the Berlin bourgeoisie, Stresemann long retained a vivid affection for his environment, where men of middling origins aspired to higher things by reading the German classics but directed their education to practical affairs. His doctoral dissertation of 1900 was an exercise in nostalgia; it was on the bottled-beer industry—his father's trade—and described small business as a way of

[4] "Groener was the most overrated man in the Weimar Republic." Felix Gilbert, in conversation with the author. It is time that such an opinion be at last publicly recorded.

[5] Meinecke expressed this fantastic estimation of German politics in 1930 in a letter to his daughter and son-in-law, Sabine and Carl Rabl, October 30, 1930. *Briefwechsel*, 128.

[6] The name seems to have been coined by Professor Wilhelm Kahl, like Stresemann a member of the German People's Party. Henry Ashby Turner, Jr., *Stresemann and the Politics of the Weimar Republic* (1963), 112.

life threatened by giant combines. In his early ventures into politics, too, he followed his father: wholly accepting the Empire, enthusiastic about German militarism, touched with the peculiar liberalism—mildly constitutionalist, vehemently imperialist—that had marked the revolutionaries of 1848. When the war came, Stresemann, then in the Reichstag, lent his considerable eloquence to the war aims of the government; he was an uncritical, unmitigated annexationist, demanding a vast colonial empire in Africa, most of Belgium, and an Eastern Europe detached from Russia and subjected to German influence. Count Kessler, who came to know him well, likened the Stresemann of those years to one of Sternheim's less attractive dramatic personages: conventional, politically ambitious, corrupted by industry and old-German cant.[7] The German collapse and the German Revolution depressed and disconcerted him; when he helped to form his new party, the *Deutsche Volkspartei*, he and his associates made their continued loyalties plain. "I was a monarchist," Stresemann wrote on January 6, 1919, "am a monarchist, and shall remain a monarchist."[8] His political line—and it was nothing more than that—now became the need for cooperation with an undesirable regime that had come to power in an unfortunate revolution and accepted a shameful peace treaty; this cooperation would save the country from civil war and dismemberment, and keep the way open for a possible restoration. At the time of the Kapp Putsch in 1920, Stresemann apologized for right-wing subversion and kept close connections with politicians and officers working for some form of monarchy.

Then something happened to Stresemann: history. It was not a dramatic conversion; it was perhaps not even a conscious process, but rather a conscious policy of gradual political adjustments for the sake of his party which masked an unconscious fading of old loyalties and growth of new connections: as early as 1919 Kessler subtly saw Stresemann as a "problematic phenomenon."[9] Certainly to the day

---

[7] *Tagebücher*, 396.
[8] Quoted in Turner, *Stresemann*, 30.
[9] *Tagebücher*, 138.

in August 1923 when he became Chancellor of the Republic, and beyond, Stresemann intimated his persistent hope for a restoration. But, just as his earlier pronouncements in defense of Weimar had smacked of political insincerity, his royalist pronouncements of the later years had a perfunctory air about them; the viciousness of the extreme right had taught Stresemann the virtues of Weimar, the exigencies of foreign and domestic politics had made him into a responsible statesman.

In January 1923, Arnold Brecht talked to Stresemann, trying to win him over to his plan for a seventy-fifth anniversary celebration of the Revolution of 1848, the liberal revolution of the Paulskirche in Frankfurt, which had fathered the flag that had become the flag of Weimar. "When he hesitated (for he immediately saw, of course, that such a celebration would bring the colors black, red, gold to center stage) we reminded him that once, as a student, he himself had carried the black-red-gold flag at a celebration for the victims of March. We showed him a newspaper clipping about it. He then consented laughingly and heartily, obviously much taken with the plan and especially enthusiastic about the historic support which, he was sure, it would lend his policy of active collaboration with the Weimar coalition. There, and at that moment, Stresemann was won over emotionally to the Weimar Republic. The previous two years, with the fall of Social Democratic predominance on the one hand, and the assassination of ministers and the lust for dictatorship on the other, had made him into a *Vernunftrepublikaner*. But now he was touched at the heart. Now more than tactical opportunism, more than mere reason, came into play. As we sat with him in conversation about the Paulskirche, he suddenly looked once more like that young idealistic student who had carried the black-red-gold flag in honor of those who had fallen in the March days. His secret attachment to the democratic Republic shone from his eyes. The Stresemann of the Wilhelminian policy of expansion—Stresemann the First, one might say, who had still supported the Kapp Putsch—had long been dying. Stresemann the Second was born, no longer a mere *Vernunftrepublikaner,* but—even if he could not plainly tell this to the members of his own party—in the game with all his heart."[10] Brecht's version of the scene sounds a little sentimental, but then with these rational republicans one could never be quite sure: their republicanism had its reasons which their reason did not know.

II

The *Vernunftrepublikaner* placed their reason in the service of reconciliation: they sought to reconcile classes with each other, parties with the state, Germany with the rest of the world—and themselves to republicanism. But there were other men of reason in Weimar, not intellectual republicans but republican intellectuals, who placed their reason in the service of criticism: they sought to uncover the arcana of government, the secrets of the unconscious, the legends of history. Nothing, no one, not even Bismarck, was safe from them.

There was neither novelty nor courage in criticizing the regime of Emperor William II—in fact, it had become fashionable to make the Emperor a scapegoat—but then, in the time of the Republic, Bismarck himself came under attack: between 1925 and 1930 Johannes Ziekursch, a university professor and neither a Jew nor a Socialist, published a political history of the Empire from 1871 to 1918 in which he attacked Bismarck's authoritarianism and charged him with responsibility for the disasters that overtook his creation.[11] After this— did not the Weimar Republic still live in Bismarck's shadow?—everything was possible. In fact, it was in 1930, the year of Ziekursch's third volume and of Brüning, that Erich Fromm, then an orthodox Freudian, offered a psychoanalytical account of the rise of the Christ dogma and in passing took issue with Troeltsch's attempt to "explain away" the class basis of early Christianity.[12] And it was in 1930 that

[10] Brecht, *Aus nächster Nähe*, 399–400.
[11] *Politische Geschichte des neuen deutschen Kaiserreiches*, 3 vols. (1925– 1930).
[12] Now available in Fromm, *The Dogma of Christ and Other Essays on Religion, Psychology, and Culture* (1966 ed.), 1–95.

the brilliant young historian Eckart Kehr published his provocative doctoral thesis, *Schlachtflottenbau und Parteipolitik*, which laid bare, in relentless and unimpeachable detail, the domestic economic sources of Germany's naval policy during the critical years from 1894 to 1901.

Eckart Kehr's tragically short career—he died in 1933 at the age of thirty—illustrates the high price a heretic had to pay, even in the Republic. His family swarmed with powerful figures in the intellectual establishment of the late Empire, but, shaken by war and defeat, he rebelled against the Prussian conservatism of his immediate environment; by heritage an insider, his experience and temperament made Kehr into an outsider determined to compel the university world to grant him recognition. His studies of the intimate relations of business leaders, industrialists, and foreign-policy-makers in the Empire forced him to the conclusion that profit had been a far more significant incentive for German imperialism than grandiose thoughts about the German mission. Writing the dissertation had had a "revolutionizing effect" on him; he had begun, after all, with "political history and philosophy," but he discovered that social structure and economic interests influenced political decisions in ways that pious historians had always denied, or, rather, never seen. His articles, which appeared in rapid succession in the late 1920s, were as scandalous as his book; they dealt, in biting language but irreproachable scholarship, with such touchy subjects as the rise of the Prussian bureaucracy, the class struggles in the early Empire, the social and financial foundations of foreign policy, the sociology of the Reichswehr.

Predictably, Kehr's fellow historians did not know what to do with him. His articles were noticed, his book had some respectful and respectable reviews, but for the most part, it was a handful of young students in Germany and American progressive historians like Charles Beard who appreciated Kehr's true value. For the rest, there was patriotic denunciation and worried head-shaking; Hermann Oncken called Kehr the *"enfant terrible"* of the profession; even Friedrich Meinecke, one of Kehr's teachers and one of his strongest, most disinterested supporters, called him, more in friendly warning than in serious disapproval, "a complete Nihilist" who believed that "to understand all is to criticize all."[13] And this, of course, was precisely the point.

III

Kehr was a lonely operator, the *Steppenwolf* of the German historical profession. In contrast, his fellow critics, committed like him to the proposition that to understand all is to criticize all, generally joined in schools or institutes, huddling together for warmth, mutual support, and informed self-criticism. Surely there is nothing especially German, or Weimar-Republican, about the founding of institutes. New disciplines, seeking to clarify their purpose, train their personnel in their own way, and propagate their findings, have often created institutions separate from, or only loosely affiliated with, old centers of higher learning. What is special about the institutes of the Weimar Republic is above all the quality of the work that was done in them.

At first glance, except for housing a high proportion of Jews, these institutes seem to have had little in common: the Kulturhistorische Bibliothek Warburg in Hamburg did its work in peaceful obscurity; the Psychoanalytische Institut in Berlin, though as unpolitical as the Warburg Institute, aroused much opposition among the members of the psychological guild; the Deutsche Hochschule für Politik attempted to establish a consensus among men of goodwill in all parties, and explicitly excluded only Communists and Nazis; while the Institut

[13] Hans-Ulrich Wehler, "Introduction," to Eckart Kehr, *Der Primat der Innenpolitik: Gesammelte Aufsätze zur preussisch-deutschen Sozialgeschichte im 19. und 20. Jahrhundert* (1965), 3–4. The transmission of Kehr's work to America is an interesting instance of the influence that Weimar scholarship exerted on American intellectual life. Beard had his attention drawn to Kehr by his German son-in-law, Alfred Vagts; after the Second World War, Franz Neumann advised his students at Columbia University to read Kehr (advice which all his students of course followed), and reinforced his advice by referring to Kehr's articles appreciatively in his *Behemoth* (see *Behemoth*, 203, 206, 477, 488–489).

für Sozialforschung in Frankfurt was a center for leftist Hegelians persuaded that Weimar was only a way station to socialism. But for all their differences, they were members of a real community of reason devoted to radical inquiry, open to ideas impossible or scandalous to traditional practitioners, and committed, all of them, not so much to Weimar institutions, but, with their lack of piety, their ruthless modernity, their search for reality through science, to the Weimar spirit.

While in retrospect the Warburg Institute appears as one of the greatest glories and most characteristic expressions of the Weimar spirit, its founder was a loyal monarchist, and the institute itself the intensely personal creation of one man, the realization of an obsessive wish. Rich, scholarly, extraordinarily sensitive and intermittently psychotic, Aby Warburg was haunted by the survival of classical antiquity in the civilization of the West. The subject had long engaged the attention of scholars, but not with the urgency and refined discrimination that Warburg himself brought to it; the precise shape of classicism, its precise impact on the Renaissance, seemed to him not dry scholastic matters but matters almost of life and death. There was in him, Panofsky has written, "an enormous tension between the rational and the irrational" which induced in him "not a romantic split, but a fascinating combination of brilliant wit and dark melancholy, the keenest rational criticism and most empathetic readiness to help."[14] It was Warburg's special achievement to recognize—I am tempted to say, re-experience—the full range of the classical heritage, which was, for him, more than serene temples and Latin poems; it was dark as it was light, and its legacy was superstitious beliefs and magical practices quite as much as sculpture and poetry. Warburg's models— Burckhardt, Nietzsche, and Usener—set his problem and suggested its solution: the study of the survival of the classical heritage demanded a broad view of cultural history, an appreciation of the Dionysian aspects of life, and close attention to man's religious experience.

For thirty years, Warburg traveled, wrote highly original essays on the art and thought of the Renaissance and the Reformation, and

[14] "A. Warburg," *Repertorium für Kunstwissenschaft,* LI (1930), 3.

collected a library of impressive diversity. In 1918, with the defeat, he fell ill, and two years later he broke down and went to a Swiss sanatorium. But he left his library, which, in the charge of Fritz Saxl, was affiliated with the new University of Hamburg. Saxl and Erwin Panofsky both held university posts, but they did most of their writing and teaching in the Warburg Library, which soon acquired a wide reputation through its monthly lectures—later printed for general distribution—and its other publications.

Ernst Cassirer's association with the institute shows the Warburg style at work. Cassirer, already a well-known philosopher, had been appointed to the chair of philosophy at Hamburg; he moved there in October 1919, and then, sometime in the following year, he went to see the Warburg Library. It was, in Hamburg as elsewhere, a bewildering time. "Although the war had been lost by Germany," Fritz Saxl recalled later, "the air was full of hope. The collapse of material power had produced a strong and favourable reaction in the intellectual field." The founding of Hamburg University and the appointment of Cassirer were obviously part of the reaction; Cassirer "lent a peculiar dignity to the young arts faculty, and an ever-growing number of students came to his courses, eager for the truth and for learning, after the many deceptions of the war years." It was in this atmosphere that Cassirer visited the Warburg Bibliothek. "Being in charge of the library," Saxl recalls, "I showed Cassirer around. He was a gracious visitor, who listened attentively as I explained to him Warburg's intention in placing books on philosophy next to books on astrology, magic, and folklore, and in linking the sections on art with those on literature, religion, and philosophy. The study of philosophy was for Warburg inseparable from that of the so-called primitive mind: neither could be isolated from the study of imagery in religion, literature, and art. These ideas had found expression in the unorthodox arrangement of the books on the shelves.

"Cassirer understood at once. Yet, when he was ready to leave, he said, in the kind and clear manner so typical of him: 'This library is dangerous. I shall either have to avoid it altogether or imprison myself here for years. The philosophical problems involved are close to my own, but the concrete historical material which Warburg has collected is overwhelming.' "[15] But this rebuff was not a rejection of the library. It was Cassirer's way of protecting his own work in progress from being swamped by the massive confirmation he knew was on its shelves; he was then working on the first volume of *Die Philosophie der symbolischen Formen*, conceived wholly independently of, yet wholly congruent with, Warburg's philosophical ideas.

Cassirer did not resist long; he returned to the institute and remained its most prolific author. And, appropriately enough, the first full-length "study" published by the Warburg Institute, in 1922, was Cassirer's *Die Begriffsform im mythischen Denken*; indeed, his best work of the twenties—the three volumes of the philosophy of symbolic forms, his essay on language and myth, and his great book on Renaissance philosophy, this last dedicated to Warburg—was done under its auspices. He did not work alone; he was surrounded by productive art historians, philosophers and philologists: Eduard Norden's *Die Geburt des Kindes*, Percy Schramm's *Kaiser, Rom und Renovatio*, Paul Lehmann's *Pseudo-antike Literatur des Mittelalters*, Erwin Panofsky's *Idea, Dürers "Melancolia I," Hercules am Scheidewege*—all now classics in their field, were all Warburg studies.

The austere empiricism and scholarly imagination of the Warburg style were the very antithesis of the brutal anti-intellectualism and vulgar mysticism threatening to barbarize German culture in the 1920s; this was Weimar at its best. Warburg's celebrated formula that Athens must be recovered over and over again from the hands of Alexandria was more than an art historian's prescription for the understanding of the Renaissance, with its painful struggles with alchemy and astrology; it was a *philosophe's* prescription for life in a world threatened by unreason. "Warburg," said one who knew him well, "believed in the power of reason; he was an *Aufklärer*, precisely because he knew the

[15] Fritz Saxl, "Ernst Cassirer," *The Philosophy of Ernst Cassirer*, ed. Paul Arthur Schilpp (1949), 47–48. For confirmation, see Toni Cassirer, *Aus meinem Leben mit Ernst Cassirer* (1950), 106 ff.

heritage of daemonic antiquity so well. Lessing's *Laocoön* had been the great influence on his youth, and he felt a deep obligation to the German Enlightenment of the eighteenth century."[16]

But the influence of the Warburg Institute, if profound, was narrow; all its survivors testify to its serene isolation. German right-wingers looking for *Kultur-Bolschewiken* found no material for suspicion in the Warburg Institute's publications on the world view of St. Augustine, the contents of medieval encyclopedias, or the iconography of a Dürer engraving.

It was different with those other students of myth, the psychoanalysts, for the myths they studied were the—often unacknowledged —possessions of everyone. The Psychoanalytical Institute in Berlin, which had begun as a branch of the International Association in 1910, became independent in 1920, complete with clinic and training facilities—a decisive step, as Freud recognized, toward creating a body of well-trained analysts.[17] To judge from the names of those who trained and were trained in Berlin—Sandor Rado, Franz Alexander, Karen Horney, Otto Fenichel, Melanie Klein, Wilhelm Reich—the institute participated in that sense of excitement so characteristic of Weimar culture, and its founder, Max Eitingon, its chief training analyst, Hanns Sachs, and its imaginative theoretician, Karl Abraham, were quite as remarkable as the psychoanalysts they trained. It was a rigorous school, and stiff; Rudolph Loewenstein, who was analyzed in Berlin by Hanns Sachs, found it "cold, very German." But even Loewenstein, with all his reservations, thought Sachs splendid ("a true empiricist") and Rado brilliant ("a magnificent teacher" and an "extraordinary intelligent man"). And, in addition to the excitement generated by the local talent, there was one unforgettable incursion by the Founder himself; at the Berlin Congress of 1922, the last he ever attended, Freud read a paper, "Some Remarks on the Un-

---

[16] Gertrud Bing, *Aby M. Warburg* (1958), 29. For the Warburg formula see his "Heidnisch-antike Weissagung in Wort und Bild zu Luthers Zeiten" (1920), *Gesammelte Schriften*, 2 vols. (1932), II, 491–492, 534.

[17] Sigmund Freud, "The Resistances to Psycho-Analysis" (1925), *The Standard Edition of the Complete Psychological Works of Sigmund Freud*, XIX (1961), 213–224.

conscious," which those present never forgot. It was in this paper, Loewenstein recalls, that Freud "introduced a whole new approach, a revolution in analysis," the "structural theory" of "the superego, the ego, and the id." The lecture was, Loewenstein says, "one of the greatest esthetic, scientific-esthetic experiences I've ever had in my life."[18]

However magnificent, such experiences had a limited public; in Germany, as elsewhere and perhaps more than elsewhere, psychoanalysis was viewed with considerable suspicion. Ironically enough, it was the war that called psychoanalysis to the favorable attention of a hostile profession; psychiatrists approached German analysts to administer rapid cures to shell-shocked soldiers that they might be fitted for combat once again, an access of pragmatic interest Abraham found unwelcome. "I did not like the idea," he wrote Freud, "that psychoanalysis should suddenly become fashionable because of purely practical considerations. We would rapidly have acquired a number of colleagues who would merely have paid lip-service and would afterwards have called themselves psychoanalysts. Our position as outsiders," he concluded, in obvious relief, "will continue for the time being."[19]

There were few signs of change, but Abraham greeted each of them optimistically; he was asked, on occasion, to address meetings of psychiatrists, and in 1920 he even wrote a long piece for *Die neue Rundschau,* the Fischer Verlag's highly esteemed monthly, expounding the general principles of psychoanalysis. "Berlin," Abraham told Freud in October 1919, "is clamoring for psychoanalysis."[20] But the clamor remained muted. For some time there were rumors that Abraham would be appointed *ausserordentlicher Professor* in psychoanalysis at the University of Berlin, but, as Freud rightly foresaw, nothing came

[18] "The Reminiscences of Rudolph M. Loewenstein," Oral History Collection, Columbia University (1965), 19–25.

[19] Abraham to Freud, October 27, 1918. *A Psycho-Analytical Dialogue: The Letters of Sigmund Freud and Karl Abraham, 1907–1926,* ed. Hilda C. Abraham and Ernst L. Freud, tr. Bernard Marsh and Hilda C. Abraham (1965), 279–280.

[20] Abraham to Freud, October 19, 1919. *Ibid.,* 292, and see *ibid.,* 299–300, 305. Abraham's article was "Die Psychoanalyse als Erkenntnisquelle für die Geisteswissenschaften," *Neue Rundschau,* XXXI, part II (1920), 1154–1174.

of it. "Intellectuals" and "liberal advanced people," Loewenstein reports, looked upon analysis "with some interest" if with not much favor, and the general attitude remained one of hostility; medical students or young physicians studying and undergoing psychoanalysis kept this to themselves for fear that they would not get, or would lose, desirable positions.[21] Many intellectuals, all across the political spectrum, continued distrustful: Ricarda Huch, historian, essayist, poet, a decent and intelligent conservative, was so hostile that even though she was present at the meeting at which Freud's name had been proposed for the Goethe Prize, she "totally forgot" this—an amusing instance of a Freudian mechanism used to repress Freud himself. When a psychiatrist sent her a book "on Freud and against Freud," she found it "very fine" but not sharp enough.[22] And from the left Eckart Kehr sniped at psychoanalysis as a bourgeois ideology inducing conformity and inviting escape from real social problems.[23]

But as time went by, there were more and more of those liberals and intellectually advanced people who, according to Loewenstein, were open to the Freudian teaching. Felix Gilbert remembers productions of Kleist's plays stressing the unconscious, father figures, and other notions borrowed from Freud, and he and his circle read Freud and Jung seriously; "Freud," he writes, "was our 'daily talk.'" There may have been "few practicing analysts in Germany at that time, but Freud as an intellectual event had certainly permeated the entire intellectual scene." In 1929 Paul Tillich affirmed that the "philosophy of the unconscious, initiated by Freud," was "daily" growing in influence;[24] and in the following year the Berlin Institute proudly issued a brochure detailing the first ten years of its work, listing its lecturers, analyzing its program, offering, a little naïvely, a statistical survey of the percentage of cures, and featuring a characteristic preface by

[21] "Reminiscences of Loewenstein," 32.

[22] Marie Baum, *Leuchtende Spur: Das Leben Ricarda Huchs* (1950), 329–330, 335–336.

[23] "Neuere deutsche Geschichtsschreibung" (a lecture given in Chicago in 1932), in *Der Primat der Innenpolitik*, 254–268.

[24] "The Protestant Message and the Man of Today," in *The Protestant Era*, ed. and tr. James Luther Adams (1951), 190.

Freud, short, lucid, and humane, which described the three functions of the Berlin Institute: "First, to make our therapy available to that large group of people who suffer under their neuroses no less than the rich, but are in no position to meet the costs of their treatments; second, to found a place where psychoanalysis may be taught theoretically and the experiences of older analysts transmitted to students eager to learn; and finally, to perfect our knowledge of neurotic illnesses and our therapeutic techniques through application and experimentation under new conditions."[25]

All this was promising, but the growth of understanding was halting; it was marked by professional squabbles and by widespread public ignorance, even among—often especially among—the educated, who found it hard to distinguish among Freud, Adler, and Jung, and who often preferred Jung, with his supposed spirituality, to Freud, with his rejection of religion—a legacy, as Ernst Robert Curtius put it, of Freud's naturalism which would be overcome only after this final version of Enlightenment thought had been overcome as well.[26] Curtius was a brilliant and perceptive scholar; as this comment makes plain, a small elite apart, in depth psychology at least, the outsider remained the outsider.

IV

Unlike the art historians and the psychoanalysts, the republican intellectuals practicing political science were directly, deliberately—I am tempted to say defiantly—involved in the political life of the Republic and sought to influence its course—or, rather, those who were setting its course.

Political science had been a victim of the German Empire. German *Staatswissenschaft* of the 1850s and 1860s had made pioneering investigations into comparative government and public administration.

[25] *Zehn Jahre Berliner Psychoanalytisches Institut (Poliklinik und Lehranstalt)*, ed. German Psychoanalytical Society (1930), 5.
[26] *Deutscher Geist in Gefahr* (1932), 24–25.

But with the advent of Bismarck's Second Reich, political scientists, like other liberals, came to concentrate on the relatively harmless branch of political science, public law, which trained submissive officials rather than free intellectuals. The study of "social and political reality," Franz Neumann wrote later, from his American vantage point, "found virtually no place in German university life. Scholarship meant essentially two things: speculation and book learning. Thus what we call social and political science was largely carried on outside the universities." Of course, Neumann continues, there was one exception: Max Weber, who possessed "a unique combination of a theoretical frame" combined with "a mastery of a tremendous number of data, and a full awareness of the political responsibility of the scholar." Yet Weber had little influence at home. "It is characteristic of German social science that it virtually destroyed Weber by an almost exclusive concentration upon the discussion of his methodology. Neither his demand for empirical studies nor his insistence upon the responsibility of the scholar were heeded." It is "in the United States," Neumann significantly concludes, "that Weber really came to life."[27]

The impulse for reform emerged from desperate practical need. Even before 1914, but with greater urgency during the war, a few German publicists, historians, and public officials, appalled by the political ignorance of statesmen and public alike, turned their attention to the École Libre des Sciences Politiques in Paris, a school, they believed, that had been the center of "the intellectual and national reconstruction" of France after its debacle in 1871.[28] Friedrich Meinecke, Friedrich Naumann, Carl Becker, who was to become *Kultusminister* in the Republic, Richard von Kühlmann, a highly placed and cultivated official in the foreign office, and Ernst Jäckh, an energetic, persuasive journalist, joined to seek ways of educating the unpolitical German in political affairs. They won over Robert Bosch, who supported his progressive convictions with munificent philanthropies, and early in 1918 founded a Staatsbürgerschule, with Naumann as its presi-

[27] Neumann, "The Social Sciences," 21–22.
[28] Ernst Jäckh, *Weltsaat: Erlebtes und Erstrebtes* (1960), 82.

dent. Naumann provided the rhetoric: Germans needed "education to politics," a training that would be provided by men and women in public life, and offer not indoctrination or slogans but insight. "The people," he argued, "is thirsty for political and socio-political truth and clarity," and a free school—free from the pressure of the state or private donors—must satisfy that thirst.[29]

Naumann died in August 1919; Ernst Jäckh became his successor. But Jäckh, whose only son was killed at the end of hostilities, the only victim in his unit, on his only day at the front, had ambitious plans born from great grief, and he transformed Naumann's "political school" into the Deutsche Hochschule für Politik. It opened in October 1920, beginning modestly with 120 students; by 1932, the last year of the Republic, it had more than 2,000 students, of whom over 500 were regularly matriculated. The course of study developed gradually, through experience. There were outside lectures, seminars, and a regular program. The faculty, both full- and part-time, was enthusiastic and first-rate. It included the philosopher Max Scheler; Theodor Heuss was director of studies for the first five years of the Hochschule; Arnold Wolfers and Hans Simons taught political science, Albert Salomon sociology; Sigmund Neumann was in charge of the newspaper archives; Franz Neumann, then a young trade-union lawyer in Berlin, was among its occasional lecturers. And from the beginning, the Hochschule cultivated its ties to scholars and foundations abroad; in the course of the twenties, Charles Beard, Nicholas Murray Butler, G. P. Gooch, and André Siegfried came to perform; and in 1931 Hajo Holborn came to the Hochschule from Heidelberg, filling a chair for History and International Relations given by the Carnegie Endowment.

The program concentrated on political science in its broadest sense: political history, political sociology, foreign and domestic policy, "cultural politics" which included courses on the press, and the theory of the legal and economic foundations of politics. In its time, and in its place, the Hochschule was a radical departure. It began as an evening

[29] Theodor Heuss, *Friedrich Naumann: Der Mann, das Werk, die Zeit* (1937), 538–542.

school, and never ceased to attract men and women of a type that had never enjoyed higher education before: trade-union officials, white-collar workers, journalists, as well as diplomats and foreign students from many countries. Traditionally, schools of higher learning had accepted only graduates of a *Gymnasium* holding the coveted certificate —the *Abitur*. But by 1930—and this, too, was revolutionary—only a third of the students at the Hochschule für Politik had graduated from *Gymnasium*, another third had left the *Gymnasium* two years early— attaining the so-called *Sekundareife*—while the last third had only attended the free secondary schools—the *Volksschulen*—a kind of lower education that had normally foreclosed all access to academic training. And the Hochschule was radical also in its independence; the board of trustees accepted from the German Government no more than 20 percent of its budget, and from the Prussian Government only its building. And when a group of industrialists under the leadership of the magnate Alfred Hugenberg offered to support the school generously on condition that they control its program and name as its director the conservative revolutionist historian Martin Spahn, the trustees refused. It was only natural that in 1933 Joseph Goebbels should take the Hochschule under his personal supervision.[30]

With its deliberately cultivated ties to high government officials— ties which did not compromise its autonomy but marked its readiness to participate in the shaping of policy—and with its attempt to float, as it were, above parties—among its regular professors was the "Young Conservative" Max Hildebert Boehm, whose specialty was *Deutschtumspolitik*, the study of Germans on and beyond the frontiers drawn at Versailles, in a word, *irredentism*—the Deutsche Hochschule für Politik stood on the ground of bourgeois liberalism. This was too radical for many Germans. It was not radical enough for the political scientists and political theorists in the Institut für Sozialforschung in Frankfurt, for that institute was securely in the hands of Marxists.

If we read the bland histories of the International Institute of Social Research—as it came to be called in exile—written in the mid-1930s for American consumption, histories where unpleasant words like

30 Jäckh, *Weltsaat*, 88.

"Marx," "dialectic," "class struggle," and even "bourgeois" do not appear, we are tempted to compare its professors to characters in Bertolt Brecht's prose writings, and indeed to Brecht himself: telling their audience what it wants to hear and what, in their judgment, it is fit to absorb. For there can be no doubt: the Frankfurt Institute was left-Hegelian to the core. Founded in 1923 with several private endowments, and affiliated with the University of Frankfurt, the institute did not really begin to function until 1924, when the veteran Socialist Carl Grünberg took the directorship. In his lecture at the festivities inaugurating the Institut für Sozialforschung, Grünberg energetically stressed its function as a research institute—a function which, in Grünberg's candid logic, was revolutionary. Most institutes, he argued, train "mandarins," social functionaries. That is understandable and just; the state needs loyal servants. But the Frankfurt Institute, he insisted, would train not servants but students of the state; by stressing the role of research, and minimizing the roles of teaching and technical training, it would seek not to dull the capacity of the students for criticism but to sharpen it; it would teach them to understand the world, and, through understanding, change it. There are pessimists in the world, Grünberg said, prating of the decline of the West; but there are many, and "their number and influence is steadily growing," who not merely "believe, wish, and hope" that a new social order will come, but who are "scientifically convinced" that this order will be "socialism," and that this is the time of "transition from capitalism to socialism." "I may assume that it is well known," Grünberg added, "that I, too, hold this view. I, too, belong among the adversaries of the historically outmoded economic, social, and legal order and among the partisans of Marxism." To be sure, Grünberg reassured his listeners, his Marxism was a commitment neither to a party line nor to dogmatism; the students would be free. But there could be no question: the solution to pressing social questions offered in the institute would be Marxist.[31] Nothing could be plainer than that.

For all his avowed radicalism, or perhaps despite it, Grünberg's

[31] Carl Grünberg, *Festrede, gehalten zur Einweihung des Instituts für Sozialforschung . . . Juni 22, 1924,* Frankfurter Universitätsreden, XX (1924).

reign was less effective than that of his successor, Max Horkheimer, who became director of the institute in 1931, when Grünberg retired after a long illness. Even under Grünberg's directorship, two major volumes had been published under the auspices of the institute: Henryk Grossmann's *Das Akkumulations- und Zusammenbruchsgesetz des kapitalistischen Systems,* in 1929—*The Law of Accumulation and Collapse of the Capitalist System,* which, in the American bibliography of the institute, appears a little less provocatively as *The Law of Accumulation* in *the Capitalist System*—and Friedrich Pollock's *Die planwirtschaftlichen Versuche in der Soviet Union, 1917–1927,* in the same year. With Horkheimer, the pace increased. His inaugural lecture, though more Aesopian than that of his predecessor, gave adequate clues to the attentive listener. Grünberg, Horkheimer said, had mainly cultivated "the history of the labor movement" and assembled a splendid library; but there were new tasks ahead: social philosophy must move beyond mere intellectual dispute to real effectiveness. This could be achieved only through a turn to empirical investigation in which "philosophers, sociologists, economists, historians, and psychologists could join in permanent collaboration."[32] Horkheimer hinted that this would not be a passive empiricism, an acceptance of things as they were; his rejection of metaphysical dogmatism and philosophical apologies, coupled with his demand for an understanding of the relations among the economic life of society, the psychological development of the individual, and changes in cultural life, and his free references to Hegel, made it obvious enough that the Frankfurt Institute would not surrender the Marxism that Grünberg had proclaimed.

Whatever Horkheimer's precise meaning, his intentions were brilliantly realized in a magazine, the *Zeitschrift für Sozialforschung,* founded in 1931, which published in its brief German phase—abruptly terminated in the spring of 1933—some important articles: Hork-

---

[32] Max Horkheimer, *Die gegenwärtige Lage der Sozialphilosophie und die Aufgaben eines Instituts für Sozialforschung,* Frankfurter Universitätsreden, XXXVII (1931).

heimer himself wrote on a variety of philosophical subjects; Erich Fromm sought to develop a social psychology on Freudian ground; Henryk Grossmann wrote on Marx, Leo Loewenthal on the sociology of literature, Theodor Adorno on the sociology of music; while others, like Herbert Marcuse, Walter Benjamin, Franz Neumann, Paul Lazarsfeld, and Otto Kirchheimer, lectured at the institute, did reviews or research, and published in journals sympathetic to its philosophical style. It was a group of powerful intellects.

V

But was it a group of powerful intellectuals? That is quite a different question. Their influence was undeniable, but it is most likely that it was greater abroad than at home, more pervasive after than during the Weimar Republic. For while these men may have been the heart of the Weimar spirit, they were not at the heart of public affairs; they met, cultivated, and sometimes influenced insiders without really becoming insiders themselves.

Nothing illuminates the quality of that inside more strikingly than a look at the academic life of the period. "When I came in the spring of 1918 to the University of Breslau," Franz Neumann reports, "its celebrated economist—in his very first lecture—denounced the Peace Resolution of 1917 (peace without annexation and indemnities) and demanded the incorporation of Longwy and Brie, the transformation of Belgium into a German protectorate, the German colonization of large stretches of Eastern Europe and overseas colonies. The still more celebrated professor of literature, after having paid homage to Kantian idealism, derived from that philosophy the categorical imperative of a German victory, a German monarchy, and substantially the same peace terms. When I came to Leipzig in the fall of 1918, the economics professor thought it necessary—in October 1918—to endorse the peace terms of the Pan German Union and of the General Staff, while the historian proved conclusively that democracy was an essentially non-German form of political organization, suitable for the materialistic Anglo-Saxons, but incompatible with the idealism of the Germanic race. When I transferred to Rostock in the summer of 1919, I had to organize students to combat anti-Semitism openly preached by university professors. When I finally landed in Frankfurt, the very first task with which I was faced was to help protect a newly appointed Socialist university professor from attack—political as well as physical—by students secretly supported by a considerable number of professors."[33]

Berlin was equally infected. On November 15, 1922, Count Kessler attended a celebration in honor of Gerhart Hauptmann's sixtieth birthday at the University of Berlin, "New auditorium [*Aula*]," he wrote in his diary, "solemn, somewhat michelangelesque hall with an ugly mural by Arthur Kampf. Hauptmann sat on the speaker's stand, between Ebert and Löbe. Some professor of literature, I think his name was Petersen, gave a colorless, tiresome address, followed by a few further professorial essays. . . .

"The only speakers who had anything to say were a student and Löbe. The student spoke with so much fire and youthful freshness that he overwhelmed the audience. Only one professor, standing next to me, with gilded spectacles and in general corresponding to the prototype of the *Boche*, who could barely master his rage through the whole ceremony, gave evidence of his displeasure by mumbling something. Hauptmann read a speech, short, not very profound, but happily pronouncing decisively in behalf of humanity and reconciliation.

"The most remarkable thing about the festivities was the grotesquely narrow-minded conduct of students and professors. The Berlin fraternity council solemnly resolved—I believe with a majority of two to one—not to participate in the Hauptmann celebration because Gerhart Hauptmann is no longer to be considered a reliable German, after professing himself a republican! And I hear from Sam Fischer that the above-mentioned Petersen who gave the official address had been to see him two days before to ask him to disinvite Ebert, since it would not be agreeable to the university to have the republican chief of state

[33] Neumann, "The Social Sciences," 15–16.

appearing before it. And when Fischer refused, Petersen asked him at least to disinvite Löbe, for, after all, two Social Democrats at once were a little too much!

"At the end of the celebration d'Albert played the Appassionata—beautifully. Whereupon once again one of the professors sitting next to me distinguished himself by whispering to his neighbor discontentedly: 'That was of course the pianist's own composition, wasn't it?' Beethoven seems to be at home in the University of Berlin as little as Ebert."[34] Whatever most Germans hungered for, evidently it was not reason, whether in its conciliatory or its critical form.

[34] *Tagebücher,* 347–348.

III / *THE SECRET GERMANY:*

Poetry as Power

I

"On a hot spring noon of the year 1913, a young student was walking through the main street of the town of Heidelberg. He had just crossed the Brunngässlein and noticed how the customary stream of pedestrians who usually strolled to the University and back from the Ludwigplatz, in casual noisy conversation and irregular groups, on sidewalk and in the street, now were crawling lazily over the red-hot pavement, exhausted by the unaccustomed heat. As all at once these tired people seemed to pull themselves together; with elastic carriage, light step, a solitary man came walking along—all stepped aside that nothing might encumber his progress, and, as though floating, as though winged, he turned the corner, toward the Wredeplatz.

"The spectator stood motionless, rooted to the spot. A breath from a higher world had brushed him. He no longer knew what had happened, hardly where he was. Was it a man who had stepped through the crowd? But he was distinguished from all the men among whom he had walked, by an unconscious loftiness and an easy power, so that beside him all pedestrians appeared like pale larvae, like soulless stick figures. Was it a god who had divided the bustling throng and hastened, with easy step, to other shores? But he had worn man's clothing, though of an unusual kind: a thin yellow silk jacket fluttered around his slender body; a large hat sat on his head, strangely light and alien, and thick brown hair welled up under it. And in his hand

TWO SCENES FROM *The Cabinet of Dr. Caligari* (1920)

The Expressionist horror film that made history, with sets by three Expressionist artists: Hermann Warm, Walter Röhrig, and Walter Reimann. Werner Krauss is the insane Dr. Caligari, Conrad Veidt the somnambulist Cesare whom Caligari incites to murder.

WALTHER RATHENAU AT CANNES IN EARLY 1922

German foreign minister and martyr to right-wing assassins in 1922, Rathenau, aesthete, millionaire, statesman, Utopian, and Jew, reveals something of his problematic personality in this photograph.

TROOPS RESTORING ORDER IN THE CITY OF DRESDEN IN 1923

Between 1918 and 1923, and 1929 and 1932, there were many such scenes, in many cities.

A BAKER RECEIVING HIS PAY DURING THE PERIOD OF HIGH INFLATION

These scenes, which reached a ludicrous crescendo in the summer and fall of 1923, are comical only in retrospect.

there twirled a small, thin cane—was it the staff of Mercury, was it a human switch? And the countenance? The spectator recalled single features only indistinctly; they were chiseled, and the pallor of the cheeks contributed to arousing the impression of strangeness, statuesqueness, divinity. And the eyes? Suddenly the spectator knew: it was a beam from these eyes that had enchanted him; quick as lightning a look had darted toward him, had penetrated his innermost being, and had strolled on with a slight, fleeting smile. And now the certainty arose: if it was a man, then—Stefan George."[1]

It was indeed Stefan George, poet and seer, leader of a tight, humorless, self-congratulatory coterie of young men, a modern Socrates who held his disciples with a fascination at once erotic and spiritual—though this Socrates, who picked his collection of Alcibiades at least in part for their looks, was handsomer than his antique model. Stefan George was king of a secret Germany, a hero looking for heroes in an unheroic time. The impression he made on Edgar Salin in 1913, an impression the young man recorded on that day, was not at all unusual; there was a certain type of German to whom George was simply irresistible.

Stefan George died in voluntary Swiss exile in 1933, unwilling to lend his prestige to the triumphant Nazis whom he despised as ghastly caricatures of his elusive ideal. Friedrich Gundolf, his best-known disciple, the handsomest of his young men and the most productive, had died before him, in 1931, but most of the others survived him, some as Nazis, some as the victims of the Nazis, some in sullen silence, some in exile. Sorcerer's apprentices, they could not exorcise the spirits they had helped call up.

Like most of the elements making up the Weimar spirit, the George circle, too, antedated the Republic, and drew on sources both German and foreign. Born in 1868, George had turned away from a culture he despised, to Baudelaire, cursed poet cursing his time, to Mallarmé, experimenter, musician in words, and prophet, and to German out-

---

[1] Edgar Salin, *Um Stefan George: Erinnerung und Zeugnis* (2nd ed., 1954), 11–12. Salin insists that this portrait was not a later elaboration, but based on a letter written that day. *Ibid.*, 303.

siders – to Hölderlin, the passionate classicist, and to Nietzsche, the vehement advocate of a new pagan aristocracy. In his journal of poetry and polemics, the *Blätter für die Kunst,* founded in 1892, and in his carefully staged conversations with his young men, Stefan George developed his program and sought an audience for his delicately chiseled poetry. His task, as he saw it, was to perpetuate cultural values—the George circle expended much energy expounding Goethe and translating Shakespeare and Dante—and to renew the aristocratic sense of life. It was Nietzsche's task: to be the good European, presiding over a transvaluation of values. But unlike Nietzsche, George did not choose to be alone; it was the heart of his method to build a secret empire for the sake of the new Reich to come, to find strength and possible inspiration in warm friendships and among the choice spirits of the past.

It was an elitist program pushed to the very limits of elitism; the secret Germany was a club to which new members were elected, and for which they were trained, one by one. Many called, few were chosen; some, like Hofmannsthal, fitted into the circle briefly, then left. It was an exclusive, solemn little troop—survivors report gaiety, but the hundreds of photographs of the George circle show not a smile among them—dedicated to service of the master, who repaid his beloved followers with emotional verses of—to mere outsiders—embarrassing warmth. Yet for all his frenetic appeal to quality and to the choice nature of the individual specimen, for all his cultism, Stefan George himself was not a racist. Gundolf's wartime fervor left him cold. Walter Mehring's savage portrait of George, therefore, misses the mark: Mehring shows him playing the harp on the Olympus of Teutonic war poets, while his *"geliebten Siegfried-Lustknaben"*— those lovely boys who served the pleasures of older men—marched off to battle.[2] In fact, George feared and loathed the war precisely because it was killing off his young men. These German prophets— gravediggers of the Republic all, whether consciously or unconsciously —were often remarkably intelligent about the stupidity of their competitors: George about the patriots, and Oswald Spengler, who was

[2] Mehring, *Die verlorene Bibliothek* (1964 ed.), 151.

stupid about so much else, about George. "The fundamental weakness of George," he wrote in 1917, "(quite apart from the fact that the 'circle' has turned him into a sacred fool) is his lack of intelligence."[3]

However grievous this lack, the George circle was incredibly busy. It did translations, polished verses, published esoteric and polemical essays on literary criticism, cultivated meaningful eccentricities in dress and typography, and, perhaps most important, combed history for worthy subjects—for select spirits who, had they lived in Stefan George's time, would surely have belonged to Stefan George's circle. Gundolf celebrated Caesar, Goethe, and Shakespeare, Ernst Bertram discovered new meaning in Nietzsche, Max Kommerell exalted Goethe and Herder into leaders of culture. These biographers were performing rituals; they did not analyze, they proclaimed their subjects, treating them as founders, as judges, as supermen shrouded in myth, who, through their lives, shamed twentieth-century Germany, that new iron age. In 1930 Eckart Kehr noted and deplored a "Plutarch Renaissance," and cited Gundolf's frenetic biography of Caesar as a leading example of this "historical belles-lettrism." The popularity of Plutarch among the George circle, and indeed among a wider public, seemed to him symptomatic of disorientation; Plutarch had written of gods and heroes, of gigantic individuals, often inaccurately, and now modern Plutarchs, with the same contempt for precision, were offering a hungry public new giants to worship. Emil Ludwig, and other bestselling biographers of the Ullstein world, smoothly fitted into this pattern; Ludwig calmly announced that he preferred graceful, unreliable storytelling to the cold accuracy of the expert. The biographers in the George circle were often themselves experts, but they did not choose experts as their subjects; they chose whole men.[4]

The most notable biography produced in the George circle was Ernst Kantorowicz's book on the great thirteenth-century Hohen-

---

[3] Spengler to Hans Klöres, January 6, 1917. *Briefe, 1913–1936,* ed. Anton M. Koktanek (1963), 63.

[4] "Der neue Plutarch: Die 'historische Belletristik,' die Universität und die Demokratie," *Die Gesellschaft,* VII, part 2 (1930), 180–188; the quotations from Ludwig are on 185, 187 (see *Der Primat der Innenpolitik,* 269–278).

staufen Emperor Frederick, *Kaiser Friedrich der II*. The text volume appeared in 1927; the second volume, which detailed the sources and analyzed technical problems, in 1931. The biography aroused immediate controversy and found a remarkably wide audience—an audience it fully deserved. It was, as Felix Gilbert has written, "a breath of fresh air in the muffiness of medieval history"; the "young people of all political shades (even Kehr!)" greeted it as "a work of opposition against the medieval establishment." The well-known medievalist Karl Hampe, who profoundly disagreed with Kantorowicz, was yet moved to concede him "exemplary mastery" of the material, patience with detail, and the kind of insight given only to the knowledgeable scholar.[5]

Kantorowicz, then, was no crude propagandist; he was, in fact, not a propagandist at all. But he poured into his biography all of his experience and all of his expectations. By origin a Jew, by vocation a Prussian officer, Kantorowicz had joined the *Freikorps* after the war and taken up arms against the left; to him, the Republic was the triumph of mediocrity, a leaderless age. He was an accomplished scholar, but as a member of the George circle he professed contempt for the cold positivism of modern scientific scholarship, and sought historical understanding of great men, and historic moments, not through analysis but through vivid intuitions. Emperor Frederick—a superman who had defied all authority, voraciously tasted all of life, and become a legend in his own time—was an obvious subject for such a historian.

In one respect, as even hostile reviewers conceded, Kantorowicz's *Weltanschauung* served him well: rationalist historians had slighted the myths surrounding Frederick II, and Kantorowicz was ideally equipped to recognize them, and to understand their role in thirteenth-century politics. But he was not content with detecting and penetrating myths. In a day when there were no more emperors, Kantorowicz said in his curt prefatory note, a "secret Germany" yearned for "its emperors and heroes." And the body of his book offered that secret

[5] "Das neueste Lebensbild Kaiser Friedrichs II.," *Historische Zeitschrift,* CXXXXVI (1932), 441–475.

Germany much palatable nourishment: Kantorowicz's Frederick II is the father of the Renaissance, a ruler rivaling the stature of Alexander the Great. He revived the classics, attained dizzying heights of the human spirit, embodied primeval forces, was strong, alert, vigorous despite all his intellect, and in his combination of qualities superior even to Caesar and Napoleon, German to his core. He was dead and yet alive, waiting to redeem a German people as yet incapable of grasping his true semidivine greatness. Kantorowicz did more than report medieval legends; his language, in its hyperbole, its shimmering vagueness, its ecstatic approval, conveys a highly tendentious—I am tempted to say erotic—engagement with its subject, and implies belief in these legends as deep truths, relevant to a suffering Germany. Kantorowicz put much reliable history into his biography, but that made his myth all the more persuasive to the educated, all the more dangerous to the Republic. It was history as political poetry.

It is impossible to measure the following for such books, or of the George *Kreis* as a whole; George's disciples exaggerated their influence. But there were many who found it seductive; it was a fresh wind in the stuffy atmosphere of the universities, and an exciting alternative to the routine cant of the politicians. Theodor Heuss later recalled that "the great works of historical prose that came out of the Stefan George circle became very important to me." Heuss never felt any real enthusiasm for the master himself; all the esoteric mumbo-jumbo (*Drum und Dran*) of the circle, all the "self-conscious verbal constructions" of its poetry, disturbed him. But, he confessed, the "works of Friedrich Gundolf, from his magnificent Shakespeare book on," and the historical writings of Wolters, Kommerell, and the others meant a great deal to him: "What was decisive in my estimate was not what one could learn from George, though that was not negligible, but the high standards his circle imposed."[6] If even Heuss was taken into camp—and the hysterical bombast of these biographies is nearly intolerable today—the seductiveness of the George style must have been nothing less than overwhelming.

[6] Heuss, *Erinnerungen,* 354.

II

While his competition with the dead was formidable, among Stefan George's living competitors there was only one poet, Rainer Maria Rilke, who could rival him in influence. Unlike George, Rilke was unencumbered by a formal coterie; one could join the Rilke cult by simply reading him. And everyone read him. Young soldiers went to their death with his verses on their lips; all the youth movements, which played such a prominent role in German life before and during Weimar, made him into one of their favorite poets; they recited him by the campfire and printed him in their magazines. He greatly impressed his fellow artists; Thomas Mann recognized him, "of course," as a "lyrical phenomenon of the highest rank."[7] In his last years, and after his death in 1926, Rilke became the dubious beneficiary of German literary criticism, a kind of writing that (with rare and honorable exceptions) was less a criticism than a celebration, intuitive in method and overblown in rhetoric, a making and staking of grandiose claims, a kind of writing mired in sensibility and pseudo-philosophical mystery-making. Rilke, as Walter Muschg has caustically but justly said, became "the idol of a generation without men." The publication of his letters, "most of them written, with violet ink, to ladies," called forth a "herd of male and female enthusiasts—*Schwärmer und Schwärmerinnen,*" until at last "the Rilke-fever grew into a world-wide fanatical sect." But however foreigners might respond, it was worse at home. Only a handful of radicals ridiculed his preciosity, and lampooned his sentimentalizing of the poor—"Have you ever shivered in an attic?" Kurt Tucholsky asked[8]—while nearly everyone else deified him. Rilke's famous late poems, the *Sonnets to Orpheus* and the *Duino Elegies,* poured out in February 1922 in a creative fit, are difficult, "in parts barely comprehensible in the original," and this made them into "the ideal support for amateurish,

---

[7] Mann to B. Fucik, April 15, 1932. *Briefe, 1889–1936,* 316.
[8] "Auf dem Nachttisch," March 25, 1930. *Gesammelte Werke,* ed. Mary Gerold-Tucholsky and Fritz J. Raddatz, 3 vols. (2nd ed., 1967), III, 392.

pseudo-religious needs which appropriated Rilke and distorted him into a kind of lyrical Rasputin behind whom the poet disappeared." Inevitably, Rilke was raised into the heavens as a seer and a saint, "a bringer of a message and founder of a religion," a unique figure who had conquered and discredited the intellectuality that had dominated the West for a millennium. This, concludes Muschg, in a happy if untranslatable phrase, was "youth-movement mysticism—*Wandervogelmystik*."[9]

These are savage judgments, but they must not be dismissed as the hindsight of a disenchanted observer seeking for causes of the Nazi triumph over Germany. Contemporary sources offer striking confirmation. On February 20, 1927—and I shall confine myself to this representative instance—Stefan Zweig gave a speech in Rilke's memory, "Farewell to Rilke," in Munich. He spoke at length, and with a flowery hyperbole surprising even for a memorial meeting. But then he was mourning a poet—a *Dichter*. Rilke, Zweig told his listeners, was a true *Dichter*: "This word, this primeval-sacred, this bronze-weighty and highly immodest word, which our questionable age confounds all too easily with the lesser and uncertain notion of the author —*Schriftsteller*—the mere writer, fully applies to him. He, Rainer Maria Rilke, he was a poet, once again and anew, in that pure and perfect sense in which Hölderlin invokes him, the 'divinely reared, himself inactive and slight, but looked upon by the ether, and pious.'" He was a poet full-time: "We know of no hour in which he was not a *Dichter*"; every letter he wrote, every gesture he made, his smile and his handwriting, testify to his mission. And it was this "inviolable certainty of his mission that made us his, from our youth on, and reverential to him." How did he begin to deserve this "illustrious name" of *Dichter*? Let no one touch upon this mystery. Perhaps it was "the last reverberation of ancient-aristocratic blood, tired after many generations, unrolling itself once more in this, the last of them" —though, in fact, Rilke's claims to old, noble ancestry were wholly imaginary and pure snobbery. But whatever the truth, Zweig mused,

---

[9] Walter Muschg, *Die Zerstörung der deutschen Literatur* (3rd ed., 1958), 215–216.

no one can fully explain the origins of a poet, "that incomprehensible stranger among men, in whom the thousand-year-old language rises once again, so new, as though it had not been chattered to death by millions of lips and ground down in millions of letters, until the day He comes, the One, who looks upon all things past and emerging with his surprised, his colorfully-enveloping, his dawnlike look." No, Zweig went on, "mundane causalities can never explain how, in the midst of thousands of dull beings only one becomes a poet," but Rilke did become that poet, and there was no one in the audience who did not carry in his unconscious some stanza, or a word, from his work, some "breath of his music." It had been nothing less than "marvelous" for the younger generation to see the growth of this poet, rising from timid beginnings to the height of lyrical poetry, then rising above that, twice again, to start anew, ever more heroically, seeking God in ever-widening circles. Only now, after his death, had the significance of his last difficult poems been revealed: "In earlier days, ourselves surprised, we could hardly grasp the meaning contained in those last poems"—but the very difficulty that would later strike Muschg as a crippling defect was, to Stefan Zweig, a divine gift. Rilke, he said, no longer addressed mere living men in the *Duino Elegies;* he was holding converse "with the other, with the beyond of things and feelings."[10] These effusions are instructive because they are not simply a mechanical eulogy; they stood, in all their calculated imprecision, all their unashamed hyperbole, for a style of thinking that many Germans recognized, enjoyed, and, in fact, found indispensable in talk about poets and poetry.

To Rilke's credit it must be said that he was the most reluctant of prophets, and when he issued warnings to his correspondents, he was not adopting the seductive pose that seeks to attract while appearing to repel; he was being faithful to his own convictions. He was besieged by letters from strangers. "What letters!" he wrote to a friend in the summer of 1921. "There are so many people who expect from me—I don't know quite what—help, advice; from me, who finds

---

[10] "Abschied von Rilke," in *Begegnungen mit Menschen, Büchern, Städten* (1937; 1956 ed.), 59–73, *passim.*

himself so perplexed before the pressing urgencies of life! And even though I know they deceive themselves, that they are mistaken—still I feel (and I don't think it's out of vanity!) tempted to communicate some of my experiences to them—some fruits of my long solitude." There are lonely girls and young women, and "then all those young working people, most of them revolutionaries, who have come out the state prisons disoriented, and blunder into 'literature' by composing intoxicated and evil poems. What shall I say to them? How can I lift up their desperate hearts . . . ?"[11] For all his self-conscious isolation, all his careful cultivation of European aristocrats, Rilke had a social conscience and a sense of his own limits. And he was thoroughly aware of the differences between life and poetry. He saw (as he put it in a letter of 1922) great danger in the confusions of his age, which "had so often understood the call of art as a call *to* art"; thus the artistic activity of the time, far from positively affecting life, had called more and more of the young away from life.[12] Clearly Rilke was a better man than his disciples, who wanted little more than to worship him and glean from his poems a way of life and a religion, and the truth about him was on the whole more attractive than the legends that formed around him so rapidly. Rilke could have applied to himself what he said about Rodin, whom he had known intimately and for whom he had worked for some time: "Fame, after all, is no more than the quintessence of all the misunderstandings collecting round a new name."[13]

The truth about Rilke was that he was a poet of remarkable powers —critics of all persuasions agree that he extended the range of the German language and elicited new melodies from it, that he was a master of metaphor and striking imagery. And, especially in his early years, he saw his poetry as the fruit of hard work and the tireless

---

[11] Rilke "*à une amie*," in French (summer 1921?). *Briefe*, 2 vols. (1950), II, 245. I owe this reference to F. W. van Heerikhuizen, *Rainer Maria Rilke: His Life and Work* (1946; tr. Fernand G. Renier and Anne Cliff, 1951), 347.

[12] Rilke to Rudolf Bodländer, March 13, 1922. *Briefe*, II, 333. (See Heerikhuizen, *Rilke*, 349–350.)

[13] Quoted in Hans Egon Holthusen, *Rainer Maria Rilke: A Study of His Later Poetry* (tr. J. P. Stern, 1952), 8.

gathering of experience. "Verses," he wrote in his novel *The Note-book of Malte Laurids Brigge,* "are not, as people think, feelings (those one has early enough)—they are experiences. For the sake of a verse one must see many cities, men, and things, one must know the animals, feel how birds fly, and know the gesture with which the little flowers open in the morning."[14] One must know much more: Rilke's assignment to the poet as consumer of experience is very demanding; it includes the knowledge of children and of the dying, of nights of love and of listening to the sea. True, in his later years Rilke was more ready than before to credit inspiration; he had hallucinations and heard voices, but even the fantastic outpouring of poetry in February 1922 was the compressed expression of lines and images he had been carrying in his head, and noted in his notebooks, for as long as ten years. The late Rilke was still working hard, but his work had become largely unconscious.

And the truth about Rilke, finally, was that he had no system. Like many writers who write a great deal and without systematic intentions, he contradicted himself. Like most poets, who write after all to make poetry and not philosophy, he embodied attitudes but belonged to no school; his magnificent gift for language paved the way to music rather than to logic. One could read Rilke just for pleasure, bathing in his images; one could read Rilke as the poet of alienation, or as the celebrant of a pagan universe in which human feelings and inanimate things, love and suffering, life and death, compose themselves into a harmonious whole. This last—the harmonizing of life and death—was particularly prominent in his mind. "In my *Elegies,*" Rilke wrote in an important letter just a year before his own death, "affirmation of life and affirmation of death are shown to be one."[15] Indeed, he had made this point, powerfully, in the first of his elegies: Angels, it is said, often do not know whether they walk among the living or the dead.

[14] Interestingly enough, Stefan Zweig quotes these lines in his speech ("Abschied von Rilke," 62–63), without drawing any serious conclusions from them.

[15] Rilke to Witold Hulewicz, November 13, 1925. *Briefe,* II, 480. (See Hans Egon Holthusen, *Rainer Maria Rilke in Selbstzeugnissen und Bilddokumenten* [1958], 152.)

The eternal stream carries all ages along with it, through both realms, drowning out both:

> Engel (sagt man) wüssten oft nicht, ob sie unter
> Lebenden gehn oder Toten. Die ewige Strömung
> reisst durch beide Bereiche alle Alter
> immer mit sich und übertönt sie in beiden.[16]

Yet even this preoccupation was a purely personal search rather than legislation for others. Rilke's private pantheism could be enjoyed; it did not need to be imitated. In his poems, one thing became something else with such ease and yet, with his discipline and precision, such lucidity—cities hold out their arms to the traveler, a man becomes not like but actually is the sea—that everything appears animated with the same breath and joins in a single organic unity. Rilke had what Freud said he did not have: the oceanic feeling. This equipped him to write lyrics, and letters, of great beauty, to paint verbal pictures and compose melodious lines which, as Stefan Zweig rightly said, remained unforgettable. That should have been enough, but to his enthusiasts, swamped in spirituality, it was not enough.

III

For all their commitment to modernity—and Rilke in particular, once he had found his own voice, joined the company of other great moderns like Valéry and T. S. Eliot—Stefan George and Rainer Maria Rilke were haunted by their German past. They dutifully, and sometimes sincerely, admired the prescribed classics of the Goethe epoch, but their real discovery was Hölderlin, nearly forgotten until they rescued him from oblivion. Hölderlin appeared in histories of German literature as the acquaintance of Goethe and Schiller, an interesting lyrical poet who had written a strange epistolary novel, *Hyperion,* and the fragment of a tragedy, *The Death of Empedocles,* and who belonged, rather vaguely, among the Graecophiles who had

[16] "First Elegy," *Sämtliche Werke,* 6 vols. (1955–1966), I, 688.

flourished in Germany in the classical age. It was also known that he had done most of his poetic work before or around 1800, and had then broken down and vegetated on in pathetic madness until 1843. He had few readers, though distinguished ones; but neither Dilthey nor Nietzsche could bring him back into the consciousness of the German public—that was to be done by his ecstatic worshipers in the twentieth century.

Perhaps the most intrepid pioneer of the Hölderlin Renaissance was Norbert von Hellingrath, a faithful member of the Stefan George circle, who rediscovered some of Hölderlin's late works, reinterpreted Hölderlin's difficult hymns, and started a critical edition of Hölderlin's writings. Stefan George himself, as Edgar Salin puts it in the approved manner, was too mature to receive Hölderlin as a "shaping and forming and coloring power," but he did "experience the profound affinity" of the newly discovered poems: "It was as if a curtain had been drawn from the holy of holies and the still unutterable offered itself to view."[17] In other words, George and his followers read Hölderlin with enthusiasm, reprinted him in their collections, and made propaganda in his behalf.

Rilke, as it happened, supported the George *Kreis* in this work. He had come to Hölderlin in large measure through Hellingrath, whom he had met in 1910, and whose work he followed closely; by 1914 he could apostrophize the magnificent Hölderlin—*"du Herrlicher"*—in some exalted verses, and thus spread the good news to a wider public. The public was ready during, and even more after, the war. In the Weimar period, literati like Stefan Zweig further popularized him in biographical-critical essays, while the scholars did their part with their dissertations. For his readers in the youth movements, Hölderlin was a preacher of integration in a world of fragmentation; time and again they would repeat Hyperion's lament: "It is a hard saying, and yet I say it because it is the truth: I can conceive of no people more dismembered than the Germans. You see workmen but no human beings, thinkers but no human beings, priests

[17] Edgar Salin, *Hölderlin im George-Kreis* (1950), 13.

but no human beings, masters and servants, youths and staid people, but no human beings."[18] Such sentiments acquired peculiar poignancy in the 1920s, when Germany was, if not literally dismembered by the Peace of Versailles, certainly separated from some German-speaking territories. Besides, the story of Hyperion, a modern Greek who participates in an eighteenth-century rebellion against Turkish rule, appealed to those Germans deeply resentful of the "foreign oppression" under which, they thought, their country labored during the Weimar period. Other readers found Hölderlin deeply satisfying in other ways; the George enthusiasts, joined by the philosopher Heidegger, appreciated Hölderlin's exalted view of the poet's mission, his call for a new god, and, by implication, a new Germany. And the George circle liked nothing better than Hölderlin's discovery of the kinship between classical Greece and modern Germany, their fateful link; as one of them wrote, they gloried in "Hölderlin's overbold proclamation, incomprehensible to a whole century, of the essential Greek-German—*Griechendeutschen*."[19] But Hölderlin was no one's private property; he was, as Felix Gilbert remembers, "the one German literary figure whom all German intellectuals" admired, "from the right" all the way "to the extreme left"; and what they especially admired was his "appeal for a new wholeness of life."

Here, indeed, was the secret of Hölderlin's appeal to a beset and bewildered twentieth-century Germany: Hölderlin had been one of the first to state rather darkly what was to become a poetic, philosophical, sociological, and political commonplace—that the modern world was fragmenting man, breaking him apart, estranging him from his society and his real inner nature. The hero of Hölderlin's *Empedocles* is, in his author's explicit words, "a mortal enemy of all one-sided existence," inclined "by his temperament and his philosophy" to a "hatred of civilization—*Kulturhass*," miserable and suffering even amid pleasant circumstances precisely because they

---

[18] Walter Z. Laqueur, *Young Germany: A History of the German Youth Movement* (1962), 5.

[19] Berthold Vallentin, *Winckelmann* (1931), in *Der George-Kreis*, ed. Georg Peter Landmann (1965), 370.

are particular, not universal.[20] When he leaps into Aetna, he chooses his "free death" quite explicitly, as a privilege open only to beings like himself, and as a testimony to the wholeness that is no longer possible. For Empedocles, as for his author, suicide is a brooding preoccupation, almost, one might say, a way of life.

This kind of feeling about the world, in which, as with Rilke later, life and death are intertwined and almost indistinguishable, had an enormous appeal to the poetic souls of Weimar. Hölderlin's madness —he lived longer in the night of madness than in the short daylight of sanity—was, to his most devoted twentieth-century readers, another form of death, and not some mere mental breakdown but a commentary on civilization and a confirmation of his "philosophy." This alone would have made the twentieth-century revival of Hölderlin significant, but beyond this, it was part of a widespread passion for such disinterments. The Hölderlin revival was accompanied by the revival, among others, of Kleist and Büchner. The late Wilhelminian Empire, it seems, specialized in such rediscoveries, as though the cultural ground of its own day were treacherous, not a place on which to stand or build. And in this, too, Weimar culture was a continuation and confirmation of a movement that had begun before, following the rediscoveries of the 1900s to their logical or emotional conclusion.

Kleist was hardly a forgotten man; his stories found their readers in the nineteenth century, and his plays a few, though not many, producers. Nietzsche coupled Kleist with Hölderin as a victim of pretentious cultivation—that cursed German *Bildung*—as practically all later writers would couple Kleist with Hölderlin as eminently deserving, and at last slowly receiving, his due. It was not until after Nietzsche ceased writing, until the turn of the century, that scholars began to gather Kleist's writings into dependable critical editions, study Kleist's life through all the surviving documents, and debate Kleist's meaning for his time and, more important, their own. As the dramatist and critic Hermann Bahr, a lifelong champion of Kleist,

[20] The so-called "Frankfurter Plan" of *Der Tod des Empedokles,* in Friedrich Hölderlin, *Werke,* ed. Fritz Usinger (n.d.), 341.

put it in 1927: "During my childhood the memory of Kleist had been almost extinguished; in school we barely heard his name: it was not part of *'Bildung'* to know him. His time came only after 1870. Scherer and his pupils remembered him. Otto Brahm wrote about him and did not forget him after he took over the management of the *Deutsches Theater*. But despite all this, Kleist did not yet become popular. Only during the world war, indeed only after the war, did the nation begin to recollect him, about the same time that there was the first glimmer of a Goethe-dawn. To the new youth which had experienced the war, Goethe was too cold, too stiff; for them, he did not have enough chaos in him. This youth felt itself gravely troubled by an experience it could not grasp, and, demanding clarification of an unjust misery, it found consolation in Kleist, who, after all, continually presses for clarification of his bewildering fate. Indeed, more than that: in his works Kleist had given shape and expression to a human type—the Prussian—of which the nation became aware only through him and in him. He survives not merely as a poet, but his poetry walks in our midst, incarnate."[21]

This is extravagant but not far from the truth. In the Weimar period Kleist scholarship became a passion, the cult a crusade. The great directors of the Weimar theater revived Kleist's plays, trying out a whole spectrum of interpretations ranging from the psychoanalytical to the patriotic, the sentimental to the Expressionist. Playwrights and critics piled up essays: Thomas Mann, Stefan Zweig, and others like them obsessively returned to Kleist, almost as if he haunted them. During the fourteen years of the Weimar Republic, at a rough count over thirty books were published on Kleist—more, it would seem, than had been published in the whole preceding century. In 1920 Kleist received the supreme accolade: a society founded to honor his memory. The *Kleist-Gesellschaft* could boast of a most distinguished and diversified group of officers and sponsors, including the greatest living classicist, Ulrich von Wilamovitz-Möllendorf, famous *Dichter*

---

[21] Answer to a circular questionnaire, "Wie stehst du zu Kleist?" *Oder-Zeitung*, October 18, 1927, in *Heinrich von Kleists Nachruhm*, ed. Helmut Sembdner (1967), 440-441.

like Gerhart Hauptmann and Hugo von Hofmannsthal and younger radical playwrights like Walter Hasenclever, the philosopher Ernst Cassirer, and the best-known, highly popular Impressionist painter, Max Liebermann. A group so varied needed to agree only on its worship of Kleist, and on its conviction that "To stand by Kleist is to be German!"[22]

The only question that remained was just what it meant to stand by Kleist—which Kleist? Some readers found in Kleist the tormented Christian, others the aristocrat out of his time, still others a rebel; Thomas Mann, in contrast to all these readers, enjoyed the delicious humor of Kleist's neoclassical comedy *Amphitryon*.[23] The Nazis claimed Kleist as the pure strong German, the George circle as the poet of the lonely elite, the Communists as an early revolutionary, while his descendant Hans Jürgen von Kleist protested against all such distortions and insisted on his ancestor's right to be read, quite simply, as the "singer of the war of liberation."[24] Kleist's work was singularly plastic: everyone made of it what he needed. True, in 1925 Walter Muschg thought he detected signs of dawning understanding, but the understanding he describes was merely the old enthusiasm brought up to date. Muschg disdainfully dismissed the publications of the *Kleist-Gesellschaft* as "erudite poverty," but thought that there was real hope in "the artists among the scholars" and the "thoughtfully inclined among the poets"; both were at last replacing the "amateurish park-statue" with a worthier monument. "Kleist," he wrote, making the inescapable pairing, "by Hölderlin's side, seems to be on the way to becoming the idol of those Germans who passionately seek entrance to the deepest secret of their nation."[25]

This was meant to be reassuring; actually it was ominous. For the so-called better interpreters of Kleist only gave new respectability to the love affair with death that loomed so large over the German mind.

---

[22] *"Aufruf"* of the *Kleist-Gesellschaft*, February 1922, in *ibid.*, 410.

[23] Thomas Mann, "Kleists *Amphitryon*" (1926), now in Mann, *Essays of Three Decades* (tr. H. T. Lowe-Porter, 1947), 202–240.

[24] "Kleist und die Kleists," *Vossische Zeitung*, October 20, 1927, in *Kleists Nachruhm*, 434.

[25] Muschg in the *Neue Zürcher Zeitung*, September 13, 1925, in *ibid.*, 419.

Fritz Strich, presumably a sober literary historian, saw Kleist's tragedy, *The Prince of Homburg,* as a demonstration that only he is a hero who "possesses ripeness for death, readiness for death"; for its author, this tragedy was destiny, "converting lust for life into a blissful wish for death—*Lebenssucht in Todesseligkeit.*" And Kleist's suicide was, for Strich, an acting out in life what the tragedy had taught on the stage; his suicide was "his last creation."[26] In 1925—the very year that Muschg found ground for encouragement—Stefan Zweig portrayed Kleist as the poet fighting with his demon. "Kleist's life," he wrote, in full agreement with Strich, "is not life, but solely a hunt for the end, a gigantic hunt with its animal-like intoxication of blood and sensuality, of cruelty and horror." For Kleist, culmination was also conclusion; that masterful tragedy could have been written only by one consecrated to death: "His voluntary early death is his masterpiece quite as much as the *Prince Frederick of Homburg.*"[27] If this murkiness dominated the critics filled with the spirit of Weimar, the sentiments animating Kleist's right-wing readers can be imagined. Only three things were clear about the Kleist crusade: its intensity, its confusion, and its exaltation of irrationality—its blissful death wish.

In contrast, the Büchner revival was always a republican, or a left-wing affair; whatever ultimate philosophical meaning could be forced on Büchner's plays, his sympathy with the poor, detestation of authoritarianism, and tough-minded realism about society made it impossible for patriots and reactionaries to use him. True, Arnold Zweig, himself a consistent radical, added Büchner to that inevitable pair Kleist and Hölderlin, as one of the three "succumbing and victorious youths of German literature,"[28] but, at least in Weimar days, Büchner clearly belonged to democrats, socialists and Communists.

Unlike Kleist, Büchner had been almost wholly forgotten after his early death in 1837, at the age of twenty-three, a young revolutionary

[26] Fritz Strich, *Deutsche Klassik und Romantik* (1922), in *ibid.,* 416.

[27] Stefan Zweig, "Heinrich von Kleist," now in *Baumeister der Welt* (1951), 251, 300.

[28] Answer to circular questionnaire, "Wie stehst du zu Kleist?" *Oder-Zeitung,* October 18, 1927, in *Kleists Nachruhm,* 440.

in exile. A single play, *Danton's Death,* was alone among his works to be published in his lifetime; his other writings, the nearly complete play *Woyzeck,* the short novel *Lenz,* and the comedy *Leonce and Lena*—a remarkably large and splendidly realized body of work for one so young—came out later and aroused practically no interest at all. With one or two exceptions, no one read Büchner for decades; the first reliable edition had to wait until 1879, and it was not until the late 1880s that the young Gerhart Hauptmann discovered Büchner and shared his excitement with the public.

At first Büchner was neglected because he aroused no response; later he was suppressed because the response he might arouse was judged to be dangerous: in 1891 a Social Democratic newspaper in Berlin printed *Danton's Death,* and the editor spent four months in prison for the offense; the Berlin *Freie Volksbühne* announced the same play in 1890, but cautiously waited for twelve years before it dared to give a performance. The authorities had little use for a playwright whom the rebel Wedekind, to whom nothing was sacred, had taken up. But by 1900 the ban was broken; producers began to mount Büchner's plays, and between 1909 and 1923 there was room and demand for five editions of his collected works.[29]

Once again the Republic completed what the late Empire had begun. Carl Zuckmayer recalls that with the outbreak of the revolution, when the youth, filled with talent, excitement, and great need, looked for figures it could truly admire, Büchner became "the patron saint of this youth; a magnificent youth, rebellious, vital, and penetrated by the awareness of its public responsibility."[30] One version of a Büchner play, Alban Berg's opera *Wozzeck,* first performed in 1925, was doubly radical: it used Schönberg's twelve-tone system and *Sprechgesang* in combination with more conventional musical means, and it had as its hero—or antihero—one of Büchner's most moving characters, the poor ignorant soldier who is humiliated by his betters

[29] See Karl Viëtor, *Georg Büchner: Politik, Dichtung, Wissenschaft* (1949), 266.

[30] *Als Wär's ein Stück von mir* (1966), 272.

and betrayed by his girl, and who ends up committing murder and suicide. The fame of Berg's opera gave fame to Büchner's play. For their part, Expressionist playwrights like Ernst Toller and the young Bertolt Brecht of *Baal* filled their plays with reminiscences of the playwright they enormously admired; Brecht, said the powerful critic Alfred Kerr, is an epigone, a *"Büchneroid."*[31] Like Hölderlin and Kleist, like George and Rilke, but in his own manner, the *Dichter* Büchner was a living force in the world of Weimar.

IV

It is easy to show that the *Dichter* occupied an exalted position in Germany, but hard to diagnose what this meant. After all, the passion for poetry did not make all Germans into militarists or reactionaries; if, in August 1914, in a rapturous moment he soon regretted, Rilke could invoke the god of war and the suffering he would bring to a waiting world, there were other poets, almost as eloquent as Rilke, who damned the war and the warmakers with all the poetic power at their command. If right-wing nationalists had their poets, so did the Social Democrats. And if many saw the poet as a sublime prophet and lawgiver, there were others who saw him as the critic of society, the realist who told society how it looked to him, and the goad who might seek to improve it. What is more, the effect of poetry was neither universal nor uniform; what might arouse the adolescent to a frenzy of enthusiasm might move the adult to cool analysis or leave him in puzzlement or boredom. In Weimar as elsewhere, men compartmentalized their minds and lives, and tough-minded, thoroughly political intellectuals like Franz Neumann could quote Hölderlin without making him into their guide in the world of party struggles.

Stefan Zweig recalled the time of the First World War almost with

[31] Reviewing Brecht's "Im Dickicht der Städte," *Berliner Tageblatt*, October 30, 1924. In *Theater für die Republik, 1917–1933,* ed. Günther Rühle (1967), 567.

fondness as a time when "the word still had power," and the word he meant was the word of the poet, the sacred figure one could safely entrust with authority.[32] But things were not so simple. Men of the word tend to overestimate the power of the word. It is an old illusion, left over from neoclassical theory, that poetry and the drama have immediate and direct effects, persuading the audience to action. But for many, even in Weimar, poetry and the theatre were entertaining or civilizing forces, with no, or only indirect and subtle, effects on conviction and conduct. Whatever poets might fear—or desire— poetry was not simply propaganda. Besides, as I have suggested, the kind of poet the Germans seemed to love most lent himself to conflicting interpretations, and could be recited with approval by members of many parties. And finally, even if the poet's message was unequivocal, it is by no means certain that this message molded the reader; it was just as likely that the reader sought the message he wanted and might have in any event found elsewhere, on nonpoetic grounds. Were not the poets more mirror than cause?

It is a hard question to answer, but this much is evident: both before the Weimar Republic and during it, poetry exercised a peculiar power over the German imagination. Certainly the Germans were not alone in worshiping poets, as they were not alone in forming powerful coteries held together by bonds of conviction or homosexual love; the affairs of the Bloomsbury circle suggest that when it came to sexual eccentricities among influential young men, graduates from Oxbridge were far more active, and far more secretive, than the George circle. But the secretiveness of the English, their outward conventionality, was at least in part their salvation; precisely because they were private, they influenced the public less—at least in this area of their activity—than the ostentatious cultists in Germany.

Yet, as the memoirs, heavily laden with testimony, show over and over again, the men of Weimar were particularly susceptible to poetry. In Prague young Willy Haas, who was to become a leading film critic and literary editor in the Berlin of the twenties, greeted the appear-

[32] *Die Welt von Gestern: Erinnerungen eines Europäers* (1955 ed.), 222–223.

an⟨ ⟩ of the equally young Walter Hasenclever as nothing less than "Friedrich Schiller's fiery youths . . . reborn."[33] Martin Buber later confessed that when he first read Stefan George at eighteen, and then again at twenty-three, these were decisive discoveries for him, "two events unforgettable, perhaps incommunicable."[34] Stefan Zweig records that Hugo von Hofmannsthal's recitations left his listeners shaken and silent. It was an ineffable, utterly fascinating phenomenon: "What can happen to a young generation more intoxicating than this: to feel near, physically near, the born, the pure, the sublime poet, whom one had only imagined in the legendary form of Hölderlin and Keats and Leopardi, unattainable and already half dream and vision?"[35] The appearance of young Werfel and his Expressionist verses left a similar impression. And there were many others who found Goethe just as present, just as shaping an experience, as the recitations of some polished youth. "No contemporary *Dichter* or *Denker*," the journalist and biographer Gustav Mayer remembered, "not excepting Ibsen and Nietzsche, accompanied and guided my development more persistently than Goethe." Goaded by foreigners for dwelling on his Germanness—his *Deutschtum*—Mayer would reply by invoking the two Germanies: "I would tell them that it was not the spirit of Potsdam but the spirit of Weimar that made me a German."[36] Goethe or Hofmannsthal, Hölderlin or Rilke, it did not matter; they were all contemporaries in the German pantheon.

Taken, then, in the extended sense in which the Germans use the word *"Dichter,"* to embrace the writers of imaginative prose, Germany can be said to be the only country that could have taken seriously Shelley's famous sweeping dictum that "poets are the unacknowledged legislators of the world"—how seriously appears from Friedrich Meinecke's last book, *The German Catastrophe* (1946) where, amid the rubble left by World War II, in the midst of shame

---

[33] *Die literarische Welt: Erinnerungen* (1960 ed.), 60.
[34] Quoted by Haas, *ibid.*, 180.
[35] *Die Welt von Gestern*, 54–55.
[36] *Erinnerungen: Vom Journalisten zum Historiker der deutschen Arbeiterbewegung* (1949), 47–48.

for unprecedented crimes, the aged historian sketches a "little wishful picture": "In every German city and larger village," he writes, "we should like to see in the future a community of like-minded friends of culture which I should like best to call Goethe Communities." To these communities "would fall the task of conveying to the hearts of the listeners through sound the most vital evidences of the great German spirit, always offering the noblest music and poetry together." So many libraries have been burned that it is only in such groups that the young may have "their first access to the imperishable poems of Hölderlin, Mörike, C. F. Meyer, and Rilke at one of those regular music and poetry festal hours of the Goethe Communities which we desire as a permanent institution everywhere among us—perhaps weekly at a late Sunday afternoon hour, and if at all possible in a church. The religious basis of our poetry justifies, yes demands, its being made clear by a symbolic procedure of this kind." These readings should include selected, "right" prose, but "lyrical and thoughtful poetry" would definitely "form the kernel of such festal hours. Lyrics of the wonderful sort, reaching their peak in Goethe and Mörike where the soul becomes nature and nature the soul, and sensitive, thoughtful poetry like that of Goethe and Schiller."[37]

In the impressive literature of German self-accusation, I know of no passage more instructive and more pathetic than this. By blurring the boundaries between poetry and religion, Meinecke perpetuates that vague religiosity of the heart that had characterized so much German philosophizing since the end of the eighteenth century—since the fatal years when the poets and thinkers of the classical period thought it necessary to "overcome" the "shallow thinking" of the Enlightenment. Reading poetry in a church, at stated hours, is a notion symptomatic of an intellectual style that raises poetry to religious importance and degrades religion to poetic feeling, permitting devotees to feel cultured without being materialists, and pious without being saddled with particular Christian dogmas which, everyone knew, are mere superstitions. And what poetry? Goethe's and Schiller's above

[37] Friedrich Meinecke, *The German Catastrophe: Reflections and Recollections* (tr. Sidney B. Fay, 1950), 119–120.

all—both profoundly unpolitical writers, the first through avoiding the subject, the second through treating it as an adjunct to heroic action. Goethe's politics was apathy, Schiller's tyrannicide; neither was a mode calculated to prepare men for parliamentary compromises; both, in calling for something higher than politics, helped to pave the way for something lower—barbarism. To treat poetry as an instrument of salvation was to prescribe a dubious medicine, since it had been one of the instruments of Germany's perdition in the first place. A century and a half before Meinecke offered this despairing recipe, Madame de Staël had called Germany the land of poets and thinkers —*Dichter und Denker*. In the years between Madame de Staël and Professor Meinecke, it had become the land where poets were elevated above thinkers or, rather, where thinkers were converted into poets, much to the detriment of thinking. One of Martin Heidegger's recent interpreters unwittingly gives the game away: "There," in Freiburg, Heidegger "lives, with Hellingrath's edition of Hölderlin's works. This closeness to Hölderlin is no accident but an essential key to an understanding of Heidegger's own philosophy. For Hölderlin came from the same physical region, he faced the same spiritual problems, and he experienced more lucidly and bitterly the ultimate meaning of nothingness than any other person who could give expression to it in song. The parallel with Heidegger is close, indeed, if 'thought' is substituted for 'song'."[38] Actually, the process went in precisely the opposite direction: song was substituted for thought.

---

[38] Stefan Schimanski, "Forward," Martin Heidegger, *Existence and Being* (tr. Douglas Scott, R. F. C. Hull, and Alan Crick, 1949), 9.

IV / THE HUNGER FOR WHOLENESS:
Trials of Modernity

I

The poets did not speak for themselves alone. Their critique of politics and their call for wholeness were guaranteed a wide audience, in part because poets had high authority, but in part also because they confirmed, and beautifully expressed, ideas that had been powerful in Germany's past and continued to be powerful during the Weimar years. There was deep, widespread discontent with politics in the Republic. "We young students did not read the newspapers in those years," Hannah Arendt has recalled. "George Grosz's cartoons seemed to us not satires but realistic reportage: we knew those types; they were all around us. Should we mount the barricades for *that*?"

This rejection of politics was a new version of an old habit of mind. For over a century Germans had looked upon politics with a mixture of fascination and aversion. The enormous numbers of newspapers and the space they gave to politics—once the censor would let them—and the high rate of participation in elections strongly suggest that Germans took to politics with a passion; as soon as they could be political, they were political. Much of this restless expenditure of energy might be self-important busy work—Germans themselves liked to satirize their incurable inclination to form clubs—or the public acting out of private passions, but it was at least what is normally called political activity: political talk, canvassing, voting.

Foolish politics is still politics. But side by side with this stream of thought there ran another channel, crowded with traffic and dug deep by careful dredging—the aversion to politics, not to this or that policy, this or that party, but to politics as such.

The pursuit of politics is a habit, like all habits strengthened by practice and atrophied by disuse. Germans had little practice in politics. The authoritarian states of the eighteenth and nineteenth centuries, large or small, had lived largely under the fiat of their rulers; there were few newspapers, and the newspapers there were had little political news and no political independence; only a handful of states could boast public debating societies known as parliaments. The imperial institutions that Bismarck built in 1871, by appearing to be better, made things worse; they were, as the veteran Social Democrat Wilhelm Liebknecht colorfully put it, "fig leaves for absolutism." The federalist structure of the new German Empire barely concealed the predominance of Prussia; the universal manhood suffrage for the federal parliament was badly compromised by Prussia's reactionary three-class electoral system, which kept all the power in the hands of the powerful; the Reichstag was only a shadow parliament, since the Chancellor was responsible not to it but to his Emperor. Deputies to the Reichstag were largely passive recipients of communications from those who really governed. The great Roman historian Theodor Mommsen, by his own confession a thoroughly political animal, warned against the damage that Bismarck was doing. "The decay of our representative system is certainly frightening," he wrote; the nation has contented itself with "pseudo-constitutional absolutism"; the Reichstag appears like "a building for momentary utility, to be thrown away after use"—in a word, "Bismarck has broken the spine of the nation."[1] Only a handful of others were as perceptive as Mommsen. And after Bismarck was dismissed in 1890, he left his institutions behind, to be managed by lesser men; what Meinecke would later call the "militarist-conservative combine"[2] kept

[1] These statements are quoted in Albert Wucher, *Theodor Mommsen: Geschichtsschreibung und Politik* (1956), 157, 180.
[2] See above, pp. 18–19.

control. Surely, the political mentality cannot train itself in an atmosphere of persistent frustration, or with the sense that it is all a sham. When the democratic Weimar Constitution opened the door to real politics, the Germans stood at the door, gaping, like peasants bidden to a palace, hardly knowing how to conduct themselves.

As realities usually do, these realities produced ideologies that explained and justified them. Leading German intellectuals, poets, and professors made an informal, largely tacit agreement with their state: they would abstain from criticism, even from politics in general, if the state in turn allowed them freedom to lead somewhat irregular private lives and hold rather unorthodox opinions in philosophy and religion. Schiller's celebrated call for *Gedankenfreiheit*—freedom of thought—was not so radical as it may appear. "*Gedankenfreiheit*," Hajo Holborn has written, "was directly felt as absolutely necessary, while social and political rights were regarded as perhaps desirable, but necessary only to a minor degree." In fact, "the whole intellectual movement of the German eighteenth century had as its almost exclusive aim the education of the individual, and to that it subordinated all political demands."[3] The world of the Germans—and here the poets helped, as models and spokesmen—came to be separated into the higher realm of self-perfection, *Bildung*, the achievement of *Kultur* for its own sake and free of politics, and the lower realm of human affairs, sordid with practical matters and compromises. The *Humanitätsideal* preached at the beginning of the nineteenth century by civilized men like Alexander von Humboldt was a noble ideal, and, in a sense, an education for humane politics both domestically and internationally; it served as a criticism of prevailing institutions and practices. But its dualism could easily be vulgarized, and was vulgarized, into mere sloganeering which elevated apathy into a superior form of existence and invidiously compared the traders' mentality of British and French politicians with the spirituality of the educated German. In fact, the separation from, and exaltation over, "Western" values was a prominent part of this German ideology.

[3] "Der deutsche Idealismus in sozialgeschichtlicher Beleuchtung," *Historische Zeitschrift*, CLXXIV, 2 (October 1952), 365.

Nor was this *"Vulgäridealismus"*—this vulgar idealism[4]—politically neutral; in valuing obedience and authority above debate and partisan activity, it was self-righteous, conservative, often reactionary, a valuable prop of the established order.

During the First World War, the unpolitical German found an eloquent spokesman, and fought a memorable battle, which was to reverberate through the short life of the Weimar Republic. In 1918 Thomas Mann proclaimed, both in the title and the six hundred pages of his *Betrachtungen eines Unpolitischen,* that he was an unpolitical man, and proud of it. The volume—it is really an overgrown polemical pamphlet—was a salvo in a family quarrel conducted in the open. Early in the war, still caught up in his conviction of Germany's cultural mission, Thomas Mann had written an essay reminding the Germans of a historic hero, Frederick the Great of Prussia, who, with all his faults, incarnated Germany itself; the great coalition that had formed itself against Prussia in 1756, after Frederick had invaded Saxony in the name of self-defense, foreshadowed the great coalition that had formed itself against Germany in 1914, after the Germans had invaded Belgium for the same reason. "Today, Germany is Frederick the Great"; it is "his soul that has reawakened in us."[5] The reply to this aggressive defense of German *Kultur* and German conduct came from Thomas Mann's brother Heinrich, in an essay ostensibly devoted to Zola but actually—as the glancing hits at his brother and at German policy made plain—an uncompromising condemnation of the very ideal that Thomas Mann cherished and hoped to sustain. It is Zola, Heinrich Mann argued, Zola, the republican, the democrat, the pamphleteer against injustice and exploitation, the ruthless truth-teller, the idealist, the Utopian, in a word, the enlightened civilian, who is the truly admirable model. This exchange took place in 1915; Thomas Mann's *Betrachtungen eines Unpolitischen,* begun then and published three years later, was, at least for a

---

[4] I have borrowed this happy phrase, a deliberate parody, of course, of favorite German expletives like "vulgar Marxism," and "vulgar liberalism," from Fritz Stern; see "The Political Consequences of the Unpolitical German," *History,* No. 3 (1960), 122.

[5] Kurt Sontheimer, *Thomas Mann und die Deutschen* (1961), 22.

time, the last word. Heinrich Mann appears, not by name, but by an untranslatable epithet, as the *Zivilisationsliterat*—the cultivated but shallow littérateur who is devoted to the cursed values of a rationalist, bourgeois, materialistic, superficial, optimistic civilization, who is blind to the abysses of the human soul, the mysteries of *Kultur*, the treacherous seductions of the theory of progress, the pitfalls of democracy, and who insists—and this is worst of all—on corrupting with politics the spheres of culture and the spirit. "I hate politics and the belief in politics, because it makes men arrogant, doctrinaire, obstinate, and inhuman."[6] When in the 1920s Thomas Mann underwent his conversion to the Republic and to democracy, he changed his mind about politics as well. "The political and the social," he now recognized, "are part of the humane sphere."[7] By then it was a little late, and not particularly impressive; there were many who interpreted Mann's change of front as treason or sheer irresponsibility, maliciously quoted his earlier in refutation of his later pronouncements, and refused to follow him.

Yet if Weimar needed anything, it needed rational politics. With the advent of the Republic, the possibility of political action, like the need for it, increased, suddenly and spectacularly. But the possibility was not realized, the need not filled. Not all the trouble lay with the unpolitical; many who had been unpolitical adopted politics of a kind that makes one long for a little apathy. Some mistook Expressionist declamation for a reform program; others chose murder as their favorite form of electioneering. At times the left seemed no less remote from the reality of reasonable conduct: in 1932 the men around the *Weltbühne* actually proposed Heinrich Mann for President of Germany, a proposal that Mann declined in favor of Hindenburg— against Hitler.[8] At the same time, as the memoirs—the literature of hindsight—make unmistakably clear, the unpolitical strain remained

[6] *Ibid.*, 39.
[7] *Ibid.*, 95.
[8] I agree with George L. Mosse, who writes: "When analyzing the *Weltbühne* people and Ossietzky it struck me forcibly how far removed they were from reality (trying to put up Heinrich Mann for the Presidency, for example)."

alive. Many simply could not bother to get involved. "I don't remember," writes the articulate philosopher Ludwig Marcuse in his autobiography, "if I voted in those years—and certainly not for whom."[9]

Doubtless this attitude, so widespread and so fatalistic, induced a certain distortion in perception; what was considered, in advance, to be not worth the trouble appeared to be not worth the trouble. Still, it must be said that the rejection of politics typified by Hannah Arendt and Ludwig Marcuse was more than an old attitude brought up to date; it had a good piece of reality in it. There was some reason to think the political life of the Republic a spectacle, remote and slightly ludicrous. Parliamentary debates, with their legalism and their occasional vehemence, had a curious air of unreality about them: party hacks quibbled, orated, and insulted one another while millions were hungry. Politics seemed a game to which all must contribute but which only politicians could win. Cabinet crisis followed cabinet crisis; in the less than fifteen years of Weimar, there were seventeen governments. It is true that there was more continuity than this figure might indicate: the so-called Weimar coalition, made up of cooperating ministers from the Social Democratic Party, the Catholic Center Party, and the Democratic Party, dominated several of these cabinets; and some men reappeared in cabinet after cabinet regardless of its general makeup; Stresemann, who presided as Chancellor over two cabinets, from August to November 1923, then became Foreign Minister in seven more, until October 3, 1929, the day of his death. Indeed, the Catholic Center was well named: it acted for much of the Weimar period as a parliamentary center of gravity.

Yet the changes of cabinet, coupled with the rise of extremist parties like the Nazis, suggested that the coalitions were papering over deep cracks; they were coalitions without consensus. There were too many for whom the general will seemed obscure or lacking altogether. The phenomenon of the party press did little to mitigate the divisions in

[9] *Mein zwanzigstes Jahrhundert: Auf dem Weg zu einer Autobiographie* (1960), 82.

German society; millions of voters read only the newspapers of "their" party, thus hardening attitudes they already held. The Center Party, for one, could count on about three hundred newspapers throughout the country, nearly all of them of modest circulation, all of them provincial and parochial. None of them was official—the Center had no equivalent for the Nazis' *Völkischer Beobachter* or the Social Democrats' *Vorwärts*—and they were stubbornly independent in management, but they remained dependably partisan in their treatment of political news.

There were exceptions, of course: major metropolitan dailies anxious for large circulation, and that voice of reason emanating from the provinces, the *Frankfurter Zeitung*. The *Frankfurter Zeitung* was democratic, liberal, but free of parties; its tone was reasonable, its coverage wide, its politics intelligent and wholly independent. In its makeup and its stories, it refused to adopt fashionable sensationalism. Its reporting of parliamentary events was thorough, for it had an important bureau in Berlin; its commitment to the best in modern culture emerged in its championship of modern poets and playwrights, and in the civilized reportage of Siegfried Kracauer. In 1931 its chief editor, Heinrich Simon, spoke movingly of the "other Germany" for which his newspaper stood. Recalling the work of Leopold Sonnemann, the paper's founder, Simon reminded his audience: "It is good to remember that time in which the advocates of freedom, the advocates of a humane Germany, experienced hostility and persecution. It is good to remember that these persecutions did not cause them to surrender a single iota of their convictions. Where did this courage come from? From the belief in the other Germany which, through the centuries, again and again interrupted saber-rattling self-laceration, even when force sought to condemn it to silence. This newspaper has lived, to this day, on the belief in this other Germany, in the Germany of freedom and humanity.[10] Here was the outsider, the representative of the other Germany, the Weimar spirit at

[10] Excerpts from this speech, delivered on October 29, 1931, are quoted in "Ein Jahrhundert *Frankfurter Zeitung*, begründet von Leopold Sonnemann," special number of *Die Gegenwart*, XI (October 29, 1956), 39.

its best, speaking sadly and bravely, aware that he was an outsider still. The *Frankfurter Zeitung* sought to heal the fragmentation of party-ridden Germany with reason. But this, it turned out, was not the kind of wholeness most Germans were looking for. The Nazis had a sense of this; they had a party—the National Socialist German Workers' Party—but they preferred to call it a movement—a *Bewegung*. It sounded more organic.

II

The hunger for wholeness found its most poignant expression in the youth. After the war, German youth, restless, bewildered, often incurably estranged from the Republic, sought salvation in the poets, but it also found other, more prosaic if not less strenuous guides. The youth movement, which had had its modest beginnings at the turn of the century and flourished mightily through the twenties, collected among its ranks and preserved among its graduates many would-be thinkers hunting for an organic philosophy of life.

It would be impossible to draw an ideological profile of the *Wandervogel* and their many offshoots. The youth movements had no real philosophy. Many were anti-Semitic, some accepted Jews. Many tied their members together in strong if unacknowledged homoerotic friendships, some encouraged girls to join. Many expounded a pantheistic love of nature and mystical love of the fatherland, some were casual associations devoted to healthful walks. Many repudiated attempts to introduce politics; some, especially after 1918, allied themselves with Communist, Socialist, or Nazi groups. But all *Wandervogel* except the most casual attached an enormous importance to their movement, an importance dimly felt but fervently articulated; as solemn, rebellious bourgeois—and they were nearly all bourgeois—they saw their rambling, their singing, their huddling around the campfire, their visits to venerable ruins, as a haven from a Germany they could not respect or even understand, as an experiment in restoring primitive bonds that overwhelming events and insidious forces had loosened or destroyed—in a word, as a critique of the adult world.

The rhetoric of the leading spokesmen for the youth movements betrays this high idealism, unremitting ̄ search, and incurable confusion. Many of the youth leaders hailed an idealized, romanticized medieval Germany as a refuge from commercialism and fragmentation. Hans Breuer, who compiled the songbook of the youth movement—one of the biggest best-sellers of twentieth-century Germany—insisted in his prefaces that he had gathered his folk songs for "disinherited" youth, a youth "sensing in its incompleteness—*Halbheit*—the good and longing for a whole, harmonious humanity." What, he asks, "What is the old, classical folk song? It is the song of the whole man, complete unto himself—*in sich geschlossen*."[11] The youth, singing these songs, was a self-conscious rebel against his father; indeed, Hans Blüher, first historian of the *Wandervogel* and apologist for its adolescent eroticism, explicitly said that "the period that produced the *Wandervogel* is characterized by a struggle of youth against age." Alienated sons sought out other alienated sons and formed a great "confederation of friendship."[12] To judge by these writers, the *Wandervogel* sought warmth and comradeliness, an escape from the lies spawned by petty bourgeois culture, a clean way of life unmarked by the use of alcohol or tobacco and, above all, a common existence that could rise above self-interest and shabby party politics. Leaders and followers alike used a verbal shorthand that was sign, and token, of their emotional intimacy; certain words were talismans for them, invocations with passionate resonance and almost magical powers—words like "*Aufbruch*," a rather poetic term evoking revolution, and "*Gemeinschaft*"—community.

As the philosopher Paul Natorp, full of sympathy and concern, warned as early as 1920, these aspirations and usages were of doubtful value. The facile irrationalism of the *Wandervogel*, he said, their

[11] "Vorwort," to the 10th edition of *Der Zupfgeigenhansl* (1913), in *Grundschriften der deutschen Jugendbewegung*, ed. Werner Kindt (1963), 67, 66.
[12] *Geschichte des Wandervogels*, from vol. I (1912), in *Grundschriften*, 47.

From the collection of the author

WASSILY KANDINSKY: ABSTRACTION

LITHOGRAPH, *ca.* 1925

Kandinsky, the most influential among the abstract artists, worked in the Bauhaus from 1922 to its closing in 1933; there he did some of his most effective geometric abstractions—testimony to the modernity of the Weimar spirit.

ERICH MENDELSOHN: EINSTEIN TOWER, POTSDAM, 1919

One of Mendelsohn's best-known Expressionist buildings. When Albert Einstein was taken through this observatory, he said one word—the right one: "Organic."

WALTER GROPIUS: BAUHAUS BUILDING IN DESSAU, COMPLETED IN 1926

Perhaps the most celebrated structure built during the Weimar Republic, a striking contrast, with its clear angularity, to Mendelsohn's swooping curves.

MARCEL BREUER: FIRST TUBULAR CHAIR, 1925

A splendid design, characteristic of the Bauhaus, as influential as the Gropius building in which it was produced.

search for the soul and distrust of the mind, was bound to produce false ideals and lead to antisocial behavior: "You fear the dismemberment of your being in all the piecework of human wishing and knowing, and fail to notice that you cannot achieve wholeness if you reject such large and essential parts of that which has been allotted to all mankind. You seek the indivisibility of man's being, and yet assent to its being torn apart."[13]

Natorp's warning was wasted. The unbridled neoromanticism and emotional thinking of the prewar years had not been cured by the experience of the war and the peace that followed it—these events, on which youth leaders dwelled obsessively, only compounded the confusion. The result was a peculiarly undoctrinaire, unanalytical, in fact unpolitical socialism—it was "a self-evident proposition," one observer noted, for all people in the youth movement to be Socialists.[14] Young men and women, seeking purity and renewal, were Socialists by instinct; the *völkisch*, right-wing groups demanded the "reawakening of a genuine Germanness—*deutsches Volkstum*—in German lands," while the left-wing groups called for "the restoration of a *societas*, a communally constructed society."[15] Everywhere, amid endless splintering of groups and futile efforts at reunion, there was a certain fixation on the experience of youth itself; novels about schools and youth groups exemplified and strengthened this fixation. Except for the Freudians and a few others, psychologists and sociologists studied adolescents and neglected child psychology; the concentration of their work on the youth reflected a real need and real concern, but it was, in its own way, part of the fixation it sought to understand. Flight into the future through flight into the past, reformation through nostalgia—in the end, such thinking amounted to nothing more than the decision to make adolescence itself into an ideology.

[13] "Hoffnungen und Gefahren unserer Jugendbewegung," a lecture first given in 1913; the quotation is from the third edition of 1920, in *Grundschriften*, 145.

[14] Elisabeth Busse-Wilson, "Freideutsche Jugend 1920," in *Grundschriften*, 245.

[15] See Ernst Buske, "Jugend und Volk," in *Grundschriften*, 198.

III

The leaders of the youth movements did not need to generate their own ideas; if anything, Weimar enjoyed too many ideas, variegated, mutually (and sometimes internally) contradictory, unanalyzed and often unanalyzable. It was swamped with polemics designed to expose the inferiority of republican culture to the imaginary glories of the First and Second Empire, or the imagined glories of the Third Empire to come. And for those who confined their reading to book jackets, authors provided slogan-like titles. Werner Sombart's indictment of the commercial mentality confronted, in its winning title, *Händler und Helden*, traders (the West) with heroes (the Germans); it was a characteristic product of the war, but kept its public during the 1920s. Even more remarkable, Ferdinand Tönnies' classic in sociology, *Gemeinschaft und Gesellschaft*, first published as far back as 1887, made its fortune in the Weimar Republic, with its invidious contrast between the authentic, organic harmony of community and the materialistic fragmentation of business society. Hans Grimm's novel of 1926, *Volk ohne Raum*, which was a long-lived best-seller, expressed in its very title a prevailing sense of claustrophobia, an anxiety felt, and played upon by right-wing politicians, over "inadequate living space," and the "encirclement" of Germany by its hostile, vengeful neighbors. In 1931 the *völkische* author Hans Freyer called, ecstatically, for a revolt against liberal ideas in his *Revolution von Rechts,* thus offering another striking novelty, the idea of a revolution not from its usual point of departure, the left, but from the right. Perhaps most effective was the pairing offered in the title of a three-volume work by the anti-Semite Ludwig Klages, who had in early years belonged to the George circle: his *Der Geist als Widersacher der Seele* pitted mind against soul, and assailed the intellect in the name of irrationalism. These fabricators of titles thought themselves aristocrats, but they did not disdain, in fact enjoyed coining, popular clichés.

Books spawned movements, which generally paraded before the

public covered in deliberately incongruous labels—Conservative Revolution, Young Conservatism, National Bolshevism, Prussian Socialism—ostensibly responsible attempts to get away from traditional political terminology, actually testimony to a perverse pleasure in paradox and a deliberate, deadly assault on reason. It was strange: the pundits who proudly proclaimed that they had outgrown or—a favorite word—"overcome" the traditional labels of liberal politics, "left" and "right," generally ended up on the right. Meinecke saw it precisely in 1924: "The deep yearning for the inner unity and harmony of all laws of life and events in life remains a powerful force in the German spirit."[16]

The spokesmen for this yearning were as varied, and as incongruous, as the ideas they proclaimed: Martin Heidegger was a difficult, it would seem deliberately esoteric, philosopher who clothed the revolt against reason in a new language of his own; Hugo von Hofmannsthal was an exquisitely cultivated *Literat*, who sought to hold high the flag of civilization in a time of decay; Ernst Jünger translated his experiences of adventure and war service—that half-authentic, half-mythical *Kriegserlebnis*—into a nihilistic celebration of action and death; the industrialist, economist, and Utopian Walther Rathenau turned on the industry on which his fortune rested by constructing elaborate and ambitious indictments of machine civilization and forecasting a new life; Oswald Spengler impressed the impressionable with his display of erudition, his unhesitating prophecies, and his coarse arrogance.

Among these prophets, Heidegger was perhaps the most unlikely candidate to influence. But his influence was far-reaching, far wider than his philosophical seminar at the University of Marburg, far wider than might seem possible in light of his inordinately obscure book, *Sein und Zeit* of 1927, far wider than Heidegger himself, with his carefully cultivated solitude and unconcealed contempt for other philosophers, appeared to wish. Yet, as one of Heidegger's most perceptive critics, Paul Hühnerfeld, has said: "These books, whose meaning was barely decipherable when they appeared, were devoured.

[16] *Staatsräson,* 490.

And the young German soldiers in the Second World War who died somewhere in Russia or Africa with the writings of Hölderlin and Heidegger in their knapsacks can never be counted."[17] The key terms of Heidegger's philosophy were, after all, anything but remote; more than one critic has noted that words like "*Angst*," "care," "nothingness," "existence," "decision," and (perhaps most weighty) "death" were terms that the Expressionist poets and playwrights had made thoroughly familiar even to those who had never read a line of Kierkegaard. What Heidegger did was to give philosophical seriousness, professorial respectability, to the love affair with unreason and death that dominated so many Germans in this hard time. Thus Heidegger aroused in his readers obscure feelings of assent, of rightness; the technical meaning Heidegger gave his terms, and the abstract questions he was asking, disappeared before the resonances they awakened. Their general purport seemed plain enough: man is thrown into the world, lost and afraid; he must learn to face nothingness and death. Reason and intellect are hopelessly inadequate guides to the secret of being; had Heidegger not said that thinking is the mortal enemy of understanding? The situation in which men found themselves in the time of the Republic was what Heidegger called an "*Umsturzsituation*," a revolutionary situation in which men must act; whether construction or utter destruction followed mattered not at all.[18] And Heidegger's life—his isolation, his peasant-like appearance, his deliberate provincialism, his hatred of the city—seemed to confirm his philosophy, which was a disdainful rejection of modern urban rationalist civilization, an eruptive nihilism. Whatever the precise philosophical import of *Sein und Zeit* and of the writings that surrounded it, Heidegger's work amounted to a denigration of Weimar, that creature of reason, and an exaltation of movements like that of the Nazis, who thought with their blood, worshiped the charismatic leader, praised and practiced murder, and hoped to stamp out reason —forever—in the drunken embrace of that life which is death. By no means all who read Heidegger were Nazis, or became Nazis be-

---

[17] *In Sachen Heidegger* (1961), 14.
[18] See *ibid.*, 54–55.

cause they read him; Christian existentialists or philosophers concerned with the supreme question of Being found him interesting and sometimes important. But Heidegger gave no one reasons not to be a Nazi, and good reasons for being one. "It is not without *some* justification," Paul Tillich has cautiously said, that the names of Nietzsche and Heidegger "are connected with the antimoral movements of fascism or national socialism."[19] and of these two Nietzsche was certainly far more remote from modern barbarism, both in time and in thought, than Heidegger.

I am not offering this scanty paragraph as an adequate summary of Heidegger's philosophy; I am suggesting, rather, that this is what Heidegger's readers thought, by and large, they were reading in him —and not without justice. When the Nazis came to power, Heidegger displayed what many have since thought unfitting servility to his new masters—did he not omit from printings of *Sein und Zeit* appearing in the Nazi era his dedication to the philosopher Husserl, to whom he owed so much but who was, inconveniently enough, a Jew? But the notorious address of May 27, 1933, with which Heidegger inaugurated his rectorate at the University of Freiburg, was not simply servility; it was a logical outgrowth of his philosophy, with its appeal to the *Führer* and the *Volk,* the abuse of words like "self-determination," the attack on objective science, the fervent proclamation of the powers of blood and soil, the call for an end to academic freedom in the name of higher things. The essence of the German university, he said, "arrives at clarity, rank, and power only when, above all, and at all times, the leaders themselves are the led—led by the inexorability of that spiritual mandate which forces the destiny of the German people into the stamp of its history." The mandate consists of three kinds of service: "Labor service, military service, and knowledge service—they are equally necessary and of equal rank." The will of the students and the will of the *Volk* together, mutually, must be ready for the struggle. "All powers of will and thought, all the forces of the heart and all the capacities of the body, must be unfolded through struggle, elevated in struggle, and preserved as struggle."

[19] "The Transmoral Conscience," in *The Protestant Era,* 166.

No question: "We want our *Volk* to fulfill its historical mission. We want ourselves. For the young and youngest power of the *Volk*, which already grasps beyond us, has already decided that."[20] The words may be a little obscure—though they are, with their reminiscences of editorials in the *Völkische Beobachter* and speeches by Goebbels, rather less obscure than Heidegger's normal style—but the message is plain enough.

Nothing could seem more remote from this dark antirationalism than the troubled musings on the modern world which Hugo von Hofmannsthal offered to an audience at the University of Munich in 1927, yet they have more in common than might at first appear. Hofmannsthal's address bore a strange title: "Das Schrifttum als geistiger Raum der Nation—Literature as the Spiritual Space of the Nation." Not unexpectedly, it was a highly civilized performance; its diction was elegant and its cultural purpose unimpeachable. But it was also a mystification, elusive, strenuously vague: Hofmannsthal speaks of seekers and prophets, and discerns in the Germany of his day a "conservative revolution" of a "magnitude hitherto unknown in European history." But he does not identify the seekers and prophets, and specifies the aim of the conservative revolution only as "form, a new German reality, in which the whole nation can participate." This elusiveness was itself, though perhaps not intentionally, a political act, for if the Germany of 1927 needed anything, it needed clarity, concreteness, demystification.

Yet a careful reading of Hofmannsthal's address suggests, if not a program, at least a coherent attitude. Evidently, Hofmannsthal believed that Germany failed, but needed, to be a cultural organism in which spirit and life, literature and politics, the educated and the uneducated, might join in common possession of cultural goods, in a living tradition that all could enjoy. We are "connected to a community," Hofmannsthal argued, not by physical coexistence or intimacy, but by some "spiritual adherence." Indeed, only where there

---

[20] *Die Selbstbehauptung der deutschen Universität*, Freiburger Universitätsreden No. 11 (1933), *passim*.

is "believed wholeness of existence—*geglaubte Ganzheit des Daseins*" —*there* is reality. And now, in the 1920s, there are some seekers and prophets in Germany who are groping for this reality, and in two ways. They "seek, not freedom, but connection," and they have achieved the insight "that it is impossible to live without believed wholeness," that "life becomes livable only through valid connections," that "scattered worthless individuals" must become "the core of the nation"—that, in a word, "all partitions into which mind has polarized life, must be overcome in the mind, and transformed into spiritual unity."[21] Hofmannsthal was fortunate; he died in 1929, before he saw the consequences to which fatigue with freedom and the denigration of individuality would lead.

In contrast with Hofmannsthal's dim vistas, Spengler's *Preussentum und Sozialismus*, first published in 1920 and often reprinted, is clear at least in the target of its scorn. Spengler had leaped into immediate prominence with the first volume of his *Untergang des Abendlandes*, in 1918, and retained his position as a deep thinker with *Preussentum und Sozialismus*, the first of his political pamphlets. It is one long insult to the Weimar Republic—"The revolution of stupidity was followed by the revolution of vulgarity." But it is also more than that: *Preussentum und Sozialismus* appropriates the word "socialism" to special purposes. Spengler agrees with most prophets of his day: socialism is inevitable. But there are two types of socialism—English and Prussian—and we must learn to discriminate between them, and choose. To Spengler, Karl Marx, "the stepfather of socialism," was an English Socialist—the materialist imbued with unrealistic, "literary ideals"; the cosmopolitan liberal in action. The task, clearly, is "to liberate German socialism from Marx." With frightening shrewdness, Spengler recognized that the so-called Marxist Socialist Party of Germany really contained powerful anti-Marxist and true Prussian elements: "The Bebel party had something soldierly, which distinguished it from the socialism of all other countries: clanking step of

[21] The address is conveniently reprinted in a posthumous collection of Hofmannsthal's prose writings, *Die Berührung der Sphären* (1931), 422–442.

the workers' battalions, calm decisiveness, discipline, courage to die for something higher—*Jenseitiges*." Class struggle is nonsense, and the German Revolution, the product of theory, is nonsense, too. The German instinct, which, rooted in the blood, is truthful, sees things differently: "Power belongs to the whole. The individual serves it. The whole is sovereign. The king is only the first servant of his state (Frederick the Great). Everyone is given his place. There are commands and obedience. This, since the eighteenth century, has been authoritarian—*autoritativer*—socialism, in essence illiberal and antidemocratic—that is, if we think of English liberalism and French democracy." The true German must recognize the needs of the day and, yielding to them, transform the authoritarian socialism of the eighteenth into the authoritarian socialism of the twentieth century. "Together, Prussianism and socialism stand against the England within us, against the world view which has penetrated the whole existence of our people, paralyzed it, and robbed it of its soul." The one salvation is "Prussian socialism." Here are Hofmannthal's search for community and leadership in the language of the officers' barracks.

IV

Quite naturally, almost inevitably, the searchers for a meaningful life in a meaningless Republic turned to German history, to find comfort or models there. They found what they sought; German historians were ready to join them, and German history turned out to be singularly rich in oversized heroes and memorable scenes, both of them invaluable to mythmakers. One famous scene, from which nationalist and *völkische* elements derived much inspiration, had taken place in October 1817, three hundred years after Martin Luther had nailed his theses to the church door at Wittenberg. German students, wearing old-fashioned costumes, gathered at the Wartburg, a historic and romantic spot; they shouted "*Heil*," sang patriotic songs, said fervent prayers, and burned some books. They were members of the new *Burschenschaften*, radical, nationalistic, anti-Semitic, anti-French student associations with names drawn from the legendary past: Germania, Arminia, Teutonia. They were at the Wartburg to celebrate the liberation of their country—or, rather, countries—from the alien yoke, and in their celebration they linked the reformer Luther with the general Blücher as twin liberators of the German spirit and the German land, determined to draw strength from ancient myths for the political and moral tasks before them.

This spirit survived into the Weimar Republic, drawing on a widening repertory of heroes: on Bismarck, the man of blood and iron, the tough realist who had unified the German nation by the sheer force of his will; on Frederick II of Prussia, invariably called "the Great," who with a historic display of self-discipline had grown from an effete flute player into the *Alte Fritz*, tough, sly, hard-working, in a word magnificent, gaunt from a lifetime of exhausting labor as first servant of his state; on Martin Luther, defiantly forging a new faith and a new language, doing what he must do; on Wagnerian Teutons, who had inspired eighteenth-century French lawyers as they had inspired classical Roman historians with their purity, their valor, their political prowess. It was a heady and, to susceptible spirits, a poisonous amalgam. "The younger generation," wrote Ernst-Walter Techow, one of Rathenau's assassins, in 1933, "was striving for something new, hardly dreamed of. They smelled the morning air. They gathered in themselves an energy charged with the myth of the Prussian-German past, the pressure of the present and the expectation of an unknown future."[22]

The wholehearted commitment to Weimar required the repudiation of all such mythology. By its very existence, the Republic was a calculated affront to the heroes and clichés that every German child knew, many German politicians invoked, and, it turned out, most Germans cherished. In the battle of historical symbols the republicans were at a disadvantage from the start: compared with Bismarck and other charismatic leaders, at once superhuman and picturesque, the models available to Weimar were pallid and uninspiring: the Goethe

[22] *Gemeiner Mörder?! Das Rathenau-Attentat*, 20, quoted in James Joll, *Three Intellectuals in Politics* (1960), 128.

of modern Weimar was a benign, ineffectual cosmopolitan, full of memorable observations about *Humanität,* whom everyone quoted and no one followed—"Official Germany celebrates Goethe," wrote Carl von Ossietzky in 1932, on the centenary of Goethe's death, "not as poet and prophet, but above all as opium."[23] And the revolutionaries who were supposed to inspire the republicans were the revolutionaries of 1848, with their black-red-gold flag, their well-meaning speeches, and their decisive failure. Significantly, Heinrich Heine, perhaps the least ambiguous and most vital ancestor of the Weimar spirit, had found no fitting memorial even by the end of the Republic; for seventy-five years proposals to erect a statue to him had aroused vehement tirades, unmeasured slanders, and, in the end, successful obstruction.[24]

While Weimar's need for a transvaluation of historical values was urgent, the hopes for achieving it were small; indeed, the need was great and the hope small from the same cause: the German historical craft, far from subjecting legends to criticism or the acid of humor, had long rationalized and refined them. Theodor Mommsen was a notable exception; in general, German historians had fitted easily into the imperial system. Professionally committed to a conservative view of things, more inclined to treasure established values than to urge change, they were thoroughly at home in the German university system, rejecting new men as much, and with equal vehemence, as they rejected new ideas. In 1915 the journalist and historian Gustav Mayer, a Jew and an independent political radical, applied for a job as a lecturer at the University of Berlin, and was advised to take the step by Erich Marcks and Friedrich Meinecke. Mayer, skeptical whether "the old prejudices against democrats, Jews, and outsiders" had "really lost their power over the university clique," decided to risk it; he subjected himself to humiliating examinations only to find his skepticism justified—he did not get the appointment he obviously deserved. It was not until the Weimar years that he was im-

23 *Weltbühne,* in *Ausnahmezustand,* 236.
24 For this tragicomedy see the account by Ludwig Marcuse, "Die Geschichte des Heine-Denkmals," *Tagebuch* (1932), in *Ausnahmezustand,* 227–236.

posed on Berlin University, but the dominant university clique of historians changed little.[25]

The ideology that continued to dominate the German historical profession through the twenties was tenacious in part because it had a long history of its own; it could invoke a figure as charismatic for German historians as the personages of the German past were for the German people: Leopold von Ranke. Beyond doubt, Ranke was a very great historian; it must be confessed that if German historians often took a high tone of self-congratulation, they had much to congratulate themselves on. Ranke was a pioneer in the use of archives, a master of complex materials, a splendid dramatist, and the founder of a new style of historical thinking. Ranke's central doctrines—the autonomy of the historian and his duty to understand each segment of the past from within—were of enormous service to the profession. But in the hands of German historians in the late Empire and the young Republic, the autonomy of history turned into its isolation. The segregation of history from ethics drove most German historians into a passive acceptance of things as they were, and the segregation of history from other disciplines alienated most German historians from the social sciences. For all his acknowledged historical erudition, most historians dismissed Max Weber as an "outsider";[26] for all his extravagance, the medievalist Georg von Below spoke for his fellows when he insisted that historians could "do without a new science of 'sociology.' "[27]

[25] *Erinnerungen,* 282–286, 310 ff; the quotation, with the crucial word "outsider" in English, is on p. 282.

[26] Hans Mommsen, "Zum Verhältnis von politischer Wissenschaft und Geschichtswissenschaft in Deutschland," *Vierteljahrshefte für Zeitgeschichte,* X (1962), 346–347.

[27] "Georg von Below," autobiographical sketch in *Die Geschichtswissenschaft der Gegenwart in Selbstdarstellungen,* ed. Sigfried Steinberg, vol. I (1925), 45; Below is referring to an article he had written in 1918. During the war itself he had predicted that "the monster of a major science of sociology will never be born." *Die deutsche Geschichtsschreibung von den Befreiungskriegen bis zu unseren Tagen: Geschichte und Kulturgeschichte* (1916), 102. Meinecke, whom no one could accuse of prejudice in behalf of the social sciences, conceded in 1922 that his profession had neglected disciplines from which it had had much to learn. "Drei Generationen deutscher Gelehrtenpolitik," *Historische Zeitschrift,* CXXV (1922), 248–283.

As their work shows, they did without it, and badly. What they could have learned from sociology and from political science was critical distance from the social and political structure in which they so comfortably lived. But then the whole energy of Ranke's historical thinking had been away from the criticism, and toward the sunny acceptance, of power; his celebrated insistence on the primacy of foreign policy was only a corollary of his cheerful resignation to the realities of the modern imperialistic state.

Ranke's triumph as a historian was as fateful as it had been glittering; his legacy was unfortunate. While many of his epigones were competent men—and few escaped being Ranke's epigone—they turned Ranke's pride into conceit, his diligence into pedantry, his acceptance of power into a mixture of servility at home and bluster abroad. This was perhaps less their fault than the fault of history itself—Ranke's teachings were more appropriate and less harmful to the nineteenth century than to the twentieth—but whatever the cause, the effects of these shifts were disastrous. We tend to make much of historians' efforts to revise the work of their predecessors; we make too little of the continuity of historical schools. Ranke's declared disciples before the First World War—capable historians like Max Lenz, Otto Hintze, Erich Marcks, Hans Delbrück—took Ranke's mystical belief in the nation-state and its ceaseless struggle for power and projected it onto the world as a whole: in the history of modern Europe, the great powers had, through war or diplomacy, prevented any single state from gaining hegemony. But now, they reasoned, in an age of imperialism, Germany was threatened by the hegemony of a single naval state, Great Britain. Germany, therefore, must arm and, if necessary, fight to secure its proper place among the great powers.

The consequences of such thinking were inescapable: unquestioning support for the political-military machine that was ruling the country, and an unpolitical evasion of domestic conflicts. The historians of the post-Rankean generations thus displayed a curious mixture of bloodless rationalism and half-concealed mysticism; they coolly shoved armies and frontiers across the chessboard of international politics, and, at the same time, reveled in the mysterious workings of History, which had assigned to Germany a sacred part to play, a sacred mission to perform. They subscribed to the dictum of the democratic imperialist Friedrich Naumann, who defined nationalism as the urge of the German people to spread its influence over the globe.[28] Thus, when the war came, they simultaneously defended the unrestrained use of naked power and Germany's special mission to preserve, and spread, *Kultur*, a product in which Germans apparently excelled, and which they thought they must defend against the barbarous mass society of Russia, the effete decadence of France, the mechanical nightmare of the United States, and the unheroic commercialism of England. Distinguished historians—Troeltsch, Meinecke, Hintze—lent themselves to collective volume after collective volume proclaiming to an incredulous world the superiority of German *Kultur* over the mere *civilization* of the Allied powers. Much of the substance of Thomas Mann's *Betrachtungen eines Unpolitischen* was anticipated in these manifestoes.

This type of historical thinking did not survive the revolution unchanged; even historians noticed that something had happened in 1918. But the myth-making mentality that had produced such thinking went underground and emerged in disguised form, more inaccessible than ever to unmasking or self-criticism. The traditional boasts about German *Kultur* and Germany's mission had embodied elaborate fantasies, wish-dreams sprung from deep needs, and historians in the Weimar Republic found it psychologically more economical to patch up their fantasies than to discard them. The Weimar spirit, I have said, was born before the Weimar Republic; so was its nemesis. As in the Empire, so now, too, there were exceptions and, thanks to Weimar, there

[28] Quoted in Ludwig Dehio, "Gedanken über die deutsche Sendung, 1900–1918," *Historische Zeitschrift,* CLXXIV (1952), 479–502; now as "Thoughts on Germany's Mission, 1900–1918," in *Germany and World Politics in the Twentieth Century,* (tr. Dieter Pevsner, 1959), 72–108. It is indicative of the respectfulness of German historians that in an article on Ranke published two years before (in 1950!) Dehio should still have thought it necessary to disclaim any arrogance, and profess respect for the "great men of earlier generations." "Ranke and German Imperialism," in *Germany and World Politics,* 38n.

were more exceptions than before, but the bulk of the historical profession trafficked in nostalgia, hero worship, and the uncritical acceptance—indeed, open advocacy—of apologetic distortions and sheer
lies, like the notorious stab-in-the-back legend.[29] "The full devotion
to Bismarck, and to the house of Hohenzollern," the cultural historian
Walter Goetz lamented in 1924, "produced that profound aversion
to democracy which was characteristic of German educated strata of
the period between 1871 and 1914," an aversion that survived into the
Republic, and was unhappily supported by leading historians. Respect
has its value, but now, in the 1920s, it had become a burden: "The
task of the historian is not cultivation of piety for a misunderstood
past, but the pitiless exploration of the truth." But this, Goetz argued,
was precisely what the German historical profession seemed incapable
of grasping. What Germany needed was "clarity about itself," but what
it got from its historians was yearning for the good old days, and mis-
reading of recent history; historians were investing the old military
caste with false glamor and the Republic with imaginary crimes. "Pre-
ceptors of the nation! Do you really think you are fulfilling an educa-
tional task if you command history to stop in its course and return
to an old condition?"[30]

The vehemence of Goetz's outburst betrays his despair; he must
have known that those who would listen to him did not need his
warning, and that those who needed his warning would not listen to
him. Patriotic, antidemocratic myth-making went on. "Above all,"
wrote the aged historian Karl Julius Beloch a year after Goetz's article, "I do not want to close my eyes forever before I have seen Germany rise again to its old glory. But if this should not be my lot, I
shall take with me the conviction that my people will one day remember that God, who made iron grow, wanted no slaves."[31] Beloch's
quotation of Ernst Moritz Arndt's patriotic *Vaterlandslied* only un-

[29] See above, p. 19.
[30] "Die deutsche Geschichtsschreibung der Gegenwart," in *Die deutsche Nation*, November 1, 1924, now in Goetz, *Historiker in meiner Zeit: Gesammelte Aufsätze* (1957), 415–424.
[31] Beloch's autobiographical sketch in *Geschichtswissenschaft der Gegenwart*, vol. II (1926), 27.

derlined the continuing vitality of the old Wartburg spirit. And, indeed, some of Beloch's most respected colleagues did their bit to restore Germany's glory. Felix Rachfahl was only one among many in the twenties to defend Germany's invasion of Belgium in 1914 as historically perfectly justified;[32] while von Below, coyly refusing to comment freely on the revolution and the Republic, in ostensible fear of the libel laws, did feel free to denounce democracy as "the great danger of our time," a force that was devouring and devastating the German people.[33]

These were the voices of grand old men among German historians. It is not surprising that in 1931 Hajo Holborn should note little progress toward scientific objectivity among his colleagues. "The profound transformations experienced in all areas of intellectual, political, and social life as a consequence of the world war," he wrote in the *Historische Zeitschrift*, had "scarcely touched the core of scientific historical studies." Old academic "traditions and institutions" had been powerful enough to make "criticism of customary procedures, directions and aims of historical research and writing" extremely rare; what was far more in evidence was "a certain pride" in the discovery "how few of one's inherited ideals one had to give up." All too many historians thought themselves heroes for "swimming against the stream of the times." But, Holborn warned, these "inclinations to a kind of 'Faith of the Nibelungs'" were no better than "self-satisfaction," mere symptoms of thoughtlessness and self-deception which were threatening to "become dangerous to our craft."[34]

In retrospect, Holborn's solemn strictures are even more poignant than they must have seemed in their day, for they apply to some degree to Holborn's revered teacher Friedrich Meinecke, the best-known and doubtless the most distinguished historian in the Weimar Republic.

Friedrich Meinecke is the Thomas Mann of German historical

[32] Rachfahl's autobiographical sketch in *ibid.*, 215.
[33] See Below's autobiographical sketch in *ibid.*, I, especially 44.
[34] "Protestantismus und politische Ideengeschichte," *Historische Zeitschrift*, CXXXXIV (1931), 15.

writing, and his *Idee der Staatsräson* is his *Zauberberg*, published, like the *Zauberberg*, in 1924, and written, like the *Zauberberg*, to confront recent history, to grasp the dialectical struggle of light and darkness battling one another in unappeasable conflict yet yoked together in indissoluble brotherhood. Like Mann, Meinecke was a cultural aristocrat converted to the Republic; like Mann, Meinecke was master of ponderous irony, enjoyed the subtle interplay of motives, sought the good but found evil fascinating, and from the pains of war and defeat derived the single lesson that if man is ever to conquer the daemon that is within him, he can conquer him only by looking at him unafraid, and taking his measure. Thomas Mann leaves his simple hero, Hans Castorp, on the battlefield, his chances of survival uncertain, but sustained by the hopeful question, Will from this universal lustful feast of death love arise some day? Meinecke, wrestling with *his* daemon, *raison d'état,* ends on a similar note: "Contemplation cannot tire of looking into its sphinxlike countenance, and will never manage to penetrate it fully. It can only appeal to the active statesman to carry state and God in his heart together, that he may prevent the daemon, whom he can never wholly shake off, from becoming too powerful."[35]

Die Idee der Staatsräson is literature, philosophy, and, as Meinecke himself openly confessed, autobiography; he had written it, he said, to pursue some themes he had first taken up before the war, in his *Weltbürgertum und Nationalstaat*, but the grave events of the war had given him new perspectives, while "the shock of the collapse" had pushed the central problem into the forefront, "in all its terror."[36] But the book, I must quickly add, is scholarly history as well. In more than five hundred closely printed pages, Meinecke traces the conception of *raison d'état* from the origin of modern political thought in Machiavelli, through its great representatives like Frederick the Great, to the twentieth century. And, in tracing it, Meinecke demonstrates its importance and its problematic quality; the state has its needs—maintenance and expansion of its power in a system of com-

[35] *Staatsräson,* 542.
[36] *Ibid.,* 27.

peting states—and the statesman finds himself compelled to act in ways that he, as a moral man or in private life, would condemn. Power, it seems, is dominated by a tragic duality: seeking its own good, it is committed to evil means—to cold calculation, to fraud and force.

There is much penetrating analysis here, informed by deep moral passion and great subtlety—though, strange to say, not enough subtlety. Meinecke, the master of words, is also their victim, and a victim in a way peculiarly representative of the *Vernunftrepublikaner*: for all his critical energy, Meinecke cuts short criticism by taking rhetoric for reality, and mundane psychological conflicts for philosophical difficulties.[37] His very vision of power as a tragic phenomenon is an unfortunate philosophical habit inherited from German Idealism; it gives a practical question metaphysical dignity, which must lead not to analysis but to resignation. "Hatred and revenge," he cites Bismarck, "are bad counselors in politics," but he does not stop to ask if Bismarck followed his own counsel;[38] "At least in his own eyes," he quotes Frederick the Great, "the hero must be justified," but he fails to inquire whether the word "hero" does not prejudge the issue, or whether Frederick was indeed justified in his own eyes;[39] he quotes some isolated, high-flown moral pronouncements of Treitschke's and, despite some rather severe criticisms of Treitschke's aggressiveness and crude social Darwinism, grants him "deep ethical seriousness and spiritual breadth."[40] Meinecke takes his ideal of the state—an organic unity in which rulers and ruled join—for the reality, thus assuming as demonstrated what needed to be—and could not be—proved. Caught in his presuppositions, Meinecke never saw that the tragic view of the state helped to excuse its crimes, that the poor

[37] "Meinecke's whole life work," Eckart Kehr wrote in 1928, reviewing Meinecke's *Geschichte des deutsch-englischen Bündnisproblems, 1890–1901* (1927), "is pervaded by a deliberate and disciplined self-limitation of his *Problemstellung*—the questions he asks." *Die Gesellschaft*, V, part 2 (1928), 27.

[38] *Staatsräson*, 8.

[39] *Ibid.*, 492.

[40] *Ibid.*, 506. Though far from uncritical of Treitschke, and silent on his anti-Semitism, Meinecke significantly separates him from disciples like Dietrich Schäfer, whom he rejects as truly intolerable.

had no stake in the state's growth in power or glory, that the state was not nature's final answer to the problem of human organization, and, quite simply, that the state did not always, indeed not often, represent the public interest. If Kantorowicz regressed by turning scientific questions into myths, Meinecke regressed by turning them into philosophical problems.

The complex of feelings and responses I have called "the hunger for wholeness" turns out on examination to be a great regression born from a great fear: the fear of modernity. The abstractions that Tönnies and Hofmannsthal and the others manipulated—*Volk, Führer, Organismus, Reich, Entscheidung, Gemeinschaft*—reveal a desperate need for roots and for community, a vehement, often vicious repudiation of reason accompanied by the urge for direct action or for surrender to a charismatic leader. The hunger for wholeness was awash with hate; the political, and sometimes the private, world of its chief spokesmen was a paranoid world, filled with enemies: the dehumanizing machine, capitalist materialism, godless rationalism, rootless society, cosmopolitan Jews, and that great all-devouring monster, the city. Othmar Spann, the Austrian Catholic social philosopher, whose fantasies were enormously popular in right-wing circles, offered a list of villains his readers could accept with ease: Locke, Hume, Voltaire, Rousseau, Ricardo, Marx, Darwin, filthy—*unflätig*—psychoanalysis, Impressionism, Dadaism, Cubism, and the film drama. It was this conglomerate of hostile feelings masquerading as philosophy that prompted Troeltsch in 1922, not long before his death, to warn against what he regarded the peculiarly German inclination to a "mixture of mysticism and brutality."[41]

V

Yet the Weimar situation was nothing if not complicated. Not all who, in the twenties, hungered for connection and unity were victims

---

[41] Quoted in Klemens von Klemperer, *Germany's New Conservatism: Its History and Dilemma in the Twentieth Century* (1957), 113.

of regression; a few, outnumbered and not destined to succeed, sought to satisfy their needs not through escape from but mastery of the world, not through denunciation but employment of the machine, not through irrationalism but reason, not through nihilism but construction—and this last quite literally, for this modern and democratic philosophy was formulated in their writings and carried out in their buildings by architects.

Among the most self-aware of these architects was Erich Mendelsohn, who was to build some distinguished buildings in the Weimar period, among them the Universum movie theatre in Berlin in 1927 and the Schocken department store in Chemnitz in 1928–1929. Mendelsohn insisted that the architect must unite what he called analysis and dynamics, reason and unreason: "Between these two poles—the rational and the irrational, move my nature, life, and work."[42] Certainly, he wrote to his wife, "the primary element is function, but function without sensual admixtures remains mere construction. More than ever I stand by my program of reconciliation" in which beauty and utility are joined. "Both are necessary, both must find each other." Using the convenient Hegelian term *"aufheben,"* which means at once elevating, canceling, and preserving, Mendelsohn thought that in the good building all dualisms are *"aufgehoben,"* just as they are *"aufgehoben* in every organism, creature, and work of art."[43] In 1920 Mendelsohn, still young and unknown, built an observatory and astrophysical laboratory, the Einstein Tower; he designed it, he said, out of some unknown urge, letting it emerge out of "the mystique around Einstein's universe."[44] When Albert Einstein walked through the building, he approved of it with a single, appropriate epithet—"organic."[45]

Such a philosophy seems proper to an architect like Mendelsohn, who preferred powerful curves to the straight line. But Walter Gropius, the advocate of a classical, geometric style, substantially subscribed

[42] Wolf von Eckardt, *Eric Mendelsohn* (1960), 11.

[43] Erich Mendelsohn, *Briefe eines Architekten,* ed. Oskar Beyer (1961), 57, 73.

[44] Eckardt, *Mendelsohn,* 9.

[45] Arnold Whittick, *Erich Mendelsohn* (1940), 64.

to the same philosophy. After doing some fine buildings before the First World War, Gropius was already well known when the Republic was born, but he achieved his real fame in the Bauhaus, which will always be linked with his name. Gropius opened the Bauhaus in early 1919, in Weimar, merging in the new venture two older schools, an academy of art and a school of applied arts. Clarifying and boldly advancing beyond principles first enunciated in the German Werkbund before the war, Gropius from the beginning dedicated his school to the creation of a single artistic unity—the building. Then and later he insisted that his was not merely a craft philosophy; craftsmanship was a "preparation for architecture." Nor was it simply a "functional" philosophy limited to the practical or to industry; it was explicitly an aesthetic philosophy resting on psychological investigations. "Architects, painters, and sculptors," he wrote in his opening manifesto of April 1919, "must once again recognize and grasp the multiform shape —*vielgliedrige Gestalt*—of the building in its totality and its parts." Only then will their work be filled by the "architectonic spirit" now lost in "salon art." Older schools of art "could not produce this unity," since they had separated art from craft. This must change: "Architects, sculptors, painters, we must all turn back to craft." There is no essential difference between craftsman and artist: "The artist is the craftsman in his highest form—*Steigerung des Handwerkers*." Let all, forgetting snobbish distinctions, collaborate in "the new building of the future, which will be everything together, architecture and sculpture and painting, in a single shape, rising to heaven from the hands of millions of craftsmen as a crystal symbol of a new emerging faith." Lyonel Feininger illustrated this call to a new unity with a woodcut depicting a tall, slender, secular cathedral, lit by stars.[46]

The course of studies at the Bauhaus was designed to turn this rhetoric into reality. After passing the elementary course, each student was trained in the workshop by two masters, who imparted, it was hoped, a mastery of materials as well as aesthetics, of content and

[46] The manifesto is reproduced in full in *Das Bauhaus, 1919–1933: Weimar, Dessau, Berlin,* ed. Hans M. Wingler (1962), 38–41.

form together. "A dual education of this kind," Gropius later wrote, "would enable the coming generation to achieve the reunion of all forms of creative work and become the architects of a new civilization." In 1922 Klee drew a symbolic representation of this program: a seven-pointed star is inscribed in a circular band; this band represents the preliminary training that encloses the several materials (glass, stone, wood) and the several courses (construction, color, composition) and leads to the heart of the star, another circle, in which the double aim of the Bauhaus is proudly displayed: *"Bau und Bühne—* building and stage."[47] The atmosphere of the new Bauhaus was experimental, cheerful, splendidly vigorous; one need only think of some of the teachers to recreate it: Paul Klee, Wassily Kandinsky, Lyonel Feininger, Gerhard Marcks, Oskar Schlemmer, Laszlo Moholy-Nagy, Josef Albers.

The activity of the Bauhaus was inventive and versatile; typography, furniture design, lamps, rugs, pottery, book-binding, the dance— all were treated with enormous freedom, and many of them, as we know, had lasting influence; we still sit in chairs designed by Marcel Breuer and read type faces first drawn by Herbert Bayer. The atmosphere at the Bauhaus was curious, exhilarating: the Bauhaus was a family, a school, a cooperative business, a missionary society. Neither Gropius nor the other masters believed in disciples; it was not an academy where the great teacher reproduces little editions of himself, but "a laboratory," where "students stimulated teachers" and teachers, students. Utility and beauty did not merely stand side by side; the masters strove to make them as one, though there was room for pure beauty as well; some of Feininger's, Klee's, and Kandinsky's most interesting graphic work was done at the Bauhaus. And high morale was essential not merely to creativity but to sheer survival: the appropriations for the school were meager and poverty, especially among the students, was extreme. In 1923, Walter Gropius recalls, when the Bauhaus mounted its first exhibition, there was no money for cleaning the building, and the masters' wives volunteered their

[47] See *ibid.,* 10.

services as charwomen. "The spirit," Walter Gropius has said, "was simply excellent, and some of the informal activities, like our celebrations—the *Feste*—when someone would set a theme, like 'black and white,' or 'square,' were splendid occasions."

Inevitably, there was some tension within: Johannes Itten, a painter and educator whom Gropius had imported from Vienna to conduct the all-important elementary course, was passionately and exclusively dedicated to aesthetics, and more indifferent to practical results than Gropius thought right or possible. In 1923 Itten resigned, and the preliminary course was taken over by two other great teachers, Josef Albers and Laszlo Moholy-Nagy. But with the passing of time, and with a congenial atmosphere inviting free debate, these tensions relaxed, and the Bauhaus even profited from that rather premature exhibition of 1923 on which the government had insisted against the better judgment of Gropius and others. The true enemy, in any event, was not internal dissension, but outside hostility—the political and aesthetic aversion of right-wing, tradition-bound craftsmen to the revolutionary implications of the Bauhaus' experiments and to the Bohemian conduct of its students. Gropius, aware that he was "sitting on a powder keg," strictly prohibited any political activity, and this helped a good deal. In 1925 the Bauhaus migrated from Weimar to the more congenial city of Dessau; there Gropius built his celebrated buildings—perhaps the most photographed artifacts of the Weimar period—Klee and Kandinsky continued to do their paintings, Breuer built his furniture, and the workshop designed its lamps and china and silverware, clean, sturdy, and beautiful, which made the Bauhaus as famous abroad as it was becoming notorious at home. Finally, in 1932 politics and depression drove it to Berlin, for its final twilight existence.

In the writings of his later years, Gropius simply developed the lines he had laid down in his opening manifesto of 1919: the new architecture sought for wholeness by seeking to satisfy both economic and aesthetic needs. Mechanization must be made to serve; the Bauhaus, in fact, had been designed "to avert mankind's enslavement by the machine by giving its products a content of reality and significance, and so saving the home from mechanistic anarchy. . . . Our object was to eliminate every drawback of the machine without sacrificing any one of its real advantages." True, modern man had been torn apart, but to abandon the division of labor would be not merely impossible but also undesirable. The tragedy of fragmentation was not caused by the machine or the minute subdivision of tasks, but by "the predominantly materialistic mentality of our age and the defective and unreal articulation of the individual to the community." What was needed was a frankly modern philosophy, unafraid of mechanization or of the right kind of standardization. "What we preached in practice was the common citizenship of all forms of creative work, and their logical interdependence on one another in the modern world." The "guiding principle was that artistic design is neither an intellectual nor a material affair, but simply an integral part of the stuff of life." Reason and passion here must collaborate. "It is true that a work of art remains a technical product, but it has an intellectual purpose to fulfill as well which only passion and imagination can achieve." The Bauhaus, in sum, had been a true community which, "through the wholeness of its approach," had "helped to restore architecture and design of today as a social art"; it had developed "total architecture."[48]

The language of architects is notorious for its imprecision, pretentiousness, and addiction to cliché, and Gropius himself did not always escape the temptation of playing oracle. Yet his work—the houses he designed, the products he supervised, the pupils he trained, the public he educated—gives solid, concrete meaning to his most fanciful expressions. What Gropius taught, and what most Germans did not want to learn, was the lesson of Bacon and Descartes and the Enlightenment: that one must confront the world and dominate it, that the cure for the ills of modernity is more, and the right kind of modernity. It should surprise no one that the Bauhaus survived the Weimar Republic by only half a year.

---

[48] I have drawn these quotations from Walter Gropius, *The New Architecture and the Bauhaus* (tr. P. Morton Shand, 1965 ed.), and *Scope of Total Architecture* (1962 ed.), *passim.*

V / THE REVOLT OF THE SON:

Expressionist Years

I

Next to the Bauhaus, probably the most celebrated artifact of the Weimar Republic was a film released in Berlin in February 1920, *The Cabinet of Dr. Caligari.* "There it was," Willy Haas wrote later, "that uncanny, demonic, cruel, 'Gothic' Germany."[1] With its nightmarish plot, its Expressionist sets, its murky atmosphere, *Caligari* continues to embody the Weimar spirit to posterity as palpably as Gropius' buildings, Kandinsky's abstractions, Grosz's cartoons, and Marlene Dietrich's legs. It is a film that fully deserves its immortality, an experiment that fathered a rash of other experiments. But *Caligari*, decisive for the history of the film, is also instructive for the history of Weimar, especially in its early, Expressionist years. There was more at stake here than a strange script or novelties in lighting.

Later, in American exile, the German writer and film critic Siegfried Kracauer reported the history of *Caligari* in authoritative detail. This is what happened: shortly after the war, two young men, the Czech Hans Janowitz and the Austrian Carl Mayer met, naturally enough in Berlin, and became close friends. They were both talented, fascinated with Expressionism, filled with horror at the war that had just ended, and eager to persuade others of their pacifist views. They wrote a story compounded of their own nocturnal experiences, their

[1] *Die literarische Welt,* 103.

despair at the war, and their imagination, the story of the mad, powerful Dr. Caligari, who exhibits his somnambulist, Cesare, at fairs. Wherever Caligari goes, death follows: an official who has snubbed him is found dead, and when one of two young students questions Cesare about the future, Cesare predicts, correctly, that he will die at dawn. Francis, the surviving student, seeks to solve the mystery; he creeps to Caligari's wagon and is relieved to see what seems to be Cesare asleep in a box. But while Francis is at the fairground, Cesare has actually gone to kidnap Jane, Francis' girl, and carried her off. Pursued across steep hills and eerie viaducts, Cesare drops the girl and dies. Now the police examine Cesare's box and discover that it contains a dummy. The truth is becoming obvious: the hypnotized Cesare had been committing crimes at his master's bidding, walking the streets while a dummy takes his place at night. Caligari eludes arrest and takes refuge in an insane asylum. Here, where Francis has followed him, another revelation awaits the pursuer: the mad hypnotist and the director of the asylum are the same man. While Caligari sleeps, Francis and the police study his records and discover the inner connection of things: the director had become fascinated by the account of an eighteenth-century mountebank named Dr. Caligari who had induced his medium, Cesare, to commit murder; fascination had turned to obsession, and so he experimented with a somnambulist in the asylum in the Caligari manner. When Francis tries to wring a confession from the director by showing him Cesare's corpse, the modern Caligari loses all control, and is restrained only by being put into a strait jacket—the very emblem of the institution he had headed and so insanely betrayed.

Erich Pommer, who was to become one of the most influential film producers of the Weimar period, accepted the script and finally assigned Robert Wiene to direct it. Now a crucial thing happened: Over the writers' vehement objections, Wiene placed the original story into a frame, and gave the film the shape it now has; it begins and ends in the insane asylum, and at the end it is clear that the student Francis is mad, as is his girl Jane, and taking the director for the murderous Dr. Caligari is simply one of Francis' delusions. Actually, the director is a kindly man, relieved to have discovered the nature of Francis' psychosis, and happy to announce that he will be able to cure Francis at last.

The two writers' fury at this change was more than authors' vanity. The film had—and has—power still, but the message the two had wanted to convey had disappeared. The "two young *Dichter*" were Willy Haas' close friends, and, he recalls, "what they had really written around 1920—so they told me often, over and over again—was a pacifist film, a film against militarism, against military obedience in general." And then the film company made changes, "very odd and striking changes, which canceled this meaning."[2] As Kracauer shows, the authors had wanted to unmask the brutality, the utter insanity, of authority; the frame which the director had placed around their story had given authority the appearance of essential decency and generosity, and the rebellion against authority the appearance of a delusion, a form of madness. Revolutionary ideas had been turned into conformist ideas.[3]

But it remains an open question whether the original design, if left undisturbed, would have been particularly clear—the public responded to *Caligari* with uncritical enthusiasm, apparently unaware that changes had been made in the original conception. They would have been indifferent had they known, and this lack of discrimination may stand as a fair comment on the Expressionist message as a whole. Kracauer admits that the authors themselves could only offer a dubious alternative to Caligari's tyranny, the anarchy symbolized by the incessant, restless, unstructured activity of the fair. "That the two authors selected a fair with its liberties as contrast to the oppressions of Caligari betrays the flaw in their revolutionary aspirations. Much as they longed for freedom, they were apparently incapable of imagining its contours."[4]

[2] *Loc. cit.*

[3] *From Caligari to Hitler: A Psychological History of the German Film* (1947), 61–76. In writing his account, Kracauer had access to an unpublished reminiscence written by one of the film's authors, Hans Janowitz.

[4] *Ibid.*, 74.

And so, in its original conception, its final form, and its eventual triumph, *Caligari* mirrors the uncertainties and the confused thinking of the Expressionists. While the Expressionists did their best, by their lights, to serve the Revolution, they were in general revolutionary without being political or, at least, without being programmatic; their rebellion against stable forms and common sense reflected the longing for renewal, the discontent with actuality, and the uncertainty about means that marked Germany in general. The Expressionists were not a unified movement but a loosely allied band; they were rebels with a cause but without clear definitions or concrete aims. When the revolution came, Expressionists of all persuasions firmly supported it, and drew other artists into the revolutionary circle. The *Novembergruppe,* founded in December 1918, as well as the provocatively called *Arbeitsrat für Kunst,* both dedicated to disseminating art appropriate to the new age, enlisted Expressionists from all parts of the political spectrum and artists from all parts of the artistic spectrum: Emil Nolde, the mystical, racist Christian, as well as Ernst Toller, the uncomfortable Communist; Erich Mendelsohn as well as Walter Gropius. All artists, or nearly all, were seized with the quasi-religious fervor to make all things new: Bertolt Brecht and Kurt Weill, Alban Berg and Paul Hindemith, all joined the *Novembergruppe.* "The future of art," they proclaimed in December 1918, "and the seriousness of this hour forces us revolutionaries of the spirit (Expressionists, Cubists, Futurists) toward unity and close cooperation."[5]

Like the unity of the Weimar coalition, this unity did not last, fantasies of brotherly cooperation faded, but revolutionaries of the spirit continued to assault their world, sometimes with consummate, controlled artistry, often with hysterical abandon. *The Cabinet of Dr. Caligari* started a fashion in Expressionist films drenched in dim lighting, in which actors moved, much like Cesare the somnambulist, in trancelike states in front of strangely painted sets. These films, their ambitious creators hoped, would appear mysterious, endowed with

[5] Bernard S. Myers, *The German Expressionists: A Generation in Revolt* (1966 ed.), 220.

many levels of meaning. Wiene followed up *Caligari* in the same year with another fantasy wallowing in blood and unchecked impulses, *Genuine*; and two years later Fritz Lang made *Dr. Mabuse, the Gambler,* somewhat like *Caligari* a tale of extravagant crime, hypnotism, and final insanity, and, quite like *Caligari,* a film decorated with sets that had painted shadows, tilted walls, and crazy angles that might have come—but did not come—out of a Feininger painting.

For the painters went their own way, though in a similar direction. They took the strong, simple, aggressive colors, the consciously primitive craftsmanship, the passionate line, and the cruel distortion of the human figure—all discovered before the war—to new extremes. More than the film makers and far more than the poets of these years, the painters were highly individualistic; even the painters who worked together at the Bauhaus—Klee, Feininger, Kandinsky—worked in their own distinctive idiom. Max Beckmann, one of the greatest painters of the time, whose debt to the Expressionist vision is evident, proudly repudiated the label for himself; as early as 1922, in the middle of the Expressionist years, he dismissed "this Expressionist business" as a mere "decorative and literary matter." He was, he knew, a modern, but he insisted that "One can be new without engaging in Expressionism or Impressionism."[6]

The very vagueness of the name reflects the vagueness of the painters' politics in the Weimar Republic. Beckmann himself firmly said, "I have never been politically active in any way," and he denied that he had ever "busied himself with barricades."[7] And what held true for Beckmann held true for many other painters. The gentle Lyonel Feininger was one of the painters who signed a manifesto of the *Novembergruppe,* in which he joined his "voice to those who say 'yes' to all that is sprouting and becoming,"[8] and this well-meaning, inoffensive affirmation of newness and construction was characteristic:

[6] Beckmann to the publisher Reinhard Piper, quoted in Peter Selz, *Max Beckmann* (1964), 39.

[7] A statement of 1938, quoted in Myers, *German Expressionists,* 254; diary entry, September 17, 1948, quoted in Aloys Goergen, "Beckmann und die Apokalypse," *Blick auf Beckmann: Dokumente und Vorträge* (1962), 21.

[8] Hans Hess, *Lyonel Feininger* (1961), 87.

George Grosz's drawings clearly—with deliberate obviousness—embodied a distinctive *Weltanschauung* and made propaganda against fat industrialists and war profiteers; Otto Dix's sympathetic pictures of workingmen and brutal portraits of pimps and prostitutes contained an open proletarian message; Käthe Kollwitz's gloomy graphic work with its mourning mothers, its farewell to Karl Liebknecht, its starving children, its desolate victims of war and capitalist exploitation, conveyed an urgent political appeal. But most of the painters were political men mainly because their enemies called them *Kultur-Bolschewiken,* much as some Germans later discovered themselves to be Jews because the Nazi Government told them that that is what they were. In fact, the political notions of Emil Nolde—his vicious anti-Semitism, his crude hostility to French culture, both underlined by his early membership in the Nazi Party—showed that Expressionism was compatible with all sorts of politics. The Expressionists yearned for a breakthrough from convention to nature. And for Nolde, evidently, virtue and reality lay in Nordic blood and mystic attachment to the soil. In 1919 the Expressionist novelist Theodor Däubler unwittingly disclosed the danger in the movement's commitment to passion. Standing before the lithograph "Jealousy," by Edvard Munch, whose influence on the German Expressionists had been enormous, Däubler reflected: "Am I not an animal? A reality! The cycle A and O says: you can be one. The animal breaks through in Munch, as a full expression of his wholly unbroken essence. The Impressionists did not know quite what to do with it. But now, once again, we are on the track of animal categories—*Tierbestimmheiten.* Above all, what monumentality: every animal an undeniable grasping at life. A consequential self-determination. The return to the animal through art is our decision in favor of Expressionism."[9] The only difficulty was that while the Expressionists returned to the animal through art—and their animal was Marc's innocuous doe—the Nazis would return to the animal in life, choosing other animals as their models.

But this is not all. While some painters repudiated the Republic

---

[9] From *Der neue Standpunkt* (1919), in *Expressionismus: Literatur und Kunst,* ed. Paul Raabe and H. L. Greve (1960), 19.

from an extreme left-wing or extreme right-wing position, while other painters were too preoccupied with painting to vote, there was a decisive sense in which they all, wittingly or unwittingly, participated in the Weimar spirit. The ironic fate of Nolde in the Nazi period—his avid claims for recognition by the new masters, his repeated appeals to high officials to be permitted a place in the new order, all rejected with contempt by a regime that had no use for "degenerate artists" no matter where their sympathies lay—suggests that while not all Expressionists loved Weimar, the enemies of Weimar hated all Expressionists. And with good reason. There was something revolutionary about their vitality, their unremitting search for reality behind appearance. The sentimental realism that the monarchists and later the Nazis liked, the photographic naturalism and propagandist myth-making which was all they could use, were anathema to the artists of Weimar; they were lies, not art. Kirchner's stark portraits of Swiss peasants, Feininger's lyrical seascapes and churches with their lovely compositions of long straight lines and cubist planes, Klee's inspired and beautifully controlled fantasies, Kandinsky's abstractions with lines, circles, and curves mysteriously tense in their relationships— these were a unanimous repudiation of the past, an aspiration to a new reality. Beckmann spoke for them all. "What I want to show in my work," he said, "is the idea which hides itself behind so-called reality. I am seeking for the bridge which leads from the visible to the invisible."[10]

But even this is not all. Even when the painters' work was not explicitly political, or explicitly unpolitical, it reflected, as did all of Weimar, one harrowing experience—the war. The unpolitical Beckmann, the painter who had never busied himself with barricades, changed his style during the years 1915 to 1918. Born in 1884, Beckmann had grown up in the late Empire, and achieved wide recognition before 1914 with his splendid draftsmanship, his Impressionist technique, and an inherent cheerfulness that gave animation to his portraits. One famous self-portrait of 1907—and all his life he drew, etched, and painted portraits of himself, recording his momentary

[10] A statement of 1938, in Myers, *German Expressionists,* 254.

states and his spiritual progress—shows a confident, properly dressed young man with a handsome head, holding a cigarette. The war changed all that. "The war," one of his admiring critics wrote in 1921, "propelled the painter into reality."[11] His drawing became deliberately distorted; it remained realistic enough to convey the dreadful scenes he had witnessed—the wounded and dying soldiers, the corpses. And the subject matter of his paintings changed: in the midst of the war, he began—though he never finished—a large apocalyptic painting, "Resurrection," he painted a heart-rending "Descent from the Cross," and canvases innocuously entitled "The Night," but magnificently repellent in the distortions of their figures and faces, their brutal colors, and their stark lines. In 1919 he published a series of nineteen dry-points, rather misleadingly entitled "Faces"—it includes, for example, a lovely view of the Main River near Frankfurt—and he kept doing self-portraits. But they were of a different man: the eyes are large and filled with pain, the mouth is unsmiling, grim. There was nothing unconscious about his change. "Just now, even more than before the war," he wrote, "I feel the need to be in the cities among my fellow men. This is where our place is. We must take part in the whole misery that is to come. We must surrender our heart and our nerves to the dreadful screams of pain of the poor disillusioned people."[12] Whatever Beckmann liked to call himself, no one stated more eloquently than he the program, or rather the longing, of the Expressionist years.

Other art forms experienced the same evolution. Poets, dancers, composers, sculptors, even cartoonists, tried out new techniques to rescue the world from itself, or at least to express their disgust with what had happened. In their need to make themselves clear, to find their audience, artists strove to become universal men; painters wrote poetry, novelists wrote songs. Few were as talented and versatile as Ernst Barlach, who was a gifted sculptor, painter, playwright, poet, and novelist, but many aspired to emulate him. And all experimented: Expressionist poets played with language and sought to convey unprecedented intensity of feeling, unheard-of purity of conviction, by

[11] Benno Reifenberg, "Max Beckmann" (1921), in *Blick auf Beckmann,* 102.
[12] Written in 1918. Quoted in Selz, *Beckmann,* 32.

incongruous juxtapositions, tight-lipped compression, or lavish word painting. And no matter how placid their subject matter might be— some of the finest Expressionist paintings, after all, were landscapes and still lifes, some of the best Expressionist poems, love lyrics—the inherent artistic direction of their work was as subversive of established tradition as George Grosz's savage drawings of revolting plutocrats, coquettish prostitutes, and maimed veterans.

Among the most inventive, certainly the most articulate, Expressionists in early Weimar were the playwrights. Prolific and hostile—to the rules, to the audience, often to clarity—they poured out plays eccentric in plot, staging, speech, characters, acting, and direction. Sets were merely indicated; lighting left the spectator much to do; speech rose to declamation and, often, sheer yelling, as far removed from ordinary manner as possible. Characters were endowed with universality by being deprived of names and individual characteristics, and called simply "the man," "the young girl," "the soldier," "the mother"—a device that the Expressionist film borrowed to good effect. These plays had much life, little elegance, and absolutely no humor; their appeal was strident and utterly direct, a cry for help and an emphatic, impatient demand for reformation.

The names of the leading Expressionist playwrights remain familiar —they call up tragic memories, for many of them killed themselves during the Nazi period—but their plays are little performed. Yet, especially during the early years of the Republic, they overwhelmed the theatre, giving it an atmosphere of freshness, and drowning it in noise. Fortunately for these playwrights, producers and directors in the Republic were on the whole sympathetic to them. The most powerful man in the Weimar theatre was Leopold Jessner, who had been imposed on the Staatliche Schauspielhaus in Berlin as *Intendant* —a strategic post—in the summer of 1919. The Prussian *Kultusminister,* Konrad Hänisch, was a Social Democrat; so was Jessner. But this was not Jessner's sole distinction; he was an experienced director and producer, who had successfully directed Ibsen, Hauptmann, Wedekind, and Schnitzler in Hamburg and in Königsberg. In fact, the last two plays he had staged at Königsberg in 1919, before

von Hindenburg [signature]

HINDENBURG

Paul Ludwig Hans Anton von Hindenburg und Beneckendorff, second and last President of the Weimar Republic, 1925 to 1933; chaste and dignified—the general as civilian.

OSKAR KOKOSCHKA: WALTER HASENCLEVER   LITHOGRAPH, 1917

The two Expressionists, the painter and the playwright, became friends late during World War I. Both incurable lovers of humanity, only Kokoschka managed to survive the Nazis—abroad. Hasenclever killed himself in June 1940 in Southern France, hounded to death by Spanish frontier guards.

THOMAS MANN IN 1930

A belated convert to the Weimar Republic, a year after winning the Nobel Prize for Literature.

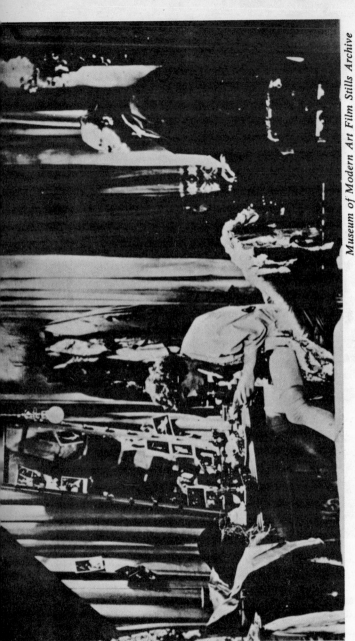

Museum of Modern Art Film Stills Archive

A SCENE FROM *The Blue Angel* (1930)

Marlene Dietrich as the cabaret singer Lola Lola, Emil Jannings as the high school teacher, Professor Unrat, who slavishly loves her. The Heinrich Mann novel of 1904, on which the film is based, is a hilarious satire on German bourgeois life; the film, adapted by Carl Zuckmayer with Mann's full consent, has satiric touches but emphasizes pathos—a remarkable and ominous change.

his call to Berlin, had been Wedekind's *Büchse der Pandora* and Kaiser's *Gas*. In Berlin he was to use his unprecedented influence with a curious mixture of daring and discretion.

The very first of his Berlin productions was, doubtless deliberately, a classic German play: Schiller's *Wilhelm Tell*. Jessner gave it an Expressionist performance, obviously intent on demonstrating the critical function of art in the new Republic. He took care to make the evening —it was December 12, 1919—as provocative as possible. He had engaged the best actors he could find—Albert Bassermann played Tell, Fritz Kortner the tyrant Gessler. The stage was dominated by what was to become Jessner's characteristic device, the *Jessnertreppe,* a jagged arrangement of bare steps on which actors could sit, which they could climb for declamation, and from which they could roll after they had been killed. The *Jessnertreppe* was an Expressionist assault on naturalism, and an Expressionist demand that the audience participate in the drama by using its imagination. Beyond this, Jessner had muted the patriotic tones of Schiller's drama by cutting a famous line about the fatherland, and converted the play into a call for revolution against tyranny. Gessler was dressed in a glittering uniform, dripping with medals, the very type of the hateful German general; his cheeks had been rouged to a furious red, to caricature the bestial Junker. The most obtuse among the spectators could not fail to guess the political message of the play before him.

Kortner records the course of the evening in his autobiography. The men of the theatre, he writes, were left-wing; they had been outraged by the murder of Liebknecht and Luxemburg, and Jessner's production was an expression of this outrage. The premiere was interrupted from the start by demonstrations in the hall. Right-wing and left were fully represented; there was yelling, whistling, stamping of feet; critics of various political directions and literary tastes stood on their seats and waved their programs at each other. Finally, Jessner, personally timid for all his radicalism, rang down the curtain, but the actors insisted that the play go on. The trumpets sounded, imitating the cadence of the ex-Kaiser's automobile, and this set off another noisy demonstration in the hall. Then Kortner, looking, he says, like an anticipation of Göring, jumped on stage, and shouted the demonstrators down. For a while there was quiet, and Bassermann could shoot the apple off his son's head to enormous applause. The curtain went down at the end of the act, and the company congratulated one another. They had celebrated too soon; the demonstrations resumed, until the yelling became deafening. And now Albert Bassermann, the refined actor, with his hoarse voice, ran through the curtain onto the stage. His unexpected appearance brought silence, and then, with a voice ringing clear for once, Bassermann shouted, *"Schmeisst doch die bezahlten Lümmel hinaus!"*—"Throw out the bums; they've been bought!" There were a few shouted disclaimers (they wanted to prove, Kortner suggests, that they were uncorrupted swine), but the resistance was over, and the play went on to a triumphant conclusion.[13] It was an Expressionist evening worthy of the production that had called it forth.

II

A style as self-consciously spontaneous and strenuously individualistic as Expressionism was not calculated to develop a single method or a single message, beyond the rebelliousness itself and the longing for communication. Even Jessner's *Wilhelm Tell*, after all, could be taken by some among the audience as a critique not so much of the Prussian General Staff as of French officers harassing Germans in the name of the Peace of Versailles. Some Expressionists recorded their sexual fears of impotence or their religious fears of nothingness; some wrote plays about their conversion to Christ or, far more frequently, to a religion of humanity. A few celebrated, most caricatured, the blessings of modern machine civilization. There were even Expressionists who glorified war and destruction as the only truly authentic human experience, but the vast majority among them execrated militarism and propagated their ecstatic vision of a regenerated peaceful humanity.

[13] Fritz Kortner, *Aller Tage Abend* (1959), 350–362.

It was this vision, therefore, that united the Expressionists more than anything else. The unlikelihood of attaining this new humanity darkened Beckmann's paintings, the hope of producing it animated the playwrights. The most remarkable Expressionist plays written late in the war, like Walter Hasenclever's *Antigone* and Fritz von Unruh's *Ein Geschlecht,* both of 1917, wrestle with the monster of war, and dimly look to a new day and a new man. With the coming of the Republic, this prophetic theme became central, and the German stage, in Berlin and in the provinces alike, a part-time pulpit. Whether they were by Ernst Toller or by Georg Kaiser, loosely based on historical incidents or dialogues carried on by abstractions in men's minds, optimistic or resigned, violently anticapitalist or simply humanitarian, their hope was always the same: that man must be converted through suffering and living—as the playwrights themselves had been converted by a war they had originally welcomed like everyone else—that man must be purified and give birth to a higher species.

In their search for this new humanity, the Expressionists offered the public many heroes: the stranger, the sufferer, the suicide, the prostitute. But there was one theme that pervades their work: the son's revolt against the father. And here art comments quite directly on life: it would be simplistic to interpret the November Revolution as just one thing, but it was also, and significantly, a rebellion against paternal authority.

The first successful play to embody this theme was Hasenclever's *Der Sohn*, prophetically written in 1914. It is a pathetic drama pitting a tyrannical father against a son yearning to be free. The father beats the twenty-year-old boy, continually humiliates him, and is in the end defeated by the strength of his son. But the strength is borrowed; the boy is helped to maturity by a motherly *Fräulein,* and, while in the last act he threatens to shoot his father, he need not take responsibility for his threat: his father dies at his feet, the victim of a stroke.

For all its pathos—and what can one say of a revolution in which the tyrant, as it were, anticipates the slave's bid for freedom?—Hasenclever's play set a pattern. It spoke to the younger generation.

"The literary qualities" of the play, wrote Kurt Wolff, who published it, "are not in question here. But this piece—certainly not an entertainment—was, with its father-son-conflict theme, explosive material for the generation born around 1890."[14] It was explosive because it was general. "A young English girl of Aldous Huxley's generation," Willy Haas writes, "once said to me: 'I hate my parents, and my parents hate me. That is quite all right.' It was not 'quite all right' with us. Franz Werfel suffered profoundly under this hatred of the father; in his visions he dreamed of a last blissful reconciliation between father and son in higher spheres"—and Haas himself deeply suffered under the same problem.[15] And it was so general that it became a cliché. "In that time," Carl Zuckmayer has caustically said, "the father-son conflict was demanded of every good young writer."[16] Many good and many mediocre young writers complied, and, not surprisingly, drew contradictory morals from this single theme.

The pendant to *Der Sohn* was *Vatermord*, by Arnolt Bronnen, who later, appropriately enough, became a Nazi. At first glance his play of parricide resembles Hasenclever's: here, too, a young man is harassed, intimidated, and beaten by his father, but the feeling is very different—while the young man of *Der Sohn* explicitly fights for freedom from tyranny, the young man of *Vatermord* lives in an atmosphere drenched in moral corruption, and his rebellion has purely subjective, irrationalist significance. *Vatermord* is an unappetizing play about an unappetizing family. Young Walter Fessel—the name "shackle" is surely not accidental—is timid and indecisive; he whines and begs like a child to be allowed to go to an agricultural school, while his father, a Socialist, wants him to study and fight for the rights of the workers; the boy is passive enough to be almost seduced by a homosexual school friend, but his real passion is for his mother, still young and beautiful, who hates her husband and lusts for her eldest son. As the play progresses through senseless beatings and endless disputes—all presented in a pseudo-poetic undifferentiated speech, a semistut-

---

[14] *Autoren, Bücher, Abenteuer*, 15.
[15] Haas, *Literarische Welt*, 60.
[16] Zuckmayer, *Als Wär's ein Stück von mir*, 324.

tering, highly repetitive prose, obviously designed to hypnotize the audience—the mother becomes sexually aroused and, like a bitch in heat, seeks the male that will satisfy her, first in her husband and finally, after the son has stabbed his father to death, in her son. But Walter Fessel, who has killed not the tyrant but all rational order, rejects his naked mother with a final stammering speech:

> I have enough of you.
> I have enough of everything.
> Go bury your husband, you are old,
> I am young however,
> I know you not,
> I am free.
> No one before me, no one beside me, no one above me, father
>   dead,
> Heaven, I jump on you, I am flying,
> It urges, trembles, moans, laments, must rise, swells, quells,
>   bursts, flies, must rise, must rise,
> I,
> I blossom—[17]

The strains of adolescence—the burden of schooling and the stirring of sex—had long attracted German writers of the modern movement; Wedekind's pioneering *Frühlings Erwachen* is, after all, crudely put, a play about puberty. In the early days of the Republic, Hermann Hesse gave these themes a psychoanalytical twist, while Franz Werfel encouraged the son's rebellion against the authoritarian father in both poems and novellas: it was in 1920 that Werfel published his short novel of successful filial rebellion, *Nicht der Mörder, der Ermordete ist schuldig—Not the Murderer, the Victim Is Guilty*—an unfortunate saying which the Nazis were to use much later, in a rather different context and with a different meaning. And it was the year before, in 1919, that Franz Kafka wrote, though he did not mail, his celebrated letter, a wounded son's indictment, to his father.

For many, the conflict went deeper than mere personal antagonism; it came to symbolize the political situation, or even the world's destiny. "Father and son," exclaims a character in Kaiser's play

[17] Bronnen, *Vatermord* (1925 ed.), 96.

Koralle, "strain away from one another. It is always a struggle of life and death."[18] And in the turmoil of the Weimar scene, writers agreed neither on the meaning of the father-son conflict nor on its proper outcome. Socialists and republicans favored the son's bid for rational freedom against irrational authority; but there were many, hostile to rebellion, who sided with the father.

For this second group, the history of young Frederick of Prussia was the perfect subject. The story was well known and thoroughly attested; myth here obtains the support of history. Frederick, still crown prince, defies his uncultivated martinet of a royal father; he would rather play the flute and write French poems than drill troops. He concerts with his friend Katte to run away, but the pair are betrayed, and the king takes his revenge. For a long time he is determined to execute his son along with his son's friend, but good sense and the pleading of his advisers induce him to change course slightly: Katte will be executed before the crown prince's eyes, and Frederick, after a long hard penance, will be restored to the royal grace.

In the versions by right-wing writers, the father holds all the good cards: King Frederick William I is coarse and cruel, his decision to have his son executed reveals a streak of obstinacy and vindictiveness that is hardly praiseworthy; but the king is, after all, the finest Prussian type: honest, frugal, upstanding, passionately devoted to the welfare of the country that God has entrusted to him. If he is harsh, he is at least manly; if he is narrow, he embodies qualities that matter—loyalty, public service, piety. The son is intellectually superior, but he has effeminate leanings, yet he—we know it from history—will grow into greatness. But who can say that he would have become Frederick the Great if he had not gone through this purgatory, if he had not learned to bow down before his father, and take the royal burden upon himself by becoming precisely like his father?

The work that represents this genre most nakedly is a play by Joachim von der Goltz, which places the meaning of young Frederick's drama, though in itself obvious enough, into its very title: it is called

[18] Quoted in Jethro Bithell, *Modern German Literature, 1880–1938* (2nd ed., 1946), 444.

Vater und Sohn. It holds no surprises: the division into acts is traditional, as is the management of the action; speech is naturalistic, filled with soldierly humor; characters are straight from the fairy-tale storehouse of a military nation—at moments of extreme tension, generals weep, while other characters face the mighty king in virile confrontation. When the flight has been discovered, and Frederick William I raves that both young men must be beheaded, Buddenbrok, a general and the king's close companion, steps forward: "If His Majesty wants blood, let him take mine. (*He tears open his military coat.*) That other [that is, young Frederick's] you won't have, as long as I may speak a word." The king: "Buddenbrok!!" Buddenbrok *"calmly"*: "My King and Lord . . ." And so forth. And in the final scene the young prince humiliates himself, as he is ordered to do, before his father and his father's companions, dryly, merely following orders, when the king suddenly melts, and comments on the prince's pallor *"in a transformed soft voice."* This is enough; young Frederick *"meets the king's look and suddenly, deeply moved, drops to his father's feet"*: "Father, forgive!" And the father forgives.

This was the kind of drama that conservative and *völkische* circles could appreciate; indeed, among its many admirers was Stresemann. Goltz's play was saluted for its "manliness"; it reminded some critics of Kleist—which was, in the inflamed political situation of Weimar, a tendentious compliment, since Kleist's plays were being widely revived to serve the cause of militant nationalism. Goltz himself was hailed as a writer whose roots were deep in the soil, a soil called *"Volk, Deutschtum."*[19] The "Fridericus" films that UFA began to produce in 1922 and continued to produce right to the end—*Fridericus Rex, The Mill of Sans Souci, The Chorale of Leuthen*—were a usually trashy but always popular tribute to Goltz's work.

The presidential campaign of 1925 re-enacted the son-father conflict in reality, and on a larger stage. The election of Hindenburg was the consequence of miscalculations and sectarian self-serving political decisions—of Socialist timidity, Communist obstructionism, and the

[19] See the excerpts from reviews printed on the back cover of *Vater und Sohn* (published 1921, 1922 ed.).

endless stupid cleverness of bourgeois politicians. But it was symbolic as well. It is true that Hindenburg did not even muster a majority, but more than 14½ millions voted for the aged "hero of Tannenberg," conveniently forgetting that he had begged for an armistice late in 1918 and left the burden of responsibility for the peace to others. Hindenburg smelled of the old order; he had been sold to the public in a demagogic campaign as the great man above parties, as the near-mystical representative of the German soul, the very embodiment of traditional values—in a word, as a sturdy paternal figure. With his election, the revenge of the father had begun.

VI / THE REVENGE OF THE FATHER:

Rise and Fall of Objectivity

I

To the intense disappointment of his promoters, President Hindenburg took his responsibilities seriously. He acted positively like a civilian, like the President of a Republic he intended to protect rather than subvert. There were skeptics who took the election as a portent of worse things to come; Meinecke feared for the Republic and placed his hope in hope itself, while Kessler thought that Hindenburg's elevation would bring "one of the darkest chapters of German history."[1] They were right, of course, though not immediately. Meanwhile most Germans, living from day to day, preferred enjoying the new, calmer atmosphere to speculating about an uncertain future. By 1925, in fact, the German atmosphere was calmer than it had been since the revolution and the war; Hindenburg's correct conduct did not produce, it reflected a lowering of the political temperature. In politics as in art, the time for revolutionary experimentation appeared to be over.

This parallel course of Weimar culture and Weimar politics is too obvious to have gone unnoticed.[2] Culture was in continuous, tense interaction with society, an expression and criticism of political realities. This mixture of intimacy and hostility between art and life is characteristic of all modern society; in Weimar, where old centers of

[1] Kessler, *Tagebücher*, 439; Meinecke, *Politische Schriften*, 384.
[2] See, for example, Garten, *Modern German Drama*, 171; Kracauer, *From Caligari to Hitler*, 165.

power—the universities, the bureaucracy, the army—had resisted outsiders while the theatre, publishing, and journalism were largely in outsiders' hands, it was particularly marked. The three lives of the Bauhaus—venturesome trials at the beginning, secure accomplishment in the middle years, and frantic pessimism at the end—are expressive of the three periods of the Republic itself. The time from November 1918 to 1924, with its revolution, civil war, foreign occupation, political murder, and fantastic inflation, was a time of experimentation in the arts; Expressionism dominated politics as much as painting or the stage.[3] Between 1924 and 1929, when Germany enjoyed fiscal stabilization, relaxation of political violence, renewed prestige abroad, and widespread prosperity, the arts moved into the phase of *Neue Sachlichkeit*—of objectivity, matter-of-factness, sobriety. And then, between 1929 and 1933, the years of disastrously rising unemployment, government by decree, decay of middle-class parties, and resumption of violence, culture became less the critic than the mirror of events; the newspaper and film industries ground out right-wing propaganda, the best among architects, novelists, or playwrights were subdued or silent, and the country was inundated by the rising tide of *Kitsch,* much of it politically inspired.

The Expressionist mood had been under criticism during the Expressionist years. "The Expressionists," Hajo Holborn has said, "wanted a new culture, but few others wanted a new culture, and those who did went over to Germanic Socialism." As early as 1918 Max Weber had called Expressionism a "spiritual narcotic," paired it with irresponsible mysticism, and demanded a new *Sachlichkeit*, as being "the only road to authenticity and the education of conscience—*Schamgefühl*."[4] And Rainer Maria Rilke, though sympathetic and sensitive to the new, and ready to acclaim the lyrical poetry of Expressionists like Heym and Werfel, thought in 1919 that Expressionism was a spectacular but unfortunate diversion. He could understand its

[3] The term "political expressionism" is, I think, Hannah Arendt's.
[4] Quoted in "Ein Jahrhundert *Frankfurter Zeitung," Die Gegenwart*, XI (October 29, 1956), 15.

origins, but he did not believe in its call for "fraternity"; it seemed to him a self-contradictory and ultimately destructive cry of despair. "It is so comprehensible that people have become impatient—and yet, what do we need more now than patience? Wounds need time, and are not healed by having flags planted in them." True progress was the work of "the carpenter, simply back at his plane, the smith back at his hammer, the merchant calculating and figuring once more"—these were the real revolutionaries. There were honest men among the Expressionists, no doubt, but for the most part these "shocking and importunate" personages were "diverting our attention from the tender growth of what will really, gradually, appear to be the future."[5] Even those who had begun as Expressionists were soon beset by doubts: Carl Zuckmayer's first play, *Am Kreuzweg*, produced by Jessner in 1920, was pure Expressionism, declamatory and difficult, yet in 1922 Zuckmayer expressed his distaste for a style he thought alien to life, artificial, hysterical, worn out, and greeted the fresh talent, Bertolt Brecht: "There is a poet! A new tone. A power of speech and form which sweeps all that stale Expressionism into the ashcan."[6] It was hardly a just verdict—the early work of Brecht owes much to Expressionist impulses—but it shows a shift of temper. By 1924 Paul Kornfeld, himself a leading Expressionist, could call for an end to Expressionism. "No more about war, revolution and the salvation of the world" he wrote. "Let us be modest and turn our attention to other and smaller things."[7] And shortly after, Rudolf Kayser, editor of the *Neue Rundschau*, announced that "now after the exorbitant, gushing —*verströmten*—ecstasies, the tendency toward a new reality and objectivity—*Sachlichkeit*—is becoming palpable in all areas of life."[8] The time for a slower pace was at hand.

The years of *Neue Sachlichkeit* were good years for the arts, but

[5] Rilke to Anni Mewes, September 12, 1919. *Briefe*, II, 157–158.
[6] *Als Wär's ein Stück von mir*, 365.
[7] Garten, *Modern German Drama*, 173.
[8] Wolfgang Grothe, "*Die neue Rundschau* des Verlages S. Fischer," *Börsenblatt für den deutschen Buchhandel*, Frankfurter Ausgabe, XVII (December 14, 1961), 2236.

the men who first used the name were aware of its ambiguity. Gustav Hartlaub, the director of the Mannheim Museum who is credited with inventing the term, related the new mood "to the general contemporary feeling in Germany of resignation and cynicism after a period of exuberant hopes (which had found an outlet in expressionism). Cynicism and resignation are the negative side of the *Neue Sachlichkeit* the positive side expressed itself in the enthusiasm for the immediate reality as a result of the desire to take things entirely objectively on a material basis without immediately investing them with ideal implications."[9] Carl Sternheim's acidulous comedy of 1926, *Die Schule von Uznach*, which was subtitled *Die neue Sachlichkeit*, took exception to the new cynicism and caricatured the "realism" of progressive educators as an excuse for promoting sexual license, and Siegfried Kracauer deplored the political passivity of the new style. But there were others, like Hartlaub himself, who greeted the disillusionment inherent in the *Neue Sachlichkeit* as a long overdue corrective to the intoxication of Expressionism; he chose to call it "healthy."[10]

Whatever its ultimate meaning—and that meaning differed from artist to artist—in substance the *Neue Sachlichkeit* was a search for reality, for a place to stand in the actual world; it was the struggle for objectivity that has characterized German culture since Goethe. It called for realism in setting, accurate reportage, return to naturalistic speech, and, if there had to be idealism, sober idealism. It was a movement toward simplicity and clarity in which many of the Expressionists could join, not merely because they were weary with old modes or venally adapted themselves to new fashions or experienced outright conversion; Expressionism itself had contained impulses toward objectivity, which now gained the upper hand. Carl Zuckmayer shifted with little evident strain from the Expressionism of his *Kreuzweg,* which he was later moved to call a bad piece, "a confused, chaotic piece,"[11] to the broad naturalism of *Der fröhliche Weinberg* of 1925, a comedy that made him rich and was greeted by the relieved critics

---

[9] Quoted in Myers, *German Expressionists*, 224.
[10] *Loc. cit.*
[11] *Als Wär's ein Stück von mir*, 315.

as a timely conversion. "*Sic transit gloria expressionismi*," wrote Alfred Kerr in his celebrated laconic style.[12] Similarly, Franz Werfel, among the first of the Expressionist poets, turned toward objectivity from conviction rather than opportunism; his call for humane pacific cosmopolitanism, for plain goodness, never wavered, but his techniques developed from exuberant playfulness to meticulous precision. Around 1924 Werfel's metamorphosis was practically complete; in that year he published a major novel, *Verdi*, which portrays Verdi in the midst of an unproductive period, deeply jealous of Wagner and depressed about his own talent. It is only when he is freed from his sick admiration for that overripe seducer that Verdi can go on to the masterpiece of his advanced years, *Otello*. In style as in message, Werfel's *Verdi* reads like an awakening from Expressionism and a return to reality.

1924 was also the year that Thomas Mann published his most famous novel, *Der Zauberberg*. The book is so familiar that it requires little exposition; it deserves attention here because it occupied a strategic place in the political education of Thomas Mann, and has important symptomatic meaning for Weimar. Mann, as his private correspondence and public utterances leave no doubt, took his novel with the utmost seriousness; irony was no laughing matter for him. He was prepared to defend the novel as an aesthetic creation and, beyond that, its cultural, philosophical, indeed political validity. Obviously— a little too obviously—*Der Zauberberg* asks to be read on several levels. It is a realistic novel, the story of Hans Castorp, introduced with deliberate disingenuousness by his creator as "a simple young man," who goes to a Swiss sanatorium to visit his tubercular cousin and, contracting the disease himself, stays for seven years. The realistic side of the novel may be exhausting—it was one of Thomas Mann's cherished convictions that only the exhaustive is truly interesting—but it is superb in its own leisurely way; Thomas Mann, the cultural aristocrat and philosophical ironist happened to be a splendid story-teller and fascinating reporter, with a penetrating eye, an accurate ear,

[12] Review of *Der fröhliche Weinberg*, in *Berliner Tageblatt*, December 23, 1925, in Rühle, *Theater für die Republik*, 669.

and—perhaps surprisingly—deft, direct humor. Beyond this, *Der Zauberberg* is a representative of a favorite genre in modern fiction, the *Bildungsroman*, the story of a young man's education in, and through, life. "It is," Mann wrote, "a specifically German and thoroughly eccentric—*grund-wunderliches*—enterprise, a sort of modern version of the *Bildungsroman*," yet, "at the same time, something like a parody of one."[13] Mann did not like to be simple if it was at all possible to be complicated.

But deeper than this—beneath the realistic novel and the novel of an education—lies the symbolic novel with its "musical dialectic."[14] The sanatorium is a simulacrum of European civilization, overripe, weary with peace, ready for the dance of death, openly prosperous and secretly corrupt; its international clientele, its gossip, love affairs, dubious psychoanalyst and even more dubious bouts of occultism, above all its ambulatory patients with their ruddy cheeks and vigorous walks concealing and displaying their insidious disease—the tubercular, with their perpetual slight fever, often look healthier than the healthy—are themselves, perceptively observed, but they are also Heartbreak House. And Mann populates this sanatorium, which is Europe on the eve of 1914, with some archetypal characters, all of them voluble; it is their role to educate Hans Castorp in a majestic tug of war among the styles of thinking that have divided Europe for centuries. There is Settembrini, the unrepentant child of the Enlightenment, well-meaning, rationalist, predictable in his anticlericalism, his opposition to censorship, his optimism, the liberal who spouts clichés but remains likable because he really means them; he is Heinrich Mann, the *Zivilisationsliterat* in transparent Italian disguise. There is Naphta, the apostle of irrationalism and the inquisition, a fanatical, darkly eloquent advocate and seeker of death who ends, as he must, by suicide, at once fulfilling his philosophy and destroying his influence. Then there is Peeperkorn, a latecomer to the novel, robust, sensual, talkative but inarticulate, a pagan celebrant of enjoyment who is, ironically, a very sick man: he has come to the sanatorium as

---

[13] Mann to Felix Bertaux, July 23, 1924. *Briefe*, 213–214.
[14] Mann to Josef Ponten, January 21, 1925. *Ibid.*, 226.

a patient and, besides, he takes his phallic philosophy with such tragic seriousness that once his fears of impotence overwhelm him he must kill himself—the slave of bodily pleasures must die when his body refuses to perform. And Castorp has other teachers, less eloquent but more important than these; there is the attractive, exotic Russian patient Clawdia Chauchat who irresistibly reminds him of a schoolmate for whom he had felt a strong attachment—it is for her sake that Hans Castorp so avidly studies biology, anatomy, and physiology, and to her that he pours out all his miscellaneous scientific learning in a long, impassioned, awkward declaration of love—in French; his love for her is desperate, his possession of her brief, his debt to her enormous. And finally there is his brave cousin Joachim, the uncomplicated young officer who hates death, despises the romanticism that so irresponsibly toys with it, wants nothing more than to return to his career, to leave this place of sickness and corruption and return to life, and whom Mann kills off in one of the most moving chapters in the novel. How does Castorp awaken to the questions that matter, his questions about man and his station? Mann asks. "Not primarily through Naphta and Settembrini, but through much more sensual means, which are hinted at in the lyrical and *infatuated* essay on the organic."[15]

It is through Clawdia and Joachim, then, that Mann drives his novel to its decisive lessons and its most general significance. Since his early days, Mann had undergone a combat in his own mind, fed by his reading of the German romantics, and his admiration for Wagner, Schopenhauer, and Nietzsche: it was the old German combat between love of life and love of death, the ironic incongruity between artistic achievement and physical survival, the sickness of talent and the stupidity of health—these themes had pervaded the early works, *Buddenbrooks* and *Tonio Kröger,* which had made him famous. Young Hans Castorp, for all his simplicity, has obscure intimations of these conflicts: the healthy world of business, which awaits him in the flatland, appeals to him less than the death-ridden, problematic world of the sanatorium; his attack of tuberculosis is a symbol—in *Der Zauber-*

15 Mann to Josef Ponten, May 11, 1925. *Ibid.,* 232.

berg everything, including the number of Castorp's room, is a symbol —of his secret infatuation with death. Disease, Castorp insists to the despair of his paternal friend Settembrini, is simply more interesting than health; and much of his reading, many of his conversations in the sanatorium are directed to clarifying and developing this dubious philosophy. Mann had held it himself; even his wartime writings on politics had been informed with it. Aristocracy, he said, talking about *Der Zauberberg*, with its romanticism and love of history, is somehow tied to death—*Todesverbundenheit*—while democracy is friendly to life—*Lebensfreundlichkeit*. There is something voluptuous about the love of death, Mann concedes this now; barbarism has its advantages.[16] But against it stands the philosophy that affirms life in the face of death, cherishes reason without underestimating passion.

In *Der Zauberberg*, Hans Castorp arrives at this precarious humanism partly through instruction, largely through his own ruminations, and makes his decisive discovery on a lonely, almost mortal excursion into the snowy landscape near the sanatorium. The chapter that describes his experience, "Snow," is the high point of the novel and one of the high points of modern literature, where Mann successfully fuses all the elements of his work—realism, symbolism, philosophy—into one lucid unity. Eager to be alone with his thoughts, Hans Castorp goes skiing in the silent snow. But he is caught in a snowstorm and gets lost; weary, numbed with sips of port, the wind, and the unfamiliar effort, he falls to the snowy ground and drops into a dream. What he sees is the antithesis of his own situation, a lovely warm park, a classical landscape—Greece, doubtless—with a classical population, gay, cheerful, beautiful, dancing, walking, resting. But then a temple, severe, almost sinister, appears before him; Hans enters it, afraid. He is right to be: there he sees two hideous witches tearing a child into pieces and devouring it. Nauseated and in despair at his vision, Hans half-awakens to find himself exhausted and frozen in the snow. And he works it out: death is in life, but love—not reason— is stronger than death. "Man is master of contradictions, they exist

16 *Loc. cit.*

through him, and so he is grander—*vornehmer*—than they. Grander than death, too grand for it—that is the freedom of his head. Grander than life, too grand for it—that is the piety in his heart." But the balance is not even; Castorp resolves: "I shall not grant death dominion over my thoughts! For goodness and charity consist in this, and in nothing else." And again, emphatically: "For the sake of goodness and love, man shall not grant death dominion over his thoughts."[17] And with a tremendous effort he rouses himself and manages to get back alive.

It is a magnificent set piece, yet doubts arise. It is dramatically right for Castorp to fall again into some confusion, to have his dream and his interpretation partially fade—he is, after all, not a philosopher. But then Thomas Mann was not much of a philosopher either, though he was a great novelist. Intellectually and emotionally he had come a long way—longer than one had any right to expect: from emotional monarchist to *Vernunftrepublikaner* to a real commitment to Weimar. Yet he would not, could not, take the last step. "In his heart," the author of *Der Zauberberg* said about himself, "he is no Settembrini."[18] Yet what Weimar needed was precisely more Settembrinis—perhaps a little less naïve and a little more laconic—liberals wholly disenchanted with political myths and metaphysical *Schwärmerei*. With *Der Zauberberg*, Mann's own contribution to the *Neue Sachlichkeit*, his love affair with death was over, but he looked back to his old mistress with evident, if fading, regret.

II

Mann's *Zauberberg* was the literary event of 1924; in its first year, it sold fifty thousand copies—a vast number for a bulky two-volume novel in those days. And it was in the same year that another event took place, less widely publicized but equally significant: Bertolt

[17] *Der Zauberberg*, 2 vols. (1924), II, 259–260.
[18] Mann to Joseph Ponten, May 11, 1925. *Briefe*, 232.

Brecht, already a well-known playwright, and halfway between his nihilistic and Expressionist experiments and a new cool, highly personal lyricism, moved from Munich to Berlin.

The move is significant because it symbolizes the growing power of Berlin in the golden mid-twenties. As Germany's largest city, as the capital of Prussia and the Empire, Berlin had been the only possible choice for capital of the Republic. And Berlin came to engross not merely government offices and party headquarters, but the leaders of culture, at the expense of the provinces. Other major cities like Munich, Frankfurt, or Hamburg struggled to keep excellence in their universities, took pride in special institutes, cultivated continued high quality in their theatres and liveliness in their Bohemian quarters. But Berlin was a magnet. After years of resistance, Heinrich Mann gave way and moved there. "Centralization," he said in humorous resignation, "is inevitable."[19] The city drew strength from its illustrious immigrants, and in turn gave strength to them. "Beckmann is unthinkable without Berlin," one of his admirers noted in 1913, while, in 1924, another admirer turned the observation around: "Beckmann," the critic Meier-Graefe said, "is the new Berlin."[20] The old Berlin had been impressive, the new Berlin was irresistible. To go to Berlin was the aspiration of the composer, the journalist, the actor; with its superb orchestras, its hundred and twenty newspapers, its forty theatres, Berlin was the place for the ambitious, the energetic, the talented. Wherever they started, it was in Berlin that they became, and Berlin that made them, famous: young Erich Kästner, who became notorious with his impudent verses before he became famous for his children's books, was fired from his post on the staff of a Leipzig newspaper and so in 1927, he recalls, he "went off, penniless, to conquer Berlin."[21]

Kurt Tucholsky wrote his affectionate chansons and nostalgic

[19] Heinrich Mann to Felix Bertaux, June 11, 1923, quoted in Klaus Schröter, *Heinrich Mann in Selbstzeugnissen und Bilddokumenten* (1967), 110.

[20] See Max Beckmann, *Leben in Berlin: Tagebuch 1908–9,* ed. Hans Kinkel (1966), editor's note, 60.

[21] Erich Kästner, "Meine sonnige Jugend," in *Kästner für Erwachsene* (1966), 528.

sketches about Berlin from the haven of Paris, but he, the native Berliner celebrating his city from a distance, was untypical. His like were greatly outnumbered by the likes of Kästner, *Wahlberliner,* men born in Hamburg or Breslau, Vienna or Prague or points east and south, who chose to live in Berlin or, rather, who found any other city intolerable. Willy Haas, born in Prague but wholly identified with Berlin, where he reviewed films and edited Rowohlt's magazine, *Die literarische Welt,* found that "the fewest Berliners I knew were real Berliners." But then, "to become a Berliner—that came quickly, if one only breathed in the air of Berlin with deep breath." Haas loved Berlin; it made him downright sentimental: "I loved the rapid, quick-witted reply of the Berlin woman above everything, the keen, clear reaction of the Berlin audience in the theatre, in the cabaret, on the street and in the café, that taking-nothing-solemnly yet taking-seriously of things, that lovely, dry, cool and yet not cold atmosphere, the indescribable dynamic, the love for work, the enterprise, the readiness to take hard blows—and go on living."[22]

Berlin, it is obvious, aroused powerful emotions in everyone. It delighted most, terrified some, but left no one indifferent, and it induced, by its vitality, a certain inclination to exaggerate what one saw. Stefan Zweig was one who projected his horror at later events onto his horror of Berlin in the time of inflation: "Berlin," he writes, "transformed itself into the Babel of the world. Bars, amusement parks, pubs shot up like mushrooms. What we had seen in Austria proved to be merely a mild and timid prelude to this witches' sabbath, for the Germans brought to perversion all their vehemence and love of system. Made-up boys with artificial waistlines promenaded along the Kurfüstendamm—and not professionals alone: every high school student wanted to make some money, and in the darkened bars one could see high public officials and high financiers courting drunken sailors without shame. Even the Rome of Suetonius had not known orgies like the Berlin transvestite balls, where hundreds of men in women's clothes and women in men's clothes danced under the benevolent eyes of the police. Amid the general collapse of values, a

[22] Haas, *Die literarische Welt,* 123.

kind of insanity took hold of precisely those middle-class circles which had hitherto been unshakable in their order. Young ladies proudly boasted that they were perverted; to be suspected of virginity at sixteen would have been considered a disgrace in every school in Berlin."[23]

There was something in what Zweig saw, but Berlin had its soberer, more respectable, yet equally striking side. It had, among others, Bruno Walter, born in Berlin, grown famous in concert and opera houses in Munich, Vienna, and Salzburg, yet always at heart a Berliner. "In his memoirs," he writes, "the English ambassador to Berlin, Viscount d'Abernon, speaks of the time after 1925 as of an epoch of splendor in the Reich capital's cultural life." He was right; it was "as if all the eminent artistic forces were shining forth once more, imparting to the last festive symposium of the minds a many-hued brilliance before the night of barbarism closed in." The accomplishments of the Berlin theatres "could hardly be surpassed in talent, vitality, loftiness of intention, and variety." Walter lists the "Deutsches Theater and the Kammerspiele, in which Reinhardt held sway," which imparted to "tragedies, plays, and comedies the character of festival plays— from Shakespeare to Hauptmann and Werfel, from Molière to Shaw and Galsworthy, from Schiller to Unruh and Hofmannsthal." Then there was "the Tribüne, under Eugen Robert," devoted to "the careful and vivacious rendition of French, English, and Hungarian comedies. And the State Theater, where "Leopold Jessner's dramatic experiments caused heated discussion." Karlheinz Martin "conducted the destinies of the Volksbühne with a genuine understanding of the artistic popularization of plays and the theater." And there were other stages, which also tried to "raise dramatic interpretative art to new levels. Actors and stage directors alike were able to display the full scope of their talents. Contemporary native and international creations as well as those of the past had their day on the boards." There were many experiments; "there were oddities, and occasionally even absurdities." But the "characteristic sign of those days was an unparalleled mental alertness. And the alertness of the giving cor-

[23] Stefan Zweig, *Die Welt von Gestern*, 287.

responded to the alertness of the receiving. A passionate general concentration upon cultural life prevailed, eloquently expressed by the large space devoted to art by the daily newspapers in spite of the political excitement of the times." Music was just as lively. "The Philharmonic Concerts led by Wilhelm Furtwängler; the 'Bruno Walter Concerts' with the Philharmonic Orchestra; a wealth of choral concerts, chamber-music recitals, and concerts by soloists; the State Opera, deserving of high praise because of *premières* such as that of Alban Berg's *Wozzeck* and Leos Janacek's *Jenufa* under Erich Kleiber's baton; the newly flourishing Municipal Opera under my guidance; the Kroll Opera under Klemperer." And a number of other institutions "matched the achievements of the dramatic stage." Add to all this "the visible arts and the outstanding accomplishments of science" and, clearly, it was a great epoch in a great city.[24]

Bruno Walter's compilation, though copious, is far from complete. Berlin was headquarters for the political cabaret, where Otto Reutter performed his own dry compositions, lampooning the Germans for their rigidity in conduct and instability in politics, where Paul Graetz and Trude Hesterberg sang Walter Mehring's satirical songs, and Claire Waldoff her proletarian ditties; Berlin the center of political journalism, the biting commentary of Carl von Ossietzky, Leopold Schwarzschild, and—usually sent in from abroad—Kurt Tucholsky; Berlin the stage for Erwin Piscator's experiment in the political theatre; Berlin the scene of Alfred Döblin's most remarkable novel, *Berlin Alexanderplatz*; Berlin the best possible town for premieres of charming trifling films, sentimental Lehar operettas, and the *Dreigroschenoper*; Berlin the city of publishing empires like Mosse and Ullstein; Berlin the city of Samuel Fischer, the great publisher, who had on his list Thomas Mann, Hermann Hesse, Gerhart Hauptmann, Stefan Zweig, Carl Zuckmayer, Alfred Döblin, Hugo von Hofmannsthal. Berlin was eminently the city in which the outsider could make his home and extend his talents. "The overflowing plenty of stimuli," the poet Gottfried Benn writes about the Jews in his autobiography, his nose for race intact, "of artistic, scientific, commercial improvisations

[24] Bruno Walter, *Theme and Variations*, 268–269.

which placed the Berlin of 1918 to 1933 in the class of Paris,
stemmed for the most part from the talents of this sector of the
population, its international connections, its sensitive restlessness, and
above all its absolute—*totsicher*—instinct for quality."[25] No wonder
there should be good Germans, like Heidegger, who looked upon
Berlin, and not the Berlin of the inflation period alone, as a modern
Babylon, and refused to live there.

But for republicans, early in the Republic and late, it was a city of
excitement and hope. "The future of Germany," Heinrich Mann said
in 1921, "is being tentatively anticipated by Berlin. The man who wants
to gather hope should look there." Berlin is a breeder of civilization,
and it, rather than laws, will finally effect the unification of Germany.
"Yes, Berlin will be the beloved capital, little though it imagined that
it would be."[26] And Zuckmayer, the republican playwright, celebrated
the republican city in his memory. Berlin, he said, "was worth more
than a mass. This city gobbled up talents and human energies with un-
exampled appetite"; it "sucked up into itself" talents real and spurious
"with tornado-like powers." In those days "one spoke of Berlin as one
speaks of a highly desirable woman, whose coldness and coquettish-
ness are widely known." She was called "arrogant, snobbish, parvenu,
uncultivated, common," but she was the center of everyone's fantasies
and the goal of everyone's desires: "Everyone wanted her, she enticed
everyone." The "man who had Berlin owned the world." It was a city
that demanded, and gave, energies: "We needed little sleep and we
were never tired." It was a city of crooks and cripples, a city of hit
songs and endless talk; with a press that was "cruel, pitiless, aggressive,
filled with bloody irony, yet not discouraging," and with criticism that
was, in the same way, harsh, nonconformist, but fair, in search of
quality, delighted with excellence. "Berlin tasted of the future, and that
is why we gladly took the crap and the coldness."[27]

[25] *Doppelleben*, in *Gesammelte Werke*, ed. Dieter Wellershoff, 4 vols. (1958–
1961), IV, 73. But then Benn makes it clear that some of his best friends were
Jews.
[26] Quoted in Ludwig Marcuse, *Mein zwanzigstes Jahrhundert*, 54.
[27] *Als Wär's ein Stück von mir*, 311–314.

III

If Berlin tasted of the future, the taste of Berlin was cruelly mistaken: there was little future left. Life would not leave art alone. True, things seemed markedly better on all fronts during those golden midtwenties: unemployment was down, wages were up, political extremism seemed played out—the Weimar Republic was getting to be a good place to live in. And gradually, precisely in these years, Germany ended her isolation and rejoined the community of nations; Stresemann's foreign policy and the sheer passage of time were paying off. In 1925 Germany, France, and other Western powers concluded the Locarno Treaty that settled Germany's western frontiers and placed Germany once more in the position of an independent power negotiating with its neighbors rather than a suppliant begging for favors. The "spirit of Locarno" became a proverbial expression for the era of reconciliation. And in the following year, in 1926, Germany entered the League of Nations.

But Weimar of those years was like the society on the magic mountain: ruddy cheeks concealed insidious symptoms. One of the most insidious of these was the cartelization of culture, on the model of the cartelization of industry. Alfred Hugenberg, a prominent member on the right wing of the right-wing German National Party, a hopelessly reactionary and politically ambitious magnate, built up an empire in the communications industry and became the strident, enormously influential voice of the counterrevolution. Officers, it was said, read only his press. Hugenberg had managed to amass dozens of newspapers all across the country, acquired the popular Berlin daily, the *Berliner Lokalanzeiger*, owned a news agency that spread the word— his word—to its numerous subscribers, and in 1927 took over the bankrupt UFA and made it into the biggest manufacturer of daydreams in the country. Personally unimpressive, Hugenberg was animated by insatiable political passions and hatreds masquerading as convictions, and his financial resources were enormous. His campaigns were predictable—against Stresemann, against Locarno, against any attempts at international understanding, against liberalism, against the Republic—but they were no less effective for their expectedness; like disciplined troops, his newspapers conducted their vicious campaigns while the master was in the Reichstag, or at party congresses, digging the grave of the Republic. Not all of Hugenberg's propagandistic efforts were so direct and blatant as the editorials in his newspapers; his UFA ground out films that helped his cause more indirectly—cheerful superficial musicals which diverted attention from politics or unemployment, historical films about German heroes with pointed allusions to the Versailles *Diktat*, and equally pointed celebrations of qualities that the men of Weimar conspicuously lacked. Hugenberg retailed not merely opinions but confusion as well, and both were equally dangerous to the Republic.

Hugenberg, to be sure, did not have a monopoly over the opinion industry; republicans had their magnates, too, the great House of Mosse and the even greater House of Ullstein. The range of the Ullstein holdings was remarkable, almost frightening. The house published books and carefully nurtured its best-selling authors, like Vicki Baum. Its weekly picture-magazine, the *Berliner Illustrirte*, claimed to be the most widely read magazine of its kind in Europe. In the profitable field of women's magazines, Ullstein's *Die Dame* was a leading journal. For middle-brow tastes, mixing well-tailored essays, frivolous short stories, racy reportage, and photographs of naked girls, there was the pocket-sized monthly *Uhu*. Housewives had the well-edited *Blatt der Hausfrau*, children the *Heitere Fridolin*, and intellectuals found their hostility to Ullstein blunted by the Ullstein magazine for intellectuals, the *Querschnitt*. There were powerful Ullstein dailies, the *Berliner Zeitung*, popularly known as the "B.Z. am Mittag," and the old respectable *Vossische Zeitung*. In 1928 the house tried its hand at a racy tabloid, fittingly called *Tempo* and quickly renamed, by Berlin wits, "*Die jüdische Hast*—Jewish nervousness." It was neither an editorial nor a popular success, but this was an exception—Ullstein was not used to failures.

Ullstein did not merely publish facile mediocrities like Vicki Baum; its list was large and varied, and the quality of its journalism generally high. "If one speaks with old Berliners today," Vicki Baum writes in her autobiography, "with those who lived through the twenties and now live elsewhere, they will sigh with profound homesickness and tell you that there is no comparison anywhere to that lively, fascinating city of Berlin in those years. Yes, and one of the hearts of the inner city was the House of Ullstein. It was a focus of liberalism. . . . To be known as a liberal and an intellectual was a high honor then, a goal infinitely desirable and worth working and struggling for. At Ullstein's this liberalism meant that the doors were wide open for the widest variety of opinions, ideas, notions, and positions. Our authors included all the colors of the rainbow, from the red of the extreme left—Brecht and Toller—across the whole scale of the Expressionist school to the antimilitarist, antiwar book, *Im Westen nichts Neues,* by the young Remarque, and over to the dark green of aged, moss-grown nativist writers—*Heimatsschriftsteller*—like Richard Skowronnek."[28] The description is not without truth, but, like everything of Vicki Baum's, it remains on the surface. Ullstein's monopolizing of outlets—and my list is only a suggestion of its vast financial power—made many writers profoundly uneasy, produced conflicts between need and conviction, and an unhealthy, eventually lethal division between those who belonged and those who did not. For a writer without a private income, the favor of Ullstein meant luxury, its indifference or disfavor, near-starvation. Before the premiere of *Der fröhliche Weinberg*, Carl Zuckmayer, who was under contract to Ullstein, asked for a small additional advance—one hundred marks—to buy his mother a present; he was turned away. After the premiere, which was an almost unprecedented critical and popular success, Zuckmayer was told that he could draw up to ten thousand marks immediately, and that right after Christmas—it was now December 23, and there was little cash about—he could of course command larger sums. And when at the celebration for his success three of the five Ullstein brothers appeared, Zuckmayer's future was, quite simply, guaranteed.[29] Kurt Tucholsky, who had worked for the house off and on for many years and felt guilty and venal for his own complaisance, ac-

---

[28] Vicki Baum, *Es war alles ganz anders: Erinnerungen* (1962), 354.
[29] See *Als Wär's ein Stück von mir*, 405–413.

curately saw the top management as cold, totally oriented toward success, and pitiless.[30] What was worse, in the time of troubles to come, it would also lack courage.

And the time of troubles was at hand. Beginning in 1929, the Republic suffered a series of traumatic blows from which neither it nor its culture was ever to recover. Gustav Stresemann died on October 3, 1929; whatever his limitations, he had been, both for republicans at home and conciliatory minds abroad, an irreplaceable force for good. Count Kessler was in Paris at the time; on October 4, he wrote in his diary: "All Parisian morning papers are reporting the news of Stresemann's death in the largest possible type. It is almost as though the greatest French statesman had died. Mourning is general and genuine. One gets the feeling that we do now have a European fatherland." And he quotes the *Times* of London: "Stresemann did inestimable service to the German Republic; his work for Europe as a whole was almost as great."[31] Then came the depression, unemployment, continual political crisis culminating in the elections of September 1930, which decimated the bourgeois parties, gave the Nazis 6½ million votes and 107 deputies in the Reichstag, and led to Brüning's semidictatorship, to government by emergency decree. Survivors like Hannah Arendt and Hajo Holborn have testified to their dismay, and their conviction that the end had come. "The German intellectual's state of mind," Franz Neumann recalled later, "was, long before 1933, one of skepticism and despair, bordering on cynicism."[32] If that was the mood of some before 1930, September 1930 saddled intellectuals with it beyond hope of recovery. When late in 1935, in English exile, Arthur Rosenberg wrote his *History of the German Republic*, he concluded it with 1930, and treated the three years until Hitler's ascent to power as an epilogue. It was a tendentious periodization of Weimar history, but it reveals more than the mood of the disillusioned and displaced historian—it points to unpleasant realities.

[30] See Kurt Tucholsky to Mary Gerold-Tucholsky, September 18, 1928. *Ausgewählte Briefe*, 488–490.

[31] Kessler, *Tagebücher*, 595–596.

[32] Neumann, "The Social Sciences," *The Cultural Migration*, 14.

By 1930, indeed even before 1930, political divisions had deepened, and debate had grown ugly, scurrilous, often issuing in real violence. Hitler's boast in September 1930 that, if he came to power, heads would roll, was grimly, if still incompletely, anticipated by clashes in the streets. In December of 1930, at the movie premiere of Erich Maria Remarque's *Im Westen nichts Neues*—which as a novel had already aroused the right with its enormous sales, and its demonstration that war was hell and that German soldiers, far from having been stabbed in the back at home, had lost the war at the front—the Nazis, under Goebbels' leadership, led riots against the film, invaded the theatre, throwing stink bombs and letting loose mice, and finally succeeded in having the film banned. In fury and prophetic despair, Carl von Ossietzky attacked the republicans for their torpor and cowardice; craven republicans, he wrote, have constructed an "especially lovely formula"; with a regretful smile, they are saying to one another: "What is one to do? The film, after all, is so bad!" But, Ossietzky objected, "this affair is political and not touched by aesthetic categories. It is completely irrelevant whether the film and the book on which it is based are works of art. The sole question is whether a deliberately moderate pacific way of thinking . . . should continue to be permitted or not." First it "was openly terrorized" by a fanatical mob "under the leadership of a clubfooted psychopath," then it was "quietly quashed in the obscure censorship office of some obscure official." The banality every German and every foreign statesman utters on every possible occasion—that peace is preferable to war—"has now in Germany attained the charm of the forbidden." Fascism had scored another victory, and liberal cowardice, which simply stays home in moments of trouble, is now bankrupt. "Fascism can be beaten only in the streets. Against the National Socialist rabble party we have only one logic: the heavy knout; to tame them, we have only one doctrine: *A un corsaire—corsaire et demi!*"[33]

It was a brave and futile cry. The Social Democrats clung to republican legality; the House of Ullstein, itself Jewish, sought to accom-

[33] Carl von Ossietzky, "Remarque-Film," *Weltbühne*, 1930, in *Ausnahmezustand*, 218, 220.

modate itself to threatening conditions by purging itself of Jews and radicals, and by adopting a patriotic, even chauvinistic tone—which dismayed its friends and did not appease its enemies. Anti-Semitism, long endemic in the universities, and a standard battle cry of right-wing parties, became more virulent than ever. In impatience and sheer disgust, a number of promising or prominent intellectuals made common cause with the Communists, joining the party or submitting to its discipline, thus mirroring, and exacerbating, the polarization of political life. Arthur Köstler, who arrived from Paris in September 1930, on the day of the fateful Reichstag elections, to join the staff of the Ullstein firm in Berlin, thought Weimar doomed, liberals and Socialists contemptible, and Communism the only hope. And Bertolt Brecht, who had been studying Marxism sympathetically since he had come to Berlin, steadily moved left. In 1928 he put his distaste for the bourgeoisie and his materialist philosophy into the *Dreigroschenoper*: Mackie Messer taunts his bourgeois audience for loving its own fat belly and the docility of the workers, and assured it that however it might try to twist the truth, this much was certain: feeding one's face came first, ethics came after that. They are imperishable lines:

> Ihr, die ihr euren Wanst und unsre Bravheit liebt
> Das eine wisset ein für allemal:
> Wie ihr es immer dreht und wie ihr's immer schiebt
> Erst kommt das Fressen, dann kommt die Moral.

But when the party criticized his cynicism and remoteness from social realities, he shifted to didactic plays, radicalized his *Dreigroschenoper* into a crudely anticapitalist movie script and novel, assailed entertainment as "culinary opera," called for a drama committed to progress, and came to advocate a philosophy of self-sacrifice unto death for the sake of the cause.

IV

This political line was not without its appeal, and the Communists, like the Social Democrats, held firm in the face of the Nazi onslaught. But neither Communists nor Socialists could ever capture a sector of the population that was growing strategically more significant week by week: the youth.

The political history of the youth in the Weimar Republic is, among its many ironies, the most poignant. As the father-son literature had shown from the beginning, there was confusion not merely over who ought to win the contest, but even over who was who. The politicized youth movement, and the student organizations, nearly all right-wing and increasingly infiltrated and then dominated by Nazis, claimed to be speaking for youth and youthfulness. As they saw it, the men who had made the Republic—the *Novemberverbrecher*—were middle-aged, not only in years but in ways of thinking; the Republic, they insisted, had been born elderly. They were both right and wrong: the Nazis were not simply reactionaries; some of their notions, whether nihilist or totalitarian, were a repudiation as much of the traditional authoritarianism of the dead Empire as of the modern democratic rationalism of the dying Republic. Some of the leaders of right-wing youth were true revolutionaries, or fellow youths intoxicated with death. To that extent, the youth were young, if fatally so, rushing, with their eyes closed, into the abyss. But whether they were demanding a *Führer* who would organize their energies and compel them to the voluptuous passivity of total obedience, a restored and purified monarchy, or a Prussian-Socialist dictatorship, they were also betraying their youth and enslaving themselves, not merely to political adventurers and psychotic ideologues, but to the old industrial-military bureaucratic machine disguised in new forms.

The Nazis were not slow to recognize the importance of the youth. The young who had so far abstained from the polls and the young who were getting ready to cast their first ballot were two sources of enormous potential voting strength for them. Both groups were hungry for action—any action, brutalized, often imbued with notions of racial purity and sheer hatred for the most conspicuous of outsiders—the Jew—and in despair over the future; after all, it had become a rueful, common joke among students to reply when they were asked what they wanted to be after they had completed their studies: "Unemployed."

There is good evidence that the young, especially the students, an-

ticipated their elders in turning toward the right. In 1930 the Social
Democratic Party reported that less than 8 percent of its membership
was under twenty-five, and less than half of its membership under
forty.[34] In the same year, General Groener declared that the "radicalization" of students—radicalization toward the right—was a serious
danger to the country;[35] and in the same year students at the University
of Jena cheered a new professor, the virulent anti-Semite Hans F. K.
Günther, who had been forced on the university as professor of a new
chair in "*Rassenkunde*—racial science." By 1930—certainly by 1931
—the students in universities and *Gymnasia*, many of whom had long
staged anti-Semitic riots against Jewish and radical professors, and
kept Jewish students out of their associations, were largely National
Socialist in sympathy; perhaps half of them were Nazis, many wholly
unpolitical, and only a few openly republican.

This rightward turn of German youth was part, and sign, of a profound malaise. There was a whole genre of novels dealing with the
suicides of young high school students—*Schülerselbstmordromane*—
and its popularity reflected widespread interest in a grave phenomenon.
In early 1929 Friedrich Torberg published a characteristic suicide
novel, *Der Schüler Gerber*, and prefaced his story with the laconic
comment that in a single week—January 27 to February 3, 1929—he
had read in the newspapers of ten such suicides. And Ernst Toller,
himself to die by his own hand in 1939, dedicated his autobiography
to "the memory of my nephew Harry who, in 1928, at the age of
eighteen, shot himself." The preface of this autobiography, dated 1933,
helplessly laments the youth "which went many ways, followed false
gods and false leaders, but steadily tried to find clarity and the laws
of the spirit."[36]

And how could they find clarity amid the general cacophony, the
conflicting appeals, the blood-tingling assemblies of the Nazis, and the
general condition of the sick Republic? The popular media, above all

[34] See Franz Neumann, *Behemoth*, 18.
[35] Quoted in George L. Mosse, "Die deutsche Rechte und die Juden," in
*Entscheidungsjahr 1932: Zur Judenfrage in der Endphase der Weimarer Re-
publik* (1965), 197.
[36] Ernst Toller, *Prosa, Briefe, Dramen, Gedichte* (1961), 26, 27.

the films, were calculated mainly to sow confusion, and it was not Hugenberg's explicit orders alone that sowed it. As early as 1927, the greatly overrated director Fritz Lang brought out the tasteless extravaganza, *Metropolis*, which would be of no importance had it not been taken so seriously and acclaimed so widely. *Metropolis* is a fantasy without imagination, a picturesque, ill-conceived, and essentially reactionary tale which has only a few good shots of mass movement and rising waters to recommend it; the film sees the class struggle as science fiction and draws the kind of conclusion that can only be called a studied lie: Metropolis is the city of the future, where brutally enslaved workers toil, often unto death, in underground factories, while a small elite of masters enjoys leisure and irresponsible pleasures on vast estates and in ornamental gardens, complete with fountains and peacocks. The son of the master goes below, to "seek his brothers," and reconcile the two strata, which never meet. But his very reasons for his social interest are rotten: he has fallen in love, naturally at first sight, with a lovely working girl who has wandered into his garden. The action is confused and not worth retelling in detail; it involves a workers' rebellion instigated by a robot who looks like the girl but is actually the tool of the masters. In destroying the machines, the workers nearly destroy themselves, but the young man and the girl rescue the workers and their children, the wicked inventor of the robot is destroyed, and in a final sentimental scene, after boy and girl are reunited, the father-and-master is induced to shake hands with a foreman—an instructive scene, with the master all cold gentleman, the worker all gauche, inarticulate, conscious of his inferior status—and the classes are reconciled. The lesson is simple: even under the worst of conditions—and conditions are at their worst in Metropolis—only an evil demon can urge strikes or revolt; the truth lies always with the mediation of the heart. It is a repulsive film, but no more repulsive than the many films to which Kracauer calls attention, in which men break down and have women comfort them; as Kracauer has noted, again and again there are scenes in which the man puts his head, helpless, on the woman's bosom.[37] The revenge of

[37] See Kracauer, *From Caligari to Hitler*, 98–99, 112, 114, 122, 157–158, 171.

the father and the omnipotence of the mother were twin aspects of the Weimar scene, both equally destructive to the youth.

Responsible republican publicists were not blind to these dangers; much has been written about those who were complacent about Hitler and the Nazification of the young, but too little about those who wrote and spoke against it until they were compelled into silence. Thomas Mann and Friedrich Meinecke were only two among many urging students toward patience, and toward an appreciation of the true freedom that comes with rationality and discipline. In 1928 the popular novelist Jakob Wassermann took up the father-son conflict in a long, tendentious novel, *Der Fall Maurizius*, which portrays the struggle of a brave adolescent boy against his cold, cruel, powerful father: the father, a prosecuting attorney, had long ago perpetrated an act of judicial injustice; the son, after diligent research, uncovers his father's crime, repudiates him—"I do not want to be your son"—and with this declaration of independence drives the father into insanity. And the boy's only close school friend attacks right-wing students for being mere puppets in the hands of unknown forces, for "allowing themselves to be shoved back and forth, like stuffed dolls, by people of whom they do not even know whether they are paid agents of reaction."[38]

To judge from the literature, by 1932 this concern had deepened into alarm. In the first six months of that year, to give only one instance, the monthly *Neue Rundschau* published no fewer than six long articles, all worried, all intelligent, all understanding of the problems of youth, all exhorting to reason and patience. Jakob Wassermann showed deep sympathy for the "hopelessness of student youth." Behind the young man, he wrote, "the war, in front of him social ruin, to his left he is being pulled by the Communist, to his right by the Nationalist, and all around him there is not a trace of honesty and rationality, and all his good instincts are being distorted into hatred." Yet, he pleaded, not all is feeling, not all action is good simply because it is action. "Not every forty-year-old is a criminal and an idiot for the simple reason that he is twenty years older than you are,

[38] Jakob Wassermann, *Der Fall Maurizius* (1928), 586, 19.

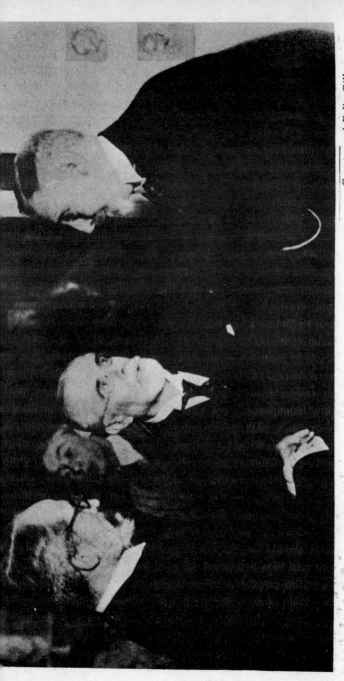

FRIEDRICH MEINECKE, ERICH MARCKS, AND HERMANN ONCKEN IN 1929

A trio of distinguished historians. Oncken and Marcks were specialists in nineteenth-century history; Meinecke, one of the most famous of *Vernunftrepublikaner*, was internationally known for his studies of the national spirit in Germany, the demonic force of *raison d'état*, and the rise of historicism.

MAX LIEBERMANN: ALBERT EINSTEIN   LITHOGRAPH, mid-1920's

In his long lifetime (1847-1935), Max Liebermann was the most famous painter in Germany; unlike his present subject, Einstein, he is now rather forgotten. A Jew and a true Berliner, Liebermann greeted the advent of the Nazis with an untranslatable remark: *"Man kann nicht soviel fressen, wie man kotzen möchte!"*—roughly, "You can't eat as much as you want to throw up." A fitting comment, not on the life, but on the death of the Weimar Republic.

not every fifty- or sixty-year-old a reactionary and enemy, not every father a fool and not every son a hero and martyr."[39] Elsewhere in the magazine Ernst Robert Curtius described the growing crisis of the university and called for a revival of humanist standards,[40] while the philosopher Ernst von Aster, in a perceptive piece, dissected what he called "the metaphysics of nationalism," in which he noted what others had noted before: that "strange connection" among the young of "revolutionary mutiny against authority and tradition" and "blind discipline toward the '*Führer*.'"[41] And in two alarming essays, the publicist and publisher Peter Suhrkamp traced the outlines, and intimated the outcome, of the father's revenge. Youth, he wrote looks back on the heroic days of its movement—before the First World War. "Their thoughts are disguised impulses; in their discussion private ideas parade as *Weltanschauung*." And they are continuing to cling to hero worship. "Without heroes they feel nothing. They resign. They take off. They have never grasped the difficulties, the dangers, and the harsh laws of reality." They are, in a word, not yet grown up. Now, in deep spiritual and economic need, they are turning anti-intellectual; they repudiate thinking as impotent, and so they are turning away from liberal parties and gathering under the umbrella of platitudes and dependence; they "love drill, and are ready for anyone who will command them." This may be natural of youth, but so far youth has never started a revolution. Yet today, Suhrkamp concludes, alienated, impoverished, ready for anything, filled with "anguish, hatred, rage, and noble indignation," youth may be ready for a real revolution. All they need is a "genuine revolutionary idea."[42]

[39] Jakob Wassermann, "Rede an die studentische Jugend über das Leben im Geiste: Zum Goethetag 1932," *Neue Rundschau*, XLIII, part I (1932), 530–544.

[40] Ernst Robert Curtius, "Die Universität als Idee und Erfahrung," *ibid.*, 145–167. This essay and others were later collected into Curtius' celebrated call to reason and culture, *Deutscher Geist in Gefahr* (1932).

[41] Ernst von Aster, "Metaphysik des Nationalismus," *Neue Rundschau*, XLIII, part I (1932), 52.

[42] Peter Suhrkamp, "Die Sezession des Familiensohnes: eine nachträgliche Betrachtung der Jugendbewegung," *ibid.*, 95–96; "Söhne ohne Väter und Lehrer: die Situation der bürgerlichen Jugend," *ibid.*, 696.

This, then, was the Weimar Republic in 1932: clear vision and political impotence, fear, suspicion, and moments of irrational hope; among the politicians of the middle, politics as usual, but with everyone else, a sense of emergency. For some—the *Vernunftrepublikaner* of the left, as Felix Gilbert has called them—the situation had aspects of high tragedy: they were alienated from the institutions they knew they must defend against the new barbarians, and, if they were bellicose at all, they were ready to fight the Nazis in the forlorn hope not of keeping things as they were, but of making, in the spirit of Weimar, something better than the Weimar Republic. Köstler, who lived at the very heart of this atmosphere, among Berlin journalists, recalls in his autobiography a joke that circulated among the editorial employees at Ullstein; a joke which, better than a lengthy analysis, conveys the reigning temper of 1932. There was once, so the story runs, an executioner named Wang Lun, who lived in the reign of the second emperor of the Ming Dynasty. He was famous for his skill and speed in beheading his victims, but all his life he had harbored a secret aspiration, never yet realized: to behead a person so rapidly that the victim's head would remain poised on his neck. He practiced and practiced, and finally, in his seventy-sixth year, he realized his ambition. It was on a busy day of executions, and he dispatched each man with graceful speed, head rolling in the dust. Then came the twelfth man; he began to mount the scaffold, and Wang Lun, with a whisk of his sword, beheaded his victim so quickly that he continued to walk up the steps. When he reached the top, he spoke angrily to the executioner. "Why do you prolong my agony?" he asked. "You were mercifully quick with the others!" It was Wang Lun's great moment; he had crowned his life's work. A serene smile spread over his face; he turned to his victim, and said, "Just kindly nod, please."[43]

A few months later, Adolf Hitler was Chancellor of Germany, and the men of Weimar scattered, taking the spirit of Weimar with them, into the Aesopianism of internal migration, into death in the extermination camps, into suicide—suicide in a Berlin apartment after a

[43] Köstler, *Arrow in the Blue: An Autobiography* (1952), 254.

knock on the door, on the Spanish frontier, in a rented flat in Paris, in a Swedish village, in a Brazilian town, in a New York hotel room. But others took the spirit of Weimar into life, into great careers and lasting influence in laboratories, in hospitals, in journalism, in theatres, in universities, and gave that spirit its true home, in exile.

/ APPENDICES

I. A Short Political History of the Weimar Republic

I. NOVEMBER 1918—JULY 1919: A TIME OF TROUBLES AND FOUNDATIONS

The Weimar Republic was proclaimed on November 9, 1918, by the Social Democrat Philipp Scheidemann. It followed upon more than four years of bloody war, with German troops, though still on foreign soil, in disarray, the General Staff frantic for peace, and the imperial administration demoralized. Reversing German advances on the Western front in the spring of 1918, the Allies had gone on the offensive in the summer, and kept the initiative. Germany's allies—Turkey, Bulgaria, and the Hapsburg monarchy—were already in a state of collapse. On September 30 Chancellor Hertling resigned and gave way, on October 4, to Prince Max von Baden, known as a liberal monarchist inclined to domestic reforms and international understanding. Prince Max appealed to President Wilson for an armistice on the basis of the Fourteen Points. The country was exhausted, weary to death of the adventure it had welcomed in August 1914 as a relief from petty civilian cares. Germany had lost 1.8 million dead and over 4 million wounded; the cost in matériel, wasted talents, maimed minds, sheer despair, was incalculable. Since the early summer of 1917, when the Reichstag had passed a resolution calling for a peace of understanding, it had been obvious that the old regime would never survive unchanged. On October 28, 1918, sailors at the Kiel Naval Base mutinied; by the first week in November some kind of revolution seemed inescapable. On November 8 the idealistic Independent Socialist Kurt Eisner proclaimed a republic in Bavaria and made himself Prime Minister; other cities and *Länder* joined his lead. On the same day, Chancellor Max von Baden firmly called for the abdication of the Emperor. The workers of Berlin were in the streets, Generals Hindenburg and Ludendorff's successor Groener joined the Chancellor's plea. William II temporized, insisting at least on the Prussian throne, but he was asking too much, and Prince Max took what his chief was unwilling to give. He made the Social Democratic leader Friedrich Ebert his successor and announced the Emperor's abdication. Some thought Scheidemann's proclamation of the Republic hasty; from Scheidemann's point of view it was barely in time —it anticipated the Spartacists, who were ready to proclaim a Soviet republic. That night, William II fled to Holland.

The Emperor and his partisans were discredited; leadership would have to come from Socialists. But what kind of Socialists? The Social Democratic party had long been a major party, but even before 1914 it had been a tense coalition, divided among radicals who took revolutionary Marxism seriously, trade unionists who wanted to forget about ideology and seek higher standards of living for the working classes, and functionaries who compromised by talking like revolutionaries and acting like parliamentarians. The decision of the party's delegation to the Reichstag on August 4, 1914, to vote for the war credits in violation of their time-honored principles, had torn this fabric apart beyond repair. By early 1917 the dissidents in the Social Democratic Party formed their own party, the Independent Social Democratic Party, and pressed emphatically for peace and socialism. They were joined in this by a small determined group of Marxist revolutionaries, led by Rosa Luxemburg and Karl Liebknecht—the Spartacists. As victory on the battlefield became more elusive and domestic discontent mounted, the Spartacists found increased support among the radicalized workers, especially the shop stewards in the factories, a tough-minded, pragmatic group set for revolution. They led strikes and, in early November 1918, founded Workers' and Soldiers' Councils on the Soviet model. And so, when Ebert found himself with a republic on his hands, he put together a temporary government of six on November 10, three from the Social Democrats and three Independents. The provisional government actually held intact for almost two months.

Since November 8 a German armistice commission had been negotiating with the Allies under the leadership of the prominent Catholic Center Party deputy Matthias Erzberger, an annexationist converted to peace. And on November 11 the war was over, even if peace had not been made. It was a promising beginning for the new regime, but the day before, Ebert had concluded another agreement that was to have fateful consequences for the young Republic. In the evening of November 10,

General Groener had called Ebert, put the army "at the disposal of his government," and asked, in return, "the support of the government in the maintenance of order and discipline in the army. The officer corps expected the government to fight against Bolshevism and was ready for the struggles. Ebert accepted the offer of an alliance."[1] Groener was, by comparison with others, moderate and responsible, but this arrangement gave the army a new entry to power and prestige, and opportunities for darker types than Groener.

The six-man government broke apart on December 27, when the Independents marched out after inconclusive arguments within the cabinet, in public meetings, and in the streets, over the future of Germany. The left wanted all power to the soviets and a complete reconstruction of society. The Social Democrats wanted a parliamentary regime and a waiting policy on social and economic transformation. There was fighting in the streets in December, and there were some dead—bitterly remembered. But on the whole the country supported the parliamentarianism of the majority Socialists. Accordingly on January 19, 1919, there was a national election for deputies to a constitutional convention to be held at Weimar; despite a Communist boycott, over thirty million Germans turned out to vote. Four hundred twenty-one seats were at stake. The Social Democratic Party led the poll with 11½ million votes and 163 seats; the Catholic Center Party, an amalgam of monarchists and mild republicans, got below 6 million votes and 89 seats; the newly founded Democratic Party, rich in distinguished bourgeois intellectuals and progressive industrialists, did extraordinarily well, totaling about 5½ million votes and 75 seats—it was this party, abundant in talent, decent in campaign methods, rational in its program, that turned out to be "the only party that lost in each election";[2] the National People's Party, the Conservatives of the Empire, unchanged in all but name, got 3 million votes and 42 seats; the Independent Socialists disappointed their following with fewer that 2½ million votes and 22 seats; while the newly founded People's Party, the party of Stresemann, big business, and right-wing leanings, got 21 seats on only 1½ million votes. The Weimar coalition had received a strong mandate.

The Assembly was solemnly opened on February 9, 1919; two days later, it elected Ebert President, and Ebert, in turn, asked Scheidemann to form a cabinet. This first full-fledged cabinet drew from the three

[1] Quoted in F. L. Carsten, *The Reichswehr and Politics, 1918–1933* (1966), 11.

[2] Fritz Stern, "The Political Consequences of the Unpolitical German," *History*, No. 3 (1960), 130.

leading parties, the Social Democrats, the Center, and the Democrats—the Weimar coalition. But the work of the Assembly was marred, though not interrupted, by disorders at home and peacemaking abroad. In Berlin, Rosa Luxemburg and Karl Liebknecht had been murdered on January 15 under revolting circumstances; in Bavaria, Kurt Eisner was murdered on February 28; by March the Social Democrat Noske, in charge of restoring order, was aided rather doubtfully by the fanatical *Freikorps*—hastily formed paramilitary organizations of ex-officers, unemployed drifters, and youthful adventurers eager to kill. The murder of Eisner produced further violence in Bavaria, then a general strike and the proclamation of a Socialist Councils' Republic; this republic was, in turn, overthrown at the end of April and the beginning of May by government troops, with savage brutality. One of the victims was the writer Gustav Landauer, a high-minded idealist and Communist, beaten to death in prison by soldiers.

In Versailles, meanwhile, a German delegation, disdainfully invited in April to accept peace terms, sought to ameliorate slightly what they could not significantly improve. Germans fulminated at the news from France; on June 20 the Scheidemann government resigned and was replaced the next day by a cabinet headed by another Social Democrat, Gustav Bauer. The new cabinet balked at only a few provisions, but the Allies were firm: the losers must sign without reservations. Faced with an ultimatum, the German Government yielded, and, on June 28, a new delegation, headed by the Social Democratic Foreign Minister Hermann Müller, signed the *Diktat*. No other course was feasible. But inescapable as it was, submission left scars that never healed.

The Versailles Treaty imposed heavy economic, political, and psychological burdens on defeated Germany. It returned Alsace-Lorraine to France, split off East Prussia from the heart of Germany by turning over West Prussia, Upper Silesia, and Posen to Poland, made Danzig a Free City, gave Belgium some small districts, left open the disposition of other border areas to later plebiscites, deprived Germany of her colonies, forbade the union of Austria with Germany, imposed military occupation on the left bank of the Rhine, reduced the German Army to 100,000 men, put an end to the General Staff, and in other ways attempted to control German militarism. Most unacceptable—certainly most inflammatory—of all the provisions were articles that deprived the Germans of that intangible thing, "honor." The treaty called for the Germans to turn over their "war criminals," including the former Emperor, for trial for "atrocities," and article 231 insisted that "Germany and her allies" accept "responsibility" for "causing all the loss and damage" to which the Allied powers had been exposed "by the aggression of her allies." And a still undisclosed amount of reparations was to be paid. The clause did not use the word "guilt," but it was quickly stigmatized as the "war guilt clause." While practically all Germans hoped for repeal, some hoped for revenge.

Despite all this, the Weimar Assembly agreed on a constitution in relatively short time—it was adopted on July 31, 1919, and became law on August 11. It enshrined a set of compromises that antagonized many and delighted few. In some respects, though, it was a perfectly straight-forward document. Germany became a democratic republic; elections to the Reichstag, the national legislative body, was by universal suffrage starting at age twenty, Germany remained a federal state, though the powers of the various *Länder* were much curtailed. The chief executive body, the cabinet, was responsible to the Reichstag. But Germany did not become a purely parliamentary regime: the Constitution gave it a strong president, elected for a seven-year term by popular elections; he was symbol at home and representative abroad, could dissolve the Reichstag, choose and dismiss the chancellor, and take charge if "public security and order are seriously disrupted or endangered." This was the notorious Article 48. In its use of devices like proportional representation, initiative and referendum, the Constitution was as modern as its democratic electorate. In the fields of economic legislation and social transformation, from which so many had expected so much, it was rather vague. It laid down fundamental rights and duties of Germans, and promised the possibility of a kind of economic parliament. But little was eventually done; the compromise between bourgeoisie and proletariat ended with a victory of the former over the latter. Still, much was done; over much protest, Germany even adopted a new flag—black, red, gold, the flag of 1848. When the delegates came home from Weimar, their Germany was in deep trouble, but the Republic was launched.

II. AUGUST 1919—DECEMBER 1923: THE TIME OF TROUBLES CONTINUES

The events of the first year of the Republic did not predetermine the fate of Weimar, but they did set its general course. The next four years stood under the signs of domestic violence and foreign intransigence, the two interacting and, to Germany's misfortune, reinforcing one another.

Chancellor Bauer gave way to his fellow Social Democrat Müller in March 1920, after the frightening but unsuccessful Kapp Putsch, and Müller then held the coalition together until June. The Kapp Putsch was the first serious attempt at a general counterrevolution. Since the acceptance of the Versailles Treaty, irreconcilables had made propaganda against the Republic and plotted for a restoration of the monarchy. On March 13, 1920, the plotters struck. A naval brigade marched on Berlin, greeted there by Ludendorff, and Dr. Wolfgang Kapp, the leader of the putsch—an East Prussian bureaucrat, significantly a civilian—appeared in the city to claim the chancellorship. Troops refused to shoot at the rebels —their fellows—and the government prudently fled. But the conspirators were inexperienced and foolish, civilian officials would not join them, and a general strike paralyzed the "new regime." After four days, Kapp and his colleagues "resigned," surrendering what they had never held. Except for Bavaria, where reactionaries kept control, the old government reasserted itself. Noske, deemed too indulgent to the military, was dropped from the cabinet, but Kapp was allowed to escape abroad, and the great purge for which Scheidemann had rightly called never took place.

On June 6, 1920, there were elections to the Reichstag; they were disastrous for republicans. The German National Party and Stresemann's People's Party emerged strong, adding millions of votes and dozens of deputies; the Democratic Party declined spectacularly, dropping to almost a third of its earlier voting strength, the Social Democratic Party polled only 5½ million votes, while the Independent Socialists showed great new strength. Another ominous development was the burgeoning of splinter parties. The Weimar coalition with 11 million votes and 225 deputies had lost control of the Reichstag; it confronted 14½ million votes and 241 seats held by a variety of other parties. Not every right- or left-wing deputy was a mortal enemy of the Republic; few of them were dependable friends. The politics of militarism, revolutionary and counter-revolutionary slogans, and direct action was on the ascendant.

After long negotiations, Konstantin Fehrenbach of the Center Party formed a cabinet, succeeded a year later, on May 10, 1921, by the first cabinet of Joseph Wirth, another Centrist, and then, late in October of that year, by Wirth's second cabinet, which survived until November 22, 1922. But problems remained intractable. In late April 1921 the Allies let it be known that German reparation payments, though sizable, were gravely in arrears, and they fixed the total sum at 132 billion gold marks, of which over 8 billion had so far been paid. The Wirth ministry, committed to fulfillment of Germany's obligations, delivered one more billion in gold. But now inflation, caused by a shortage of gold, adverse balance of payments, and the flight of capital, became worrisome. In January 1921 the German mark had stood at 45 to the dollar, through the spring and summer it had remained stable at 60, in September it had reached 100, and by the end of the year it took over 160 marks to purchase one dollar. Before that, another disaster: Matthias Erzberger was shot to death by two ex-officers. The murderers fled to Hungary, which refused to extradite them; their accomplices at home were left unmolested or acquitted. Thousands celebrated openly, shamelessly. In October the Allies, following up the plebiscite of March, and after intermittent military imbroglios, drew the new frontiers for Upper Silesia. No good solution was possible, but the solution the Allies adopted caused a cabinet crisis from which Wirth emerged to succeed himself. In his new cabinet, Walther Rathenau, that enigmatic mixture of dreamer and politician, Jew with a penchant for blond Nordics, who had been Minister for Reconstruction in Wirth's first administration, took a more prominent place. On January 31, 1922, Wirth made Rathenau his Foreign Minister. The appointment, made to prevent disasters, only caused further disasters.

Germany's foreign relations remained in a delicate condition; German failures to pay reparations on time strengthened anti-German politicians in France and England. In January 1922 the good European Aristide Briand was toppled by Raymond Poincaré, known as an inflexible advocate of the enforcement of Versailles. Rathenau's path was difficult. His domestic enemies did not help. A couplet made the rounds of right-wing meetings and student taverns: *"Knallt ab den Walther Rathenau/ Die gottverfluchte Judensau—*Shoot down that Walther Rathenau/ That cursed, Goddamned Jewish sow." Soon poetry became reality: on June 24, 1922, Rathenau was shot to death by young right-wing militants. Pursued by the police, one of the assassins was killed, a second killed himself, the third received a prison sentence of fifteen years but spent only seven years in prison—the Republic was always generous with its enemies. Some hesitant republicans now repudiated their nationalist, militarist allies—"The enemy," Chancellor Wirth exclaimed, "is on the right"—but the right, unrepentant, continued its campaign of vilification and terror. And big industry, led by the ruthless magnate, Hugo Stinnes, was regaining self-confidence; there was talk that the eight-hour day should be replaced by the ten-hour day.

In this atmosphere, Ebert sought a broadly based government, but the Social Democrats refused to countenance a cabinet that included Stresemann's conservative People's Party in it. Chancellor Wirth resigned on November 14, 1922; he was succeeded on November 22 by Wilhelm Cuno, head of the Hamburg American Line; his cabinet contained no Social Democrats. In France Poincaré continued his hard anti-German line; in England the conciliatory David Lloyd George had been succeeded in mid-October by Bonar Law; while in Italy Mussolini seized power on

October 30. It was not a favorable constellation. Poincaré pressed for the occupation of the Ruhr. The facts were clear: the Germans were not paying their reparations on time, a delay the French interpreted as deliberate sabotage. Late in December 1922 the Reparations Commission officially declared that Germany had failed to meet her obligations, and on January 11, 1923, a French-Belgian contingent occupied the Ruhr to operate the mines and the industries in behalf of the victorious powers. The French fostered separatism; the occupying troops acted with a high hand and open brutality. There were bloody clashes. The German Government counseled passive resistance. Production came to a standstill. And inflation, already a grave threat, now got out of control altogether; the disruption of trade, the disastrous decline in tax payments, all consequences of the Ruhr occupation, were more than the mark could stand. The Reichsbank tried to help, but its reserves were near depletion, and in April 1923 the dam burst: the currency dropped daily, and inflation reached fantastic dimensions—by October 1923 not millions, or billions, but trillions of marks were needed to buy a loaf of bread or mail a letter. Farmers refused to ship produce, manufacturing reached an all-time low, there were food riots, workers hovered near starvation, millions of bourgeois lost all their savings, while speculators grew rich. The resulting economic dislocation and psychological upheaval only strengthened the already pervasive distrust of the Weimar Republic.

Early in August 1923 the Social Democrats declared the need for a national coalition and, at the same time, their lack of confidence in Cuno. Cuno resigned and Ebert called upon Stresemann to form a cabinet; the first Stresemann government lasted until early October, followed by a second, which survived until the end of November. It ended passive resistance, to get production started again; and in November, under the direction of Hjalmar Schacht, the government ended the printing of money, began a ruthless economy drive, and proclaimed a new mark, the *Rentenmark,* which was "secured" by Germany's total resources. Schacht was rewarded; he became president of the Reichsbank. Stability returned, though hardships did not end.

Stresemann's conciliatory policy exasperated the right, already embittered and emboldened by French violence, local successes in Bavaria, and the general uncertainty. On the night of November 8, 1923, and the morning of November 9, Hitler, Göring, Ludendorff, and a handful of others staged a putsch in Munich. It failed; some of the conspirators were captured and tried. Ludendorff was, of course, acquitted; Hitler was convicted of high treason, but permitted to convert the trial into a propaganda feast against the Republic. His sentence was the minimum possible—five years—of which, in any event, he spent only about eight months in confinement, to emerge a significant political figure. Adolf Hitler had joined an obscure right-wing group—a small cluster of anti-Semitic, antirepublican, vaguely Socialist fanatics—in July 1919, and witnessed its gradual growth in Bavaria. By April 1920 it had formulated a program and taken a name, the National Socialist German Workers' Party, a name not without significance. For three years the Nazis fomented disorder, gave inflammatory speeches against the Republic, preached violence against Jews, and enlisted some sympathizers in high positions. When Hitler's rebellion in November 1923 collapsed, and when financial stability gradually returned, republicans breathed easier; was Hitler not, after all, just another crank? It took years before they were proved wrong.

III. DECEMBER 1923—OCTOBER 1929: THE GOLDEN TWENTIES

The assertion that happy ages have no history is a myth, and in any event the middle years of the Weimar Republic were far from happy; still the political events of this comparatively tranquil time can be rapidly summarized. Sanity seemed to be returning at home and abroad. In November 1923 the Social Democrats overthrew the Stresemann cabinet, charging that it had been gentle with right-wing subversion while acting briskly against left-wing radicalism, but the six cabinets that were to govern Germany between December 1923 and the end of June 1928 showed sturdy continuity: each had Stresemann as its Foreign Minister; four of them were led by Wilhelm Marx, the Centrist leader, as Chancellor, and two by Hans Luther, a nonpartisan public servant with conservative leanings. If it was a relatively stable period, it was also a conservative one: though they repeatedly saved it with their votes, the Social Democrats were out of the government for almost five years. Meanwhile, Poincaré was defeated in elections in May 1924, and succeeded by Édouard Herriot, another good European, sympathetic to Germany's plight. His hand was strengthened by the "Dawes Plan," named after the American banker and statesman Charles G. Dawes, which proposed the evacuation of the Ruhr, considerable reductions in reparations payments, and loans to Germany.

The German Government accepted the plan, over fierce right-wing opposition. It was always the same story: the concessions that seemed to implacable Frenchmen too great, seemed too small to irreconcilable Germans. In July 1924 the Allies met in London; in August they invited the Germans to join them, and the French reluctantly agreed to begin to evacuate some troops. After venomous Reichstag debates, Germany accepted the Dawes Plan, French troops moved out of the Ruhr—they were gone by July 1925—Germany received foreign loans, and the *Rentenmark* was replaced by the *Reichsmark*. By mid-1925 the "golden twenties" had arrived.

But then President Ebert died on February 28, 1925, and the elections for his successor brought out all the old divisions. On the first run no one received the required majority of all the votes cast; on the second run a plurality would be sufficient. And after prolonged maneuvering among the parties, after some old candidates had been dropped and new candidates brought forward, it was the aged hero of World War I, Hindenburg, who received the largest vote—14½ million, or 48 percent. His main opponent, the Centrist leader Marx, got nearly 14 million votes. It seemed a grave setback to the Republic, but Hindenburg acted quite scrupulously and, until overtaken by senility, effectively as a loyal chief executive.

As the fears of German republicans about Hindenburg waned, they waned abroad as well. Germany's isolation gradually ended. Since early 1925 Stresemann had been making overtures to the Allies, and in October France, Great Britain, Belgium, Italy, and Germany signed a treaty at Locarno, which settled the western frontiers, and called for the peaceful settlement of all further disputes. Like every other step toward fraternity, Locarno was denounced by the right in Germany, but the treaty was adopted by a narrow margin. For several years the "spirit of Locarno" guided European diplomacy. In June 1926 Germany concluded a treaty of friendship with Soviet Russia; in September Germany entered the League of Nations. Stresemann followed up these triumphs by discussions with Briand on international peace which eventuated, in 1928, in the Kellogg-Briand treaty condemning war as an instrument of national policy. It was like a handsome screen concealing unpleasant realities.

There was something masklike about German internal prosperity as well. The prosperity was real enough; German industry was modernizing its plant, business was stable, wages were relatively high, unemployment was low—it fell below three-quarters of a million in 1928. But there were hidden ominous developments: industries and businesses were merging on an unprecedented scale; governments, both federal and state, were wasting funds; the powerful industrial magnate Alfred Hugenberg, who had grown rich in the inflation, was gaining control of the opinion industries; and much of the basis of the prosperity was, after all, foreign money pumped into Germany—a source that might dry up. Reparations remained an issue. The Communists continued to refuse cooperation with

"Social Fascists"—that is, Social Democrats. The new army retained its old ideas: it wanted political influence, nationalist policies, and secret rearmament. And right-wing fanatics never weakened in their determination to overthrow a regime that was being almost suicidally indulgent with them. In September 1928 the Brandenburg section of the Stahlhelm, an extreme anti-Weimar group of veterans founded in 1918 and swollen to great size in the following years, candidly proclaimed: "We hate the present regime"; it has "made it impossible for us to liberate our enslaved Fatherland, destroy the war-guilt lie and win needed *Lebensraum* in the east. We declare war against the system which today rules the state and against all those who support this system by a policy of compromise."[3] It would be wrong to say that no one listened, but things were going too well to make such threats really terrifying.

Indeed, while the Nazis and their allies floundered and fumed—peace and prosperity were never their best times—and the Communists continued their opposition, the Social Democrats gained strength. In the last general elections to the Reichstag, in December 1924, the Socialists had held 131 seats; in the new elections, of May 1928, they raised their representation to 152. In contrast, the German Nationalists were reduced from 103 seats to 78; and the Nazis from 14 to only 12. Other right-wing and center parties lost seats as well; the time for the Socialists' return to a leading rather than supporting role had come. On June 28, 1928, Hermann Müller formed a cabinet of "personalities," distinguished individuals speaking only for themselves; most were Social Democrats. But not all: Stresemann, the indispensable man, after some hesitation agreed to serve as Foreign Minister once more. The enemies of Weimar, needless to say, did not remain silent. The sinister Hugenberg took over the leadership of the German National Party and soon made overtures to Hitler, still the pariah of German politics; among the crowd of self-appointed gravediggers to the Republic, Hugenberg has undisputed claim to front rank. The Nazis had held their first Nuremberg party rally in August 1927, spouting their racial theories and calling for a general purge of the German body politic and the German soul. But they did not merely rave; more and more the Nazi leadership found connections in respectable circles, among military men who despised the Republic, agrarians longing for a Restoration, and industrialists anxious to protect their trusts and cripple Socialist trade unions.

But in 1928 and 1929 the center of tension was still in foreign affairs. It was not until August 1929 that Briand promised to evacuate the last

[3] Quoted in William S. Halperin, *Germany Tried Democracy: A Political History of the Reich from 1918 to 1933* (1946), 366.

French troops from the Rhineland by the following year—the sore of occupation had continued to fester for over six decisive years. Earlier, in mid-December 1928, the French, British, and Germans had agreed to appoint a committee of experts to look, once again, into Germany's capacity to pay reparations. The United States agreed to join, and one of its delegates, Owen D. Young, became chairman. The experts, including Hjalmar Schacht who had acquired a reputation as a financial wizard, wrangled, privately and publicly, for half a year. On June 7, 1929, they finally signed an agreement: Germany was to be complete master over its affairs, but would continue to pay reparations on a graduated scale, ranging from 1.7 billion marks the first year to about 2.5 billion in 1966 and around 1.5 billion annually thereafter until 1988. The amount, though large, was lower than any other demand made so far; the specificity, though it now seems absurd, was designed to anesthetize passions and reduce reparations to a merely technical question. The German response was quick and wholly predictable: vehement denunciations by Hitler and Hugenberg, poisonous speeches on the right, vigorous defenses by republicans, and delay. There was even a plebiscite on the Young Plan which failed, and then Schacht, one of the signers, repudiated his earlier support; on March 7 he resigned as president of the Reichsbank, and became an unexpected recruit of the extreme right. Five days later the Reichstag finally voted to adopt the Young Plan, and Hindenburg conscientiously signed it. But then, by mid-March 1930, the architect of Germany's foreign policy, Gustav Stresemann, had been dead for over five months. In bad health for over a year, harassed by members of his own party, vilified by the Nazis and the German Nationals, he had continued to defend his policies until the end. He died on October 3, 1929, and was succeeded by Julius Curtius, a fellow member of the German People's Party—a friend and follower, but no replacement. Stresemann should not be sentimentalized; nor should we exaggerate the power of one man in the turbulent stream of history—there were forces at work in New York and Paris and Berlin that Stresemann would have been powerless to stem. Yet his death was a grievous loss; it was, if not cause, at least sign of the beginning of the end.

IV. OCTOBER 1929—MAY 1932: THE BEGINNING OF THE END

Stresemann's death dramatized the dilemma of "bourgeois, politically homeless Protestantism"[4]—that large number of voters mortally afraid of

[4] Theodor Eschenburg, "Kurze Geschichte der Weimarer Republik," *Die Improvisierte Demokratie: Gesammelte Aufsätze zur Weimarer Republik* (1963), 64.

Communists, unwilling to join the Socialists, suspicious of the Catholic Center, disoriented by the war and its aftermath and, on the whole, unimpressed by Germany's rapid recovery and renewed international prestige. Stresemann had taught these millions the virtues of collaborating with Social Democrats—a collaboration which, he had candidly said, was an affair not of the heart but of reason. With his death, the right wing of his People's Party reasserted itself, and the fragmentation of the Weimar coalition—its vital political center—continued.

It would not have become dangerous if there had not been a world economic crisis. But there was. Precarious German prosperity had already been shaken early in 1929, when unemployment rose to two million and tax collections declined. The focus of political debate became unemployment insurance, admittedly a heavy and growing burden on the government; it was a principle the Social Democrats dared not touch, and a grievance to industrialists and conservatives of all kinds, inclined to make these payments the convenient scapegoat for all of Germany's accumulating ills. Then came, late in October 1929, the stock market crash on Wall Street. Its reverberations were felt everywhere; the Great Depression was world-wide. But it was most disastrous for the least stable regime, that is, for Germany, which had lived off foreign aid far more than many Germans knew or were willing to admit. With the rush to self-protection everywhere, German exports dwindled, foreign loans to Germany were not renewed. In consequence, tax income dropped further, bankruptcies multiplied, and unemployment grew inexorably. The Social Democrats demanded an increase in unemployment premiums; the Center Party and the People's Party, now speaking for the employers, refused to go along; and on March 27, 1930, the Müller cabinet resigned. The great coalition was dead. On the next day, Hindenburg asked Heinrich Brüning to form a cabinet of personalities. Brüning, since 1929 the chairman of the Center delegation to the Reichstag, a cool, conservative Catholic with a reputation for financial expertness and no gift for oratory, promised continuation of a conciliatory foreign policy, demanded vigorous action in the economic sphere, and called, in almost bullying tones, for cooperation from the Reichstag in this emergency. His program was agricultural tariffs, higher excise taxes, government economies—deflationary policies designed to cheer conservatives and appall the workers. Yet the Nationalists remained dissatisfied; the Nazis, who took to the streets in defiance of police orders, followed a policy of obstruction; the Social Democrats and Communists naturally opposed Brüning's proposals. In the midst of growing misery, the final evacuation of German soil by French troops, on June 30, 1930, went almost unnoticed—an ironic commentary on the ephemeral quality of political passions. When no agreement on Brüning's program could be reached, the Chancellor threatened to invoke Article 48 of the Weimar Constitution; then on July 16, after a defeat in the Reichstag, instead of resigning, he invoked it. Germany was now governed by presidential decree. Faced with strenuous protests, Brüning dissolved the Reichstag, and set national elections for September 14, 1930.

Through the summer, responsible bourgeois and Socialist politicians, far from blind to the pressures exerted by the extremists, sought for some accommodation. In vain. The campaign plumbed new depths of demagogy and sheer violence, and voting on September 14 was heavy: there were 35 million voters in 1930 whereas there had been only 30 million two years before. Many of these new voters were the hitherto apathetic, brought to the polls by the general distress and the militant parties, and the young, who had turned to the right in the universities and in the streets, before their elders turned in the same direction. The Social Democrats held firm; they lost a half-million votes and 10 seats, but this still meant a parliamentary delegation of 132. The Center picked up a half-million votes and increased its seats from 78 to 87. The other parties lost disastrously, both in votes and in seats. The Communists gained over a million votes and 23 seats; they were represented in the Reichstag by 77 delegates. But the real victors were the Nazis; they climbed from 800,000 votes to almost 6½ million, from 12 seats to 107. Among the extremists, it was the extreme right alone that benefited from the condition of Weimar Germany.

Brüning governed on, until May 30, 1932, amid growing unemployment, mounting misery, rising violence, and increasing signs that the Republic was dying: for many intellectuals September 14, 1930, marked the death of the Republic. Through 1931 Hindenburg signed one emergency decree after another, controlling the price of food, regulating bank payments, reducing unemployment compensation. The Nazis made no secret of their plans for the future. When in September 1930 three lieutenants were tried for treason—they had sought to enlist fellow officers in the Nazi cause—Hitler testified for the defense, in the glaring light of full publicity, and predicted that if his "movement" should be victorious, the "crimes of November" would be avenged, and then, "indeed, heads will roll in the sand." Nazis began to commit excesses against Jewish stores; the Nazi press, skillfully led by Goebbels, preached action against republicans, democrats, Jews, Communists—"November criminals" all; Nazis interfered with the showing of Remarque's *Im Westen nichts Neues*.

Attempts to ban processions were on the whole futile, and in October 1931 the Nazis widened their hold on the right at a meeting in Harzburg attended by leading Nazis, industrialists like Thyssen and Hugenberg, military men like Seeckt, financiers like Schacht. It created a "national" front against Bolshevism—a fatal, if still rather fragile, combination uniting the power of money, political shrewdness, mob appeal, and aristocratic trimmings.

The threat was grave enough to induce the Social Democrats to support Hindenburg in the presidential elections to be held in early 1932. For the first time unemployment exceeded six million in January 1932, and anything seemed possible. But the "Harzburg Front" was not yet solid enough to unite behind Hitler's candidacy; in the vote on March 13, Hindenburg polled 18½ million votes, Hitler almost 11½ million, the Communist candidate Thaelmann nearly 5 million, and Duesterberg, the candidate of the Nationalists, 2½ million. A runoff was needed, and on April 10, 1932, Hindenburg was re-elected President of the Republic with over 19 million votes; Hitler ran a strong second with 13½ million, Thaelmann a poor third with less than 4 million votes. Three days later, the President dissolved both Nazi paramilitary associations, the Brown Shirts (the SA) and the Black Shirts (the SS), but in a series of state elections the Nazis consolidated their strength, and on May 12 General Groener, the Defense Minister responsible for the government's anti-Nazi move, was let go. Then, on May 30, Hindenburg dismissed the Brüning cabinet, persuaded by his friends and by his influential adviser, Kurt von Schleicher, that Brüning's social program smacked of agrarian socialism. His successor was the smooth, gaunt, manipulative reactionary Centrist Franz von Papen. He even looked like an undertaker.

V. JUNE 1932–JANUARY 1933: INTO BARBARISM

The rest is a story of fear, terrorism, irresponsibility, missed opportunities, and shameful betrayal. Von Papen's cabinet included the ambitious Kurt von Schleicher as Defense Minister, and a collection of aristocrats—an innovation in Weimar. "The list of appointments," S. William Halperin writes, "read so much like a page out of the German nobility's 'Who's Who?' that the public dubbed Papen and his colleagues the 'Almanach de Gotha' cabinet."[5] In addition to Junkers, the cabinet included prominent industrialists. It was as though the Revolution of 1918 had never taken place. On June 4, 1932, Hindenburg dissolved the

[5] Halperin, *Germany Tried Democracy*, 486–487.

Reichstag and called for elections in late July; on June 16 he rescinded the ban on the SA and the SS—both decisions major victories for the Nazis. The Brown Shirts and the Black Shirts had never been dormant; now they went into action wholeheartedly, and the summer of 1932 was marked by sanguinary clashes between Communists and Nazis, and Socialists and Nazis. The Socialists called it civil war, and they were right. But the government did nothing, or aided the aggressors—the title of Franz Werfel's Expressionist novel, *Not the Murderer, the Victim Is Guilty*, now took on new meaning. On July 20 von Papen, after persuading Hindenburg that the step was necessary, seized the Prussian government from the Social Democrats, and governed it as the "Commissioner of the Reich." The Social Democrats, imbued with the myth of republican legality, challenged the action in the courts, but offered no resistance.

On July 31, 1932, the elections took place and ended in a stunning victory for the Nazis: they got over 13½ million votes and 230 seats. The Social Democrats with 8 million votes and 133 seats held relatively firm, while the Communists with 5 million votes and 89 delegates and the Center with almost 6 million votes and 97 delegates made some gains. The other parties were nearly wiped out. The opposition to the Nazis remained numerous but disunited; the Nazi leadership was confident. Von Papen negotiated with Hitler, prepared to take Nazis into his government, but Hitler wanted the chancellorship or nothing. He got nothing— for the moment. Von Papen even acted forcefully for a while, making public his aversion to Hitler's political tactics and support of murder. Then, after a clash with Göring, the Nazi President of the new Reichstag, von Papen dissolved the Reichstag and called for new elections.

The elections took place on November 6, 1932, and gave new hope to the few remaining optimists among republicans. The Nazis lost 2 million votes and 34 seats in the Reichstag; they were still the strongest party with a delegation of 196, as against 100 for the Communists (who again picked up strength), 121 for the Social Democrats, and 90 for the Center, who both suffered moderate losses. But there were many, including Nazis, who interpreted the results as the beginning of a real, final decline; in mid-November, in a number of local elections, this decline seemed confirmed. Nazi brutality in talk and action had alienated many. And Hitler had other troubles: in desperate need of financial backing, he had long since surrendered all claims to the socialism incorporated in the program and the very title of his party; but there were old Nazis still imbued with their "German Socialism," their agrarian, anticapitalist, though also anti-Marxist and anti-Semitic, collectivism. In December 1932 one of the leading "Socialist" ideologists of the Nazis, Gregor Strasser, an im-

mensely shrewd organizer, resigned all his party offices; Goebbels feared
for the future and Hitler darkly hinted at suicide. He was saved by his
right-wing competitors. On November 17 Hindenburg had reluctantly
permitted von Papen, one of his favorites, to resign, but, unpopular as
von Papen was, he continued to govern until a successor could be found.
It was Schleicher who took over most of von Papen's cabinet. But no one,
left or right, trusted Schleicher, and on January 28, 1933, he resigned.

Meanwhile the dying Weimar Republic was experiencing the last and
most fateful intrigue of all. Once out of office, filled with dislike of
Schleicher and the desire to return to power, von Papen decided to use
Hitler as a kind of stalking horse. He, too, underestimated his man. He
met Hitler privately, and sought to persuade the aged Hindenburg to make
Hitler Chancellor. "The Old Man" was reluctant, but then he trusted von
Papen—a trust itself a sign of limited judgment and advanced senility—
and other trusted men around him, like his secretary Otto Meissner and
his son, Oskar, also advocated the appointment of Hitler. After Schleicher's
resignation, even Schleicher urged this course. All of Hindenburg's advisers were confident: Hitler would be kept in check by Vice Chancellor
von Papen and other reliable conservatives in the cabinet. The old man
yielded, and on January 30, 1933, he made Adolf Hitler Chancellor of
Germany. The Republic was dead in all but name, the victim of structural
flaws, reluctant defenders, unscrupulous aristocrats and industrialists, a
historic legacy of authoritarianism, a disastrous world situation and
deliberate murder.

Whatever the appearance of the Nazi seizure of power and the various
"legal" steps taken later, it was murder and nothing less. "Stressing
'legality,' " Karl Dietrich Bracher has written, "Hitler made his way into
the government not as the leader of a working parliamentary majority
coalition (as misleading apologists still suggest) but through the
authoritarian gap in the Weimar Constitution, and immediately set about
destroying the Constitution he had just taken an oath to defend. That
formally correct oath he regarded as the symbol and end of his successful policy of legality. Now the actual seizure of power began. Now the
tactics of legality had to be combined with the strategy of revolution to
form the specific technique of seizing power that in a short time was to
outplay, eliminate, or regiment all safeguards and counterforces, political,
social, and intellectual."[6] Contrasted with its cultural history, the political
history of the Weimar Republic is a depressing affair, but it is El Dorado

[6] Karl Dietrich Bracher, "The Technique of the National Socialist Seizure
of Power," in *The Path to Dictatorship, 1918–1933: Ten Essays by German
Scholars,* tr. John Conway (1966), 118–119.

compared to what followed, a history of degradation, corruption, the suppression of all living cultural forces, systematic lying, intimidation, political murder followed by organized mass murder. In the light of *that* history, it is not hyperbole but sober realism to say that the death of Weimar saw the birth of a dark age.

II. Bibliography

This bibliography, though comprehensive, makes no claim to completeness. I refer the reader to the bibliography published by the Wiener Library in London, *From Weimar to Hitler: Germany 1918–1933* (2nd, rev. and enlarged ed., 1964). Here I have concentrated on books and articles I found useful, interesting, or for some reason important. I have appended brief evaluations to most if not all the entries and, for the reader's convenience, given the titles in English wherever possible, even thought I normally used the German original. For the reader's convenience, also, I have subdivided the bibliography into sections, but these are only intended as rough divisions, imposing a degree of order on a vast pile of materials.

I. SOURCES AND DOCUMENTS

This book owes much to interviews and exchanges of letters with students and survivors of Weimar. For a list of names, see the preface, p. xv.

A. COLLECTED CORRESPONDENCE

Barlach, Ernst, *Leben und Werk in seinen Briefen,* ed. Friedrich Dross (1952).

Beckmann, Max, *Briefe im Kriege,* collected by Minna Tube (2nd ed., 1955). Shows evolution of his style.

Benjamin, Walter, *Briefe,* 2 vols., ed. Gershom Sholem and Theodor Adorno (1966).

Freud, Sigmund, *A Psycho-Analytical Dialogue: The Letters of Sigmund Freud and Karl Abraham, 1907–1926,* ed. Hilda C. Abraham and Ernst L. Freud, tr. Bernard Marsh and Hilda C. Abraham (1965). Instructive on German developments.

George, Stefan, *Briefwechsel zwischen George und Hofmannsthal,* ed. Robert Boehringer (2nd ed., 1953).

———, *Stefan George-Friedrich Gundolf Briefwechsel,* ed. Robert Boehringer (1962). Remarkably revealing of the relationship, and Gundolf's wartime chauvinism.

Goll, Iwan, and Claire Goll, *Briefe,* foreword by Kasimir Edschmid (1966).

Hofmannsthal, Hugo von, Helene von Nostitz, *Briefwechsel,* ed. Oswalt von Nostitz (1965).

———, Edgar Karg von Bebenburg, *Briefwechsel,* ed. Mary E. Gilbert (1966).

———, Arthur Schnitzler, *Briefwechsel,* ed. Therese Nickl and Heinrich Schnitzler (1964). All highly important, carefully written, showing the development of an exquisite mind, and, quite incidentally, the importance of Berlin.

Landauer, Gustav, *Sein Lebensgang in Briefen,* 2 vols., ed. Martin Buber (1929).

Mann, Heinrich, *Briefe an Karl Lemke, 1917–1949* (1963).

Mann, Thomas, *Briefe, 1889–1936,* ed. Erika Mann (1962). Though instructive, the editing is too delicate to permit a full insight.

———, *Thomas Mann–Heinrich Mann: Briefwechsel, 1900–1949* (1965). The two hostile brothers, face to face.

Meinecke, Friedrich, *Ausgewählter Briefwechsel,* ed. Ludwig Dehio and Peter Classen (1962). Important though (especially the replies of Siegfried A. Kaehler) sometimes depressing.

Mendelsohn, Erich, *Briefe eines Architekten,* ed. Oskar Beyer (1961). Articulate on his Expressionist philosophy of architecture.

Nolde, Emil, *Briefe aus den Jahren 1894–1926,* ed. Max Sauerlandt (1927).

Rathenau, Walther, *Briefe,* 2 vols. (4th ed., 1927).

———, *Politische Briefe* (1929). Of considerable importance.

Rilke, Rainer Maria, *Gesammelte Briefe,* 6 vols., ed. Ruth Sieber-Rilke and Carl Sieber (1936–1939).

———, *Briefe,* 2 vols., ed. Karl Altheim (1950). The more accessible but less complete edition.

Spengler, Oswald, *Briefe, 1913–1936,* ed. Anton M. Koktanek (1963). There is an English abridgment of this abridgment, by Arthur Helps (1966), but it is not recommended; the originals convey Spengler's mentality and working habits quite well.

Tucholsky, Kurt, *Ausgewählte Briefe, 1913–1935,* ed. Mary Gerold-

Tucholsky and Fritz J. Raddatz (1962). Though not complete, biting, often brilliant reading.

Wolff, Kurt, *Briefwechsel eines Verlegers, 1911–1963* (1966). Revealing letters of a progressive publisher who knew everyone and published some of the best.

Wolfskehl, Karl, *Briefe und Aufsätze, München 1925–1933*, ed. Margot Ruben (1966). Letters, which have much on Stefan George, are on pp. 19–181.

Zweig, Stefan: *Stefan Zweig, and Friderike Zweig: Their Correspondence, 1912–1942*, tr. and ed. Henry G. Alsberg (1954). Though not always felicitous in translation, very moving.

B. AUTOBIOGRAPHIES, DIARIES, REPORTS TO ORAL HISTORY

Alexander, Franz, *The Western Mind in Transition: An Eyewitness Story* (1960). Partly autobiography, partly biography of the psychoanalytical movement.

Baum, Vicki, *Es war alles ganz anders: Erinnerungen* (1962). Title—It Was All Quite Different—is revealing; candid, naïve, helplessly middle-brow, but gives good picture of the Ullstein industry.

Bebel, August, *Aus meinem Leben*, 3 vols. (1910–1914). Classic reminiscences by the great Social Democratic Party leader before World War I.

Beckmann, Max, *Leben in Berlin: Tagebuch, 1908–9*, ed. Hans Kinkel (1966). With excellent annotations.

Beloch, Karl Julius (see below under Steinberg).

Below, Georg von (see below under Steinberg).

Benn, Gottfried, *Doppelleben*, in *Gesammelte Werke*, 4 vols., ed. Dieter Wellershoff (1958–1961), IV, 69–176. Unconsciously revealing self-portrait by the right-wing Expressionist poet. Selected writings of Benn, under the title *Primal Vision*, ed. E. B. Ashton (1958), are available in fluent English.

Bernauer, Rudolf, *Das Theater meines Lebens: Erinnerungen* (1955). Supplies a corrective to the Jessner cult.

Bismarck, Otto von, *Gedanken und Erinnerungen*, 3 vols. (1921 ed.). Celebrated reminiscences which have been much studied; to be used with discretion.

Bonn, M. J., *Wandering Scholar* (1949). Splendid autobiography of a liberal and sensible economist.

Brecht, Arnold, *Aus nächster Nähe: Lebenserinnerungen 1884–1927* (1966). Acute observations of a highly placed democratic public servant.

Brentano, Lujo, *Mein Leben* (1931). Recollections by an influential and interesting German economist—a "Socialist of the Chair," who was both a liberal and a patriot.

Ebert, Friedrich, *Schriften, Aufzeichnungen, Reden,* ed. Paul Kampffmeyer (1926). Posthumous collection of the papers of Weimar's first president; a limited but honest and vigorous man.

Ernst, Max, "An Informal Life of M. E.," in William S. Lieberman, ed. *Max Ernst* (1961), 7–24. This autobiography is as surrealistic as are Ernst's paintings.

Graf, Oskar Maria, *Gelächter von Aussen: Aus meinem Leben, 1918–1933* (1966).

Glum, Friedrich, *Zwischen Wissenschaft, Wirtschaft und Politik: Erlebtes und Erdachtes in vier Reichen* (1964). Pious, stodgy, but helpfully detailed.

Groener, Wilhelm, *Lebenserinnerungen,* ed. Friedrich Freiherr Hiller von Gaertringen (1957). A crucially important military man in Weimar.

Grosz, George, *A Little Yes and a Big No* (1946). Worthy companion to his graphic work.

Guthmann, Johannes, *Goldene Frucht: Begegnungen mit Menschen, Gärten und Häusern* (1955). Wealthy connoisseur with excellent connections among artists and publishers.

Haas, Willy, *Die literarische Welt: Erinnerungen* (1960 ed.). Excellent, if rather brief, recollections of a critic and editor.

Hartmann, Heinz, "Reminiscences," Oral History Collection, Columbia University (1963). Some passages on the German psychoanalytical scene.

Hasenclever, Walter, "Autobiographisches," in Walter Hasenclever, *Gedichte, Dramen, Prosa,* ed. Kurt Pinthus (1963), 501–508.

Hauptmann, Gerhart, *Die grossen Beichten* (1966). Collects his earlier autobiographies, *Das Abenteuer meiner Jugend* and *Buch der Leidenschaft,* with added, hitherto unpublished material on his private life. Pretentious and disappointing, but not without value.

Heuss, Theodor, *Erinnerungen, 1905–1933* (1963). Recollections of a good German; associate of Friedrich Naumann and foe of Hitler.

Hollaender, Friedrich, *Von Kopf bis Fuss* (1965). Memoirs by a popular composer.

Jäckh, Ernst, *Weltsaat: Erlebtes und Erstrebtes* (1960). A little fanciful, but filled with valuable material on the Berlin Hochschule für Politik, and efforts at world peace.

Kästner, Erich, "Meine sonnige Jugend," in *Kästner für Erwachsene* (1966), 527–528.

Kessler, Harry Graf, *Tagebücher, 1918–1937* (1961). Invaluable; a wealthy aesthete, aristocrat, and democratic politician, Kessler wrote about everyone with enormous bite. At times the dramatist conquers the historian, but only at times. (For some criticisms, see Glum, above.) Portions of Kessler's diary have been translated by Sarah Gainham, and published in *Encounter*, XXIX, 1 (July 1967), 3–17; 2 (August 1967), 7–17; 3 (September 1967), 17–28.

Köstler, Arthur, *Arrow in the Blue: An Autobiography* (1952). Lucid on the late Weimar atmosphere.

Kortner, Fritz, *Aller Tage Abend* (1959). A great, politically conscious actor reminisces, to excellent effect.

Kühlmann, Richard von, *Erinnerungen* (1948).

Loewenstein, Rudolph M., "Reminiscences," Oral History Collection, Columbia University (1965). Short but instructive pages on psychoanalysis in Berlin to 1925.

Mann, Heinrich, *Ein Zeitalter wird besichtigt* (1945). Somewhat disappointing; the essays (see below in section II) are more interesting.

Mann, Klaus, *The Turning Point: Thirty-Five Years in this Century* (1942). Sensitive; interesting for the reactions of a brilliant, ambitious young man to the literary world around him.

Mann, Thomas, *A Sketch of my Life* (1960).

Mann, Viktor, *Wir waren fünf: Bildnis der Familie Mann* (1949). Precisely what the subtitle claims: a family portrait.

Marcuse, Ludwig, *Mein zwanzigstes Jahrhundert: Auf dem Weg zu einer Autobiographie* (1960). Strenuously informal but very instructive.

Mayer, Gustav, *Erinnerungen: Vom Journalisten zum Historiker der deutschen Arbeiterbewegung* (1949). Memoirs of a Jewish academic intellectual, author (among other books) of an important bulky biography of Engels.

Mehring, Walter, *Die verlorene Bibliothek: Autobiographie einer Kultur* (rev. ed., 1964; earlier English edition, *The Lost Library*, 1946). Lyrical reminiscences of the political poet in the form of a conversation with his beloved books.

Meinecke, Friedrich, *Erlebtes, 1862–1901* (1941).

———, *Strassburg, Freiburg, Berlin, 1901–1919* (1949). Deserve to be read in conjunction with the correspondence.

Nabokov, Vladimir, *Speak Memory* (1951). Some good pages on Berlin in the twenties.

Nolde, Emil, *Das eigene Leben* (2nd ed., Christian Wolff, 1949).

———, *Jahre der Kämpfe* (2nd ed., Christian Wolff, 1958). These two volumes take his life down to 1914; prejudiced.

Noske, Gustav, *Von Kiel bis Kapp* (1920).

————, *Aufstieg und Niedergang der deutschen Sozialdemokratie* (1947). Reminiscences, necessarily defensive, by the self-styled "bloodhound" of the Republic.

Osborn, Max, *Der Bunte Spiegel: Erinnerungen aus dem Kunst-, Kultur-, und Geistesleben der Jahre 1890 bis 1933* (1945). Recollections of an influential drama critic.

Piper, Reinhard, *Mein Leben als Verleger* (1964), incorporating two earlier autobiographies, *Vormittag* (1947) and *Nachmittag* (1950).

Rachfahl, Felix (see below under Steinberg).

Reik, Theodor, "Reminiscences," Oral History Collection, Columbia University (1965).

Scheidemann, Philipp, *Memoiren eines Sozialdemokraten,* 2 vols. (1928). Important reminiscences by a key actor in the revolution.

Schnabel, Artur, *My Life and Music* (1961). A collection of autobiographical talks given at the University of Chicago in 1945.

Schoenberger, Franz, *Confessions of a European Intellectual* (1946).

————, *The Inside Story of an Outsider* (1949). Valuable memoirs by the editor of *Simplicissimus;* the title of the latter helped me to formulate my thesis.

Steinberg, Sigfrid, *Die Geschichtswissenschaft der Gegenwart in Selbstdarstellungen,* 2 vols. (1925–1926). Part of a larger enterprise of enlisting autobiographical articles from prominent German intellectuals; this set includes the autobiographies of such historians as Karl Julius Beloch, Georg von Below, Felix Rachfahl (which I quote in the text), and many others.

Straus, Rahel, *Wir lebten in Deutschland: Erinnerungen einer deutschen Jüdin, 1880–1933,* ed. Max Kreutzberger (1961). The first German woman doctor—and a Jew—recounts her life.

Stresemann, Gustav, *Vermächtnis. Der Nachlass in drei Bänden,* ed. Henry Bernhard (1932–1923). A problematic legacy; see Hans W. Gatzke, "The Stresemann Papers," *Journal of Modern History,* XXVI (1954), 49–59.

Susman, Margarete, *Ich habe viele Leben gelebt. Erinnerungen* (1964). An intellectual, a Jew and a woman, yet close to the George circle, as well as other poets and writers.

Toller, Ernst, "Eine Jugend in Deutschland" and "Briefe aus dem Gefängnis," in Toller, *Prosa, Briefe, Dramen, Gedichte,* preface by Kurt Hiller (1961), pp. 25–234. Informal, enormously interesting recollections by the tragic Expressionist figure.

Ullstein, Heinz, *Spielplatz meines Lebens: Erinnerungen* (1961). Totally superficial, but instructive, recollections of a member of the great publishing empire, himself indifferent to publishing.

Walter, Bruno, *Theme and Variations; An Autobiography,* tr. James A. Galston (1946). Innocent, reticent, good on cultural life.

Wassermann, Jakob, *Mein Weg als Deutscher und Jude* (1921). Important testimony to an attempt to be both a German and a Jew.

Wolff, Kurt, *Autoren, Bücher, Abenteuer: Betrachtungen und Erinnerungen eines Verlegers* (1965). Informal broadcasts and essays.

Zuckmayer, Carl, *Als Wär's ein Stück von mir* (1966). Enormous in its vitality, this book covers the whole cultural and much of the political front of the twenties. Magnificent.

Zweig, Stefan, *The World of Yesterday* (1953). Important, nostalgic.

II. POLITICS, ECONOMY, SOCIETY, EDUCATION, THOUGHT

This section includes general histories, histories of specific subjects or cities, analyses of social structure and change, political thought and general philosophy, studies of the youth movements, the universities, the schools, the various specialized institutes including psychoanalysis, monographs, and biographies of leading figures.

Abraham, Karl, "Die Psychoanalyse als Erkenntnisquelle für die Geisteswissenschaften," *Neue Rundschau,* XXXI, part 2 (1920), 1154–1174. One of the first summaries of psychoanalysis addressed to the general (cultivated) public.

Anderson, Evelyn, *Hammer or Anvil* (1945). History of the German labor movement from a radical position.

Angress, Werner T., *Stillborn Revolution: The Communist Bid for Power in Germany, 1921–1923* (1963). Detailed account.

Arendt, Hannah, *The Origins of Totalitarianism* (1951).

Aron, Raymond, *German Sociology* (1936; trs. Mary and Thomas Bottomore, 1964). Brief and suggestive survey.

Aster, Ernst von, "Metaphysik des Nationalismus," *Neue Rundschau,* XLIII, part 1 (1932), 40–52. Good analysis of right-wing thought of the moment.

——, "Othmar Spanns Gesellschaftsphilosophie," *Die Gesellschaft,* VII, part 2 (1930), 230–241. Excellent, caustic study of a right-wing "thinker."

Ausnahmezustand, ed. Wolfgang Weyrauch (1966). Generous anthology culled from the *Weltbühne* and the *Tagebuch,* marred by a poetic introduction and lack of precise dates.

Baum, Marie, *Leuchtende Spur: Das Leben Ricarda Huchs* (1950).

Adulatory but not useless biography of the decent conservative writer and historian.

Below, Georg, *Die deutsche Geschichtsschreibung von den Befreiungskriegen bis zu unseren Tagen: Geschichte und Kulturgeschichte* (1916). A history of history in Germany, by a reactionary both in political and professional questions.

Bendix, Reinhard, *Max Weber: An Intellectual Portrait* (1962). More an extensive summary of Weber's vast output than a portrait, but valuable in that respect.

Bergsträsser, Ludwig, *Geschichte der politischen Parteien in Deutschland* (11th ed., by Wilhelm Mommsen, 1965). A standard work with parts IV and V of particular relevance here.

Berichte der deutschen Hochschule für Politik, VIII, No. 7 (October 1930), 113–129. Reports tenth anniversary celebrations.

Bernstein, Eduard, *Die deutsche Revolution* (1921). Sad but fair history of the revolution by an independent-minded Socialist.

Besson, Waldemar, "Friedrich Meinecke und die Weimarer Republik," *Vierteljahrshefte für Zeitgeschichte,* VII (1959), 113–129. Discriminating and critical.

Böhme, Helmut, *Deutschlands Weg zur Grossmacht* (1966). Penetrating recent analysis of Germany's rise to power in the mid-nineteenth century; uses modern techniques of investigation.

Bracher, Karl Dietrich, *Deutschland zwischen Demokratie und Diktatur: Beiträge zur neueren Politik und Geschichte* (1964). A collection of important essays by Germany's foremost modern historian. (See also below under *The Path to Dictatorship*).

———, *Die Auflösung der Weimarer Republik: Eine Studie zum Problem des Machtverfalls in der Demokratie* (1955). The opening sections of this masterly work are relevant to the end of Weimar.

———, Wolfgang Sauer, and Gerhard Schulz, *Die nationalsozialistische Machtergreifung: Studien zur Errichtung des totalitären Herrschaftssystems in Deutschland, 1933–1934* (1960). Pp. 1–368, by Bracher, deal with the structure of Weimar, its fall, the "legal" seizure of power, and the first year of Nazi rule. First-rate.

———, *Die Entstehung der Weimarer Verfassung* (1963). A short introduction followed by the Weimar Constitution.

Brackmann, Albert, "Kaiser Friedrich in 'mythischer Schau,'" *Historische Zeitschrift,* CXXXX (1929), 534–549; "Nachwort," *ibid.,* CXXXXI (1930), 472–478. A review of Ernst Kantorowicz's *Kaiser Friedrich der II.* and a reply to Kantorowicz's response.

Brecht, Arnold, *Federalism and Regionalism in Germany: The Division of Prussia* (1945). Discusses plans to break up Prussia; with maps.

———, *Prelude to Silence: The End of the German Republic* (1944).

———, "Bureaucratic Sabotage," *Annals of the American Academy of Political Science,* CLXXIX (January 1937), 48–57. The classic article on this subject.

Briefs, Goetz, "Das gewerbliche Proletariat," *Grundriss der Sozialökonomik,* Division IX, "Das soziale System des Kapitalismus," part 1, "Die gesellschaftliche Schichtung im Kapitalismus" (1926), 142–240. A pioneering part of a pioneering sociological volume, typical of the best Weimar work. (See also below, under Brinkmann, Lederer and Marschak, and Michels.)

Brinkmann, Carl, "Die Umformung der kapitalistischen Gesellschaft in geschichtlicher Darstellung," *Grundriss der Sozialökonomik,* IX, 2, pp. 1–21. (See just above.)

———, "Die Aristokratie im kapitalistischen Zeitalter," *ibid.,* 22–34. (See above.)

Bullock, Alan, *Hitler: A Study in Tyranny* (rev. ed., 1964). A very full biography.

Bussmann, Walter, *Treitschke: Sein Welt- und Geschichtsbild* (1952).

———, "Siegfried A. Kaehler: Ein Gedenkvortrag," *Historische Zeitschrift,* CLXXXXVIII (1964), 346–360.

Carsten, F. L., *The Reichswehr and Politics, 1918–1933* (German in 1964; English version, slightly different, 1966). A very valuable survey.

Cassirer, Toni, *Aus meinem Leben mit Ernst Cassirer* (1950). Sometimes petulant but usually interesting.

Conze, Werner, "Brünings Politik unter dem Druck der grossen Krise," *Historische Zeitschrift,* CIC (1964), 529–550. Excellent essay by a specialist in the late Weimar period.

Craig, Gordon, *The Politics of the Prussian Army* (1955). Fine general history; chapters 8 to 11 deal with the world war and the Republic. (See also above under Carsten.)

———, *From Bismarck to Adenauer: Aspects of German Statecraft* (rev. ed., 1965). Lucid lectures on German foreign ministers and policy.

———, "Engagement and Neutrality in Weimar Germany," *Journal of Contemporary History,* II, 2 (April 1967), 49–63. Analyzes the attitudes of some Weimar writers to politics.

Curtius, Ernst Robert, *Deutscher Geist in Gefahr* (1932). A collection of articles collected as a call to conscience, reason, and humanity, by a distinguished Swiss scholar.

Dahrendorf, Ralf, *Class and Class Conflict in Industrial Society* (4th ed., 1965). General, non-Marxist view of modern society, including Germany, by a brilliant German sociologist.

———, *Society and Democracy in Germany* (1965; tr. by the author, 1967). Severe, disciplined, honest sociological analysis of the "German question"; perhaps the best book to come out of Germany in ten years.

Dehio, Ludwig, *Germany and World Politics in the Twentieth Century*, tr. Dieter Pevsner (1959). A splendid collection of essays, generally done in the 1950s, re-examining German imperialism, Germany's sense of mission, the Versailles Treaty; includes a respectful but devastating piece on "Ranke and German Imperialism." Indispensable.

———, *The Precarious Balance: Four Centuries of the European Power Struggle* (1948; tr. Charles Fullman, 1962). Seeks to place Germany's urge for expansion in the European state system.

Dorpalen, Andreas, *Hindenburg and the Weimar Republic* (1964). A clear study.

———, "The German Historians and Bismarck," *Review of Politics*, XV, 1 (January 1953), 53–67. Assesses the large Bismarck literature.

———, "Historiography as History: The Work of Gerhard Ritter," *Journal of Modern History*, XXXIV, 1 (March 1962), 1–18.

Epstein, Klaus, *Matthias Erzberger and the Dilemma of German Democracy* (1959). An important political biography by the late German-American historian.

Eschenburg, Theodor, *Die improvisierte Demokratie: Gesammelte Aufsätze zur Weimarer Republik* (1963). A collection of political essays on Weimar by a veteran observer, largely on leading personalities like Stresemann, Papen, Brüning, and others.

Eyck, Erich, *Bismarck and the German Empire* (1963, a translation and abridgment of a larger German work).

———, *A History of the Weimar Republic*, 2 vols. (1956; tr. Harlan P. Hanson and Robert L. G. Waite, 1962–1964). Indispensable political history by an intelligent and judicious liberal.

Feldman, Gerald D., *Army, Industry and Labor, 1914–18* (1966). An excellent monograph on a neglected subject.

Fischer, Fritz, *Griff nach der Weltmacht: Die Kriegszielpolitik des kaiserlichen Deutschlands, 1914–18* (3rd, rev. ed., 1964). The celebrated controversial examination of Germany's aggressive war aims; though somewhat obsessive, thoroughly documented. (See also below under Gatzke.)

———, "Der deutsche Protestantismus und die Politik im 19. Jahrhundert," *Historische Zeitschrift*, CLXXI, 3 (May 1951), 473–518. (See also below under Holborn.)

Flexner, Abraham, *Universities: American, English, German* (1930). A pioneering comparative survey; generous but not uncritical.

Frank, Philipp, *Einstein: His Life and Times* (1947). Solid biography of Germany's greatest scientist and most famous exile.

Freisel, Ludwig, *Das Bismarckbild des Alldeutschen Verbandes von 1890 bis 1933: Ein Beitrag zum Bismarckverständnis des deutschen Nationalismus* (1964). Instructive monograph on political perception.

Frobenius, Else, *Mit uns zieht die neue Zeit: Eine Geschichte der deutschen Jugendbewegung* (1927). Ecstatic but informative; as much a symptom as a history of the youth movement. (See also below under Laqueur.)

Freud, Sigmund, "The Resistances to Psycho-Analysis" (1925). *Standard Edition of the Complete Psychological Works of Sigmund Freud*, XIX (1961), 213–224. Relevant to the situation of psychoanalysis in early Weimar. (See also above under Hartmann and Loewenstein.)

Fromm, Erich, *The Dogma of Christ and Other Essays on Religion, Psychology, and Culture* (1966 ed.). Contains Fromm's then subversive essay on Christ (1930).

———, *Escape from Freedom* (1941). A still important, though controversial, attempt to interpret the psychology of Nazism as an escape from the burdens imposed by freedom.

Gatzke, Hans W., *Germany's Drive to the West: A Study of Germany's Western War Aims During the First World War* (1950). (See also above under Fischer.)

———, *Stresemann and the Rearmament of Germany* (1954). Both are dependable studies.

Gay, Peter, *The Dilemma of Democratic Socialism: Eduard Bernstein's Challenge to Marx* (1952). An intellectual biography of the veteran Revisionist Socialist who came to oppose the war, and lived through the Weimar Republic. (See below under Schorske.)

Geiger, Theodor, *Die soziale Schichtung des deutschen Volkes* (1932). A pioneering, still valuable attempt, from an independent Marxist standpoint, to analyze Germany's social structure; especially its analysis of the rise of Nazism remains important.

Gilbert, Felix, "European and American Historiography," in John Higham, with Leonard Krieger and Felix Gilbert, *History* (1965), 315–387. A brilliant study of twentieth-century European historians, somewhat more favorable to Meinecke than I am in the text.

Goetz, Walter, *Historiker in meiner Zeit: Gesammelte Aufsätze* (1957).

Important essays on modern German historians and the modern German profession of history by a democratic cultural historian.

Goodspeed, D. J., *Ludendorff: Genius of World War I* (1966).

Gordon, Harold J., *The Reichswehr and the German Republic, 1919–1926* (1957). (See above under Carsten and Craig.)

Grabowsky, Adolf, and Walther Koch, eds., *Die freideutsche Jugendbewegung: Ursprung and Zukunft* (1920). An interesting collection of essays, including one by Paul Tillich on youth and religion, others on the relationship of youth to the state and to sex.

Groener-Geyer, Dorothea, *General Groener: Soldat und Staatsmann* (1954). Apologetic though informative; excellent appendix with documents.

Grünberg, Carl, *Festrede, gehalten zur Einweihung des Instituts für Sozialforschung . . . Juni 22, 1924*, Frankfurter Universitätsreden, XX (1924). A candid Marxist view of the Institute's function. (See also below under Horkheimer.)

Gumbel, Emil Julius, *Zwei Jahre Mord* (1921).

——, *Vier Jahre politischer Mord* (1922).

——, *Verräter verfallen der Feme* (1929).

——, *Lasst Köpfe rollen* (1932). An invaluable, wholly reliable series of studies on political assassination during the Republic.

Habermas, Jürgen, *Strukturwandlung der Öffentlichkeit: Untersuchungen zu einer Kategorie der bürgerlichen Gesellschaft* (2nd ed., 1965). An important analysis of changes in the concept and significance of public opinion.

Halévy, Elie, *The Era of Tyrannies* (1938; tr. R. K. Webb, 1965). Includes that great historian's great essay on "The World Crisis of 1914–1918: An Interpretation" (1929), pp. 209–247.

Halperin, S. William, *Germany Tried Democracy: A Political History of the Reich from 1918 to 1933* (1946). Its subtitle is just; the book is a dependable, clearly written account of political developments in the Republic. I found it useful in compiling my short history.

Hamerow, Theodore S., *Restoration, Revolution, Reaction: Economics and Politics in Germany, 1815–1871* (1958). Useful survey of German history in the period before and during Bismarck's rise to power.

Hampe, K., "Das neueste Lebensbild Kaiser Friedrichs II.," *Historische Zeitschrift*, CXXXXVI (1932), 441–475. A discriminating, critical review of Ernst Kantorowicz's great biography.

Hannover, H. and E., *Politische Justiz, 1918–1933* (1966). An unsparing analysis of "political justice" in the Weimar Republic. Depressing but essential.

Hartenstein, Wolfgang, *Die Anfänge der deutschen Volkspartei, 1918–1920* (1962). A modern monograph of the kind the Germans are now beginning to write. (See also below under Morsey.)

Heidegger, Martin, *Die Selbstbehauptung der deutschen Universität*, Freiburger Universitätsreden, XI (1933). The notorious inaugural speech Heidegger gave as rector of Freiburg after the Nazis had come to power; his apologists have spent as much time explaining it away as they have explaining his difficult philosophical thought.

Heuss, Theodor, *Friedrich Naumann: Der Mann, Das Werk, Die Zeit* (1937). An important biography of the democratic imperialist.

————, *Hitlers Weg: Eine historisch-politische Studie über den Nationalsozialismus* (1932). Ironic and prophetic.

————, *Robert Bosch: Leben und Leistung* (1946). Biography of a progressive industrialist.

Hiller, Kurt, *Köpfe und Tröpfe: Profile aus einem Vierteljahrhundert* (1950). Outspoken, delightfully frank profiles.

Hofstadter, Richard, "The Paranoid Style in American Politics," in *The Paranoid Style in American Politics and Other Essays* (1965), 3–40. Illuminating by extension for German politics, too.

Holborn, Hajo, *The Political Collapse of Europe* (1951). A concentrated, rich analysis of the political fate of Europe before and after World War I.

————, "Protestantismus und politische Ideengeschichte," *Historische Zeitschrift*, CXXXXIV (1931), 15–30.

————, "Der deutsche Idealismus in sozialgeschichtlicher Beleuchtung," *Historische Zeitschrift*, CLXXIV (October 1952), 359–384. A justly influential article concentrating on the origins of the separation of Germany from the West at the turn of the nineteenth century.

Horkheimer, Max, *Die gegenwärtige Lage der Sozialphilosophie und die Aufgaben eines Instituts für Sozialforschung*, Frankfurter Universitätsreden, XXXVII (1931). Important but already somewhat Aesopian. (See also above under Grünberg.)

————, ed., *Studien über Autorität und Familie* (1936). A famous collective volume done by the members of the Institut für Sozialforschung in French exile, with articles by Horkheimer, Erich Fromm, Herbert Marcuse, and others.

Hühnerfeld, Paul, *In Sachen Heidegger* (1961). Lucid, well-tempered, devastating critique of Heidegger.

International Institute of Social History: A Short Description of its History and Aims (n.d., 1935?).

International Institute of Social History: A Report on its History, Aims and Activities, 1933–1938 (n.d., 1939?). Both informative reports of the Institut für Sozialforschung, prepared in New York; but rather toning down its Marxist slant.

Jäckh, Ernst, ed., *Politik als Wissenschaft: Zehn Jahre deutsche Hochschule für Politik* (1931). An anniversary volume.

Joll, James, *The Second International, 1889–1914* (1955). Lucid but excessively weary in tone.

———, *Three Intellectuals in Politics* (1960). One of the three—a good essay, by the way—is Rathenau (pp. 57–129).

Jones, Ernest, *The Life and Work of Sigmund Freud,* 3 vols. (1953–1957). The last volume has some (but not enough) material on psychoanalysis in Weimar Germany.

Kampffmeyer, Paul, *Fritz Ebert* (1923). A short appreciation.

Kantorowicz, Ernst, *Kaiser Friedrich der II.,* 2 vols. (1927, 1931).

———, " 'Mythenschau,' Eine Erwiderung," *Historische Zeitschrift,* CXXXXI (1930), 457–471. A reply to Albert Brackmann's review of his great book. (See above under Brackmann.)

Kehr, Eckart, *Schlachtflottenbau und Parteipolitik, 1894–1901* (1930). The celebrated dissertation tying the German naval rearmament program to domestic economic pressures.

———, *Der Primat der Innenpolitik: Gesammelte Aufsätze zur preussisch-deutschen Sozialgeschichte im 19. und 20. Jahrhundert,* ed. Hans-Ulrich Wehler (1965). Wehler's introduction gives an appreciative biography and a vigorous—too vigorous—defense; the articles, on the Prussian bureaucracy and other touchy subjects, are often highly original and deeply penetrating.

Kessler, Harry Graf, *Walther Rathenau: Sein Leben und sein Werk* (1929; English version, 1930; see reprint [1963?] with long postscript by Hans Fürstenberg). Lucid biography of an enigmatic and profoundly contradictory statesman and Utopian.

Kiaulehn, Walther, *Berlin: Schicksal einer Weltstadt* (1958). Though a deliberately popular account of Berlin in the nineteenth and twentieth centuries, very informative and rich.

Kindt, Werner, *Grundschriften der deutschen Jugendbewegung* (1963). Intelligent and comprehensive compilation from the vast amount of writings on the youth movement; I have used it freely.

Klemperer, Klemens von, *Germany's New Conservatism: Its History and Dilemma in the Twentieth Century* (1957). An excellent survey of right-wing thinking.

Knowles, David, "The Monumenta Germaniae Historica," in *Great His-*

torical Enterprises and Problems in Monastic History (1963), 63–97. A fascinating account of nineteenth-century and early twentieth-century German historical scholarship.

Koplin, Raimund, *Carl von Ossietzky als politischer Publizist* (1964).

Krieger, Leonard, *The German Idea of Freedom: History of a Political Tradition* (1957). An important history of the relation of ideas to politics in Germany.

Krill, Hans-Heinz, *Die Ranke-Renaissance: Max Lenz und Erich Marcks* (1962). Excellent study of two Ranke epigoni and the political consequences of their work.

Krockow, Christian Graf von, *Die Entscheidung: Eine Untersuchung über Ernst Jünger, Carl Schmitt, Martin Heidegger* (1958). A comparative study of three "philosophical" irrationalists, all of whom had some affinities for the Nazis.

Kurucz, Jenö, *Struktur und Funktion der Intelligenz während der Weimarer Republik* (1967). Abstract but suggestive short analysis of the sociological situation of the intellectual in the Republic.

Lampl-de Groot, Jeanne, "Die Entwicklung der Psychoanalyse in Deutschland bis 1933," *Ansprachen und Vorträge zur Einweihung des Instituts-Neubaues am 14. Oktober 1964,* Sigmund Freud Institut, Frankfurt am Main (n.d., 1964). Very sketchy; only a beginning.

Laqueur, Walter Z., *Young Germany: A History of the German Youth Movement* (1962). A sure guide through a bewildering field.

——, and George L. Mosse, eds., *The Coming of the First World War* (1966). A series of articles.

Laue, Theodore von, *Leopold Ranke: The Formative Years* (1950). An excellent brief study.

Lederer, Emil, and Jakob Marschak, "Der neue Mittelstand," *Grundriss der Sozialökonomik,* IX, part 1 (1926), 120–141. (See above under Briefs.)

Leipart, Theodor, *Carl Legien* (1929). Biography of the outstanding German labor leader.

Lenz, Max, and Erich Marcks, eds., *Der Weltkrieg im Spiegel Bismarckischer Gedanken* (1915). A wartime patriotic collection showing how the spirit of Bismarck lived after, or was used after, his death.

Lilge, Frederic, *The Abuse of Learning: The Failure of the German University* (1948). A devastating survey.

Loewenthal, Leo, "German Popular Biographies: Culture's Bargain Counter," in *The Critical Spirit: Essays in Honor of Herbert Marcuse,* ed. Kurt H. Wolff and Barrington Moore, Jr. (1967), 267–283. An interesting content analysis of biographies by Stefan Zweig and others, showing their easy superlatives, cheap optimism, and intellectual shoddiness.

Mann, Golo, *Deutsche Geschichte des 19. und 20. Jahrhunderts* (1966 ed.). Vigorous, informal, antiauthoritarian, interesting.

Mann, Heinrich, *Essays* (1960 ed.). This edition contains his most provocative performances, including the early "Voltaire-Goethe," "Zola," which so embittered his brother Thomas, and essays done in the 1920s. Of great importance.

Mannheim, Karl, *Essays on the Sociology of Knowledge,* ed. Paul Kecskemeti (1952). A convenient collection, in translation, of some of Mannheim's most important sociological essays written during the Weimar period, surrounding his *Ideology and Utopia.*

Masur, Gerhard, *Prophets of Yesterday: Studies in European Culture, 1890–1914* (1961). Deals with a crucial period in European history; Masur's exposition is not always adequate, and sometimes, as with Freud, a caricature.

Mayer, Arno J., *Political Origins of the New Diplomacy, 1917–1918* (1959). Unconventional and authoritative diplomatic history; it analyzes the weariness of the belligerent powers.

————, *Politics and Diplomacy of Peacemaking: Containment and Counterrevolution at Versailles, 1918–1919* (1967). A sequel, just as authoritative; concentrates on the exclusion of Soviet Russia from the Concert of Powers.

Mehring, Franz, *Die Geschichte der deutschen Sozialdemokratie,* parts I and II, 2 vols. (1897–1898). Scrupulous, though wholly sympathetic history of the years 1830 to 1891 by a veteran Socialist intellectual.

Meinecke, Friedrich, *Weltbürgertum und Nationalstaat: Studien zur Genesis des deutschen Nationalstaates* (1907). From cosmopolitanism to nationalism, Humboldt to Bismarck; the book that made Meinecke's reputation.

————, *Die Idee der Staatsräson in der neueren Geschichte* (1924). There is a translation of this subtle book, by Douglas Scott, with the unsubtle and misleading title *Machiavellianism* (1965).

————, *Die Entstehung des Historismus,* 2 vols. (1936). A vigorous defense and brilliant, though to my mind not adequate, analysis of historicism.

————, *The German Catastrophe: Reflections and Recollections* (1946; tr. Sidney B. Fay, 1950). Reconsiderations, partly affecting, partly pathetic, on the German past.

———, *Politische Schriften und Reden,* ed. Georg Kotowski (1958). An important collection of talks and essays on politics.

———, "Drei Generationen deutscher Gelehrtenpolitik," *Historische Zeitschrift,* CXXV (1922), 248–283.

———, "Values and Causalities in History" (1928), tr. Julian H. Franklin, in *The Varieties of History,* ed. Fritz Stern (1956), 267–288.

Meyer, Henry Cord, *Mitteleuropa in German Thought and Action, 1815–1945* (1955).

Michels, Robert, *Political Parties: A Sociological Study of the Oligarchical Tendencies of Modern Democracy,* tr. Eden and Cedar Paul (1949 ed). The classic study in pessimism about democracy, using largely instances from the German Social Democratic Party before World War I.

———, "Psychologie der antikapitalistischen Massenbewegungen," *Grundriss der Sozialökonomik,* IX, part 1 (1926), 241–359. (See above under Briefs.)

Mitchell, Allan, *Revolution in Bavaria, 1918–1919: The Eisner Regime and the Soviet Republic* (1965). Careful, too careful, documentary study.

Modern Germany in Relation to the Great War, by Various German Writers, tr. William Wallace Whitelock (1916). Apologetics by Otto Hintze, Ernst Troeltsch, Hans Delbrück, Friedrich Meinecke: an all-star cast in a dramatic failure.

Mohler, Armin, *Die konservative Revolution in Deutschland, 1918 bis 1932: Grundriss ihrer Weltanschauungen* (1950). A very comprehensive survey of German right-wing thought in economical compass.

Mommsen, Hans, "Zum Verhältnis von politischer Wissenschaft und Geschichtswissenschaft in Deutschland," *Vierteljahrshefte für Zeitgeschichte,* X (1962), 341–372. Part of the reappraisal of German historical writing.

Mommsen, Wolfgang J., *Max Weber und die deutsche Politik* (1959). Much-needed examination of a hero; concludes that Weber was not a political liberal.

———, "Universalgeschichtliches und politisches Denken bei Max Weber," *Historische Zeitschrift,* CCI (1965), 557–612. Excellent supplement to his book; full bibliography on the Weber controversy; sees charisma as a central problem for Weber.

Morsey, Rudolf, *Die deutsche Zentrumspartei, 1917–1923* (1966). An exhaustive model monograph.

Mosse, George L., *The Crisis of German Ideology: Intellectual Origins of the Third Reich* (1964). Stresses, surveying racism, youth movements, political notions, the *"völkische"* elements.

———, "Die deutsche Rechte und die Juden," in *Entscheidungsjahr 1932: zur Judenfrage in der Endphase der Weimarer Republik*, ed. Werner E. Mosse (1963), 183–246.

Nettl, J. P., *Rosa Luxemburg*, 2 vols., (1966). An excellent extensive biography.

Neumann, Franz L., *Behemoth: The Structure and Practice of National Socialism* (2nd ed., 1944). The long introduction summarizes Neumann's interpretation of the inner structure of Weimar; an independent Marxist view of importance.

———, "The Social Sciences," in *The Cultural Migration: The European Scholar in America* (1953), 4–26. A brilliant comparative analysis of social science in Germany and America, with valuable personal reminiscences. (See also below under Panofsky and Tillich.)

Neumann, Sigmund, *Die Parteien der Weimarer Republik* (1932; ed. 1965 with preface by Karl Dietrich Bracher). Excellent, in fact indispensable survey of party politics in Weimar.

———, "Die Stufen des preussischen Konservatismus: Ein Beitrag zum Staats- und Gesellschaftsbild Deutschlands im neunzehnten Jahrhundert," in *Historische Studien*, No. 190 (1930). An important sociohistorical analysis of conservatism, to be compared with Karl Mannheim's work.

Neurohr, Jean F., *Der Mythos vom dritten Reich: Zur Geistesgeschichte des Nationalsozialismus* (1957). Good analysis of a fatal myth.

Oberschall, A., *Empirical Social Research in Germany, 1848–1914* (1965). Brief; more work is needed; but meanwhile very helpful. (See also below under Shad.)

Panofsky, Erwin, "The History of Art," in *The Cultural Migration: The European Scholar in America* (1953), 82–111. Witty comparison between ways of teaching art history in German and American universities. (See also above under Neumann, Franz, and below under Pevsner).

PEM (pseud. for Paul Erich Marcus), *Heimweh nach dem Kurfürstendamm: Aus Berlins glanzvollsten Tagen und Nächten* (1952). Nostalgic evocation of Berlin in the "golden twenties."

Pevsner, Nikolaus, "Reflections on Not Teaching Art History," *The Listener*, XLVIII, No. 1235 (October 30, 1952), 715–716. Informative memories on the German way of teaching the subject. (See also above under Panofsky.)

Pflanze, Otto, *Bismarck and the Development of Germany: The Period of Unification, 1815–1871* (1963). Excellent first volume.

————, "Bismarck and German Nationalism," *American Historical Review*, LX, 3 (April 1955), 548–566.

Plessner, Helmuth, *Die verspätete Nation: Über die politische Verführbarkeit bürgerlichen Geistes* (1959). Seeks to account for the deliberate rejection of Western in behalf of "German" values by many Germans.

Ramm, Agatha, *Germany, 1789–1919: A Political History* (1967). Intelligent, adequately detailed survey; highly recommended.

Rathenau, Walther, *Die neue Wirtschaft* (1918).

————, *Der neue Staat* (1919). Two polemical pamphlets indispensable to an understanding of Rathenau's style of thinking; the second is a vehement expression of profound disappointment in the "Revolution."

Rauschning, Hermann, *Die konservative Revolution: Versuch und Bruch mit Hitler* (1941). An important, disquieting essay by an early ally and later enemy of Hitler, claiming that the Nazis betrayed the true "conservative revolution."

Röhl, J. C. G., *Germany without Bismarck: The Crisis of Government in the Second Reich, 1890–1900* (1967). Makes excellent use of documents to illuminate a murky period.

Rosenberg, Arthur, *The Birth of the German Republic, 1871–1918* (1928; tr. Ian F. D. Morrow, 1931).

————, *A History of the German Republic* (1935; tr. Ian F. D. Morrow and L. Marie Sieveking, 1936). Both indispensable; the orientation is left-radical but independent; the grasp of the deep issues is admirable.

Rothfels, Hans, "Problems of a Bismarck Biography," *Review of Politics*, IX, 3 (July 1947), 362–380. Good contribution to a large issue.

Schieder, Theodor, ed., *Hundert Jahre Historische Zeitschrift 1859–1959* (1959). A large but disappointing collection of articles, illuminating many facets of historical writing in Germany for a hundred years without grappling with some crucial issues.

————, "Grundfragen der neuen deutschen Geschichte: Zum Problem der historischen Urteilsbildung," *Historische Zeitschrift*, CLXXXXII (1961), 1–16.

Schimanski, Stefan, "Forward," to Martin Heidegger, *Existence and Being*, tr. Douglas Scott, R. F. C. Hull, and Alan Crick (1949). Collection of four short essays by the author of *Sein und Zeit*, introduced briefly by Schimanski and at length by Werner Brock.

Schmitt, Carl, *Hugo Preuss: Sein Staatsbegriff und seine Stellung in der deutschen Staatslehre* (1930). Appreciation of the "father" of the German constitution by a supple legal theorist whose sympathies lay elsewhere. (See also below under Simons.)

Schnabel, Franz, *Deutsche Geschichte im neunzehnten Jahrhundert*, 4 vols. (2nd ed., 1937–1949). Liberal, but not "too" liberal; detailed interpretation of nineteenth-century Germany. Vol. II, 245–253, contains account of the 1817 meetings at the Wartburg.

Schorske, Carl E., *German Social Democracy, 1905–1917: The Development of the Great Schism* (1955). Brilliant, and important.

Schwabe, Klaus, "Zur politischen Haltung der deutschen Professoren im ersten Weltkrieg," *Historische Zeitschrift*, CLXXXXIII (1961), 601–634. Full of excellent—that is, awful—instances of chauvinism among German intellectuals in World War I.

Sell, Friedrich C., *Die Tragödie des deutschen Liberalismus* (1953). Tells the familiar story well.

Shad, Susanne P., "Empirical Social Research in Weimar Germany," Columbia University Dissertation (1964).

Sheehan, James J. *The Career of Lujo Brentano: A Study of Liberalism and Social Reform in Imperial Germany* (1966).

Siefert, Hermann, *Der bündische Aufbruch, 1918–1923* (1963). Discriminating study of the youth movements in the early Republic.

Simons, Walter, *Hugo Preuss* (1930).

Sontheimer, Kurt, *Anti-Demokratisches Denken in der Weimarer Republik: Die politischen Ideen des deutschen Nationalismus zwischen 1918 und 1933* (1962). Excellent survey of right-wing philosophies in the Republic.

Spengler, Oswald, *The Decline of the West*, 2 vols. (1918–1922; tr. Charles Francis Atkinson, 1926–1928).

————, *Preussentum und Sozialismus* (1919). Both vitally important—as documents.

Srbik, Heinrich Ritter von, *Geist und Geschichte vom deutschen Humanismus bis zur Gegenwart*, 2 vols. (1950–1951). Expansive in tone, conservative in philosophy.

Stampfer, Friedrich, *Die vierzehn Jahre der ersten deutschen Republik* (3rd ed., 1953). A history of the Republic by a Social Democratic publicist who went through it all himself.

Steinhausen, Georg, *Deutsche Geistes- und Kulturgeschichte von 1870 bis zur Gegenwart* (1931).

Sterling, Richard W., *Ethics in a World of Power: The Political Ideas of Friedrich Meinecke* (1958). The first full examination of the political thought of a great German historian.

Stern, Fritz, *The Politics of Cultural Despair: A Study in the Rise of the Germanic Ideology* (1961). Fine studies of three anticipators, Langbehn, Lagarde, Moeller van den Bruck.

————, "The Political Consequences of the Unpolitical German," *History*, No. 3 (1960), 104–134. Sober examination of an important topic.

Stolper, Gustav, *The German Economy, 1870–1940* (1940). Important.

Stolper, Toni, *Ein Leben in Brennpunkten unserer Zeit: Gustav Stolper, 1888–1947* (1960). Informative biography of the versatile economic historian by his widow.

Suhrkamp, Peter, "Die Sezession des Familiensohnes: Eine nachträgliche Betrachtung der Jugendbewegung," *Neue Rundschau*, XLIII, part 1 (1932), 94–112.

———, "Söhne ohne Väter und Lehrer: Die Situation der bürgerlichen Jugend," *ibid.*, 681–696. Both thoughtful analyses of the disoriented youth on the verge of chaos.

Taylor, A. J. P., *The Course of German History* (1945).

———, *Bismarck: The Man and the Statesman* (1955). Both character-istic Taylor: brilliant in writing, stimulating in ideas, eccentric in inter-pretation.

The Path to Dictatorship, 1918–1933: Ten Essays by German Scholars, tr. John Conway (1966). Radio talks by Karl Dietrich Bracher, Kurt Sontheimer, Rudolf Morsey, Hans Rothfels, and six others on political parties, antidemocratic thought, Nazi tactics. Of varying merit, but the introduction by Fritz Stern and the chronology of Weimar history in its last five years are helpful.

Thimme, Anneliese, *Gustav Stresemann: Eine politische Biographie zur Geschichte der Weimarer Republik* (1957). Severe, unsentimental, re-visionist, important.

Tietz, Georg, *Hermann Tietz: Geschichte einer Familie und ihrer Waren-häuser* (1965). The great department store and its owners.

Tillich, Paul, "The Transmoral Conscience," in *The Protestant Era,* ed. and tr. James Luther Adams (1951), 152–166.

———, "The Protestant Message and the Man of Today," *ibid.*, 189–204. Both shed light on liberal theology in the late Weimar period.

———, "The Conquest of Theological Provincialism," in *The Cultural Migration: The European Scholar in America* (1953), 138–156. Both humble and amusing, Tillich reports what theological pride was in his Germany, and what he learned in America. (See also above under Neumann, Franz, and Panofsky.)

Troeltsch, Ernst, *Spektator-Briefe,* ed. Hans Baron (1924). Collected essays on the German Revolution and world politics, 1918 to 1922; very revealing.

Turner, Henry Ashby, Jr., *Stresemann and the Politics of the Weimar Republic* (1963). A dependable investigation.

Waite, Robert G. L., *Vanguard of Nazism: The Free Corps Movement in Postwar Germany, 1918–1923* (1952).

Wassermann, Jakob, "Rede an die studentische Jugend über das Leben im

Geiste: Zum Goethetag 1932," *Neue Rundschau,* XLIII, part 1 (1932), 530–544. A novelist's plea to the youth, for reason.

Weber, Marianne, *Max Weber: Ein Lebensbild* (1926). An important biography.

Weber, Max, *Gesammelte Politische Schriften* (2nd, expanded ed., by Johannes Winckelmann, 1958). Of critical importance; Weber wrote extensively on domestic and foreign policy, and his voice was heard.

Wehler, Hans-Ulrich, ed., *Moderne deutsche Sozialgeschichte* (1966). A diversified collection of social history put together by the editor of Eckart Kehr's shorter writings; many of the essays included here, dealing mainly with nineteenth- and early twentieth-century Germany, are excellent.

Wheeler-Bennett, John W., *The Nemesis of Power: The German Army in Politics, 1918–1945* (1954). (See also above under Carsten and Craig.)

Wucher, Albert, *Theodor Mommsen: Geschichtsschreibung und Politik* (1956). An exceptional, refreshing essay in a literature overwhelmed with piety.

Zehn Jahre Berliner Psychoanalytisches Institut (Polyklinik und Lehranstalt) (1930). An anniversary volume offering details on the Institute's history and achievements.

Ziekursch, Johannes, *Politische Geschichte des neuen deutschen Kaiserreiches,* 3 vols. (1925–1930). It might not be so sensational now (though it still remains worth reading), but its independent judgment and clarity of presentation made it an event in Weimar history-writing.

III. THE ARTS

This section includes painters, graphic artists, sculptors, composers and other musicians, architects, and art history.

Barr, Alfred H., Jr., *Cubism and Abstract Art* (1936). A pioneering survey, including Germans.

Bayer, Herbert, Ise Gropius, and Walter Gropius, eds., *Bauhaus 1919–1928* (1938, reprinted 1959). Classic book accompanying a classic exhibition. (See also below under Wingler.)

Bing, Gertrud, *Aby M. Warburg* (1958). Essay on the founder of the Warburg Institute, by a close associate.

Buchheim, Lothar-Günther, *Der Blaue Reiter und die Neue Künstler-Vereinigung München* (1959).

———, *The Graphic Art of German Expressionism* (1960).

Drexler, Arthur, *Ludwig Mies van der Rohe* (1960). Brief, well illustrated.

Eckardt, Wolf von, *Eric Mendelsohn* (1960). Useful short essay.

Edschmid, Kasimir, *Über den Expressionismus in der Literatur und die neue Malerei* (1921). An important proclamation by a leading writer.

Fitch, James Marston, *Walter Gropius* (1960). Good short study.

———, "A Utopia Revisited," *The Columbia University Forum*, IX, 4 (Fall 1966), 34–39. A look at the Bauhaus now, with some sad photographs.

Goergen, Aloys, "Beckmann und die Apocalypse," *Blick auf Beckmann: Dokumente und Vorträge* (1962), 9–21.

Grohmann, Will, *Das Werk Ernst Ludwig Kirchners* (1926). Crucial; includes all but the last twelve years of Kirchner's life.

———, *Zeichnungen von Ernst Ludwig Kirchner* (1925). Equally good on the drawings.

———, *Ernst Ludwig Kirchner* (1961).

———, *Wassily Kandinsky: Life and Work* (1959). Includes an *œuvre* catalogue.

Gropius, Walter, *The New Architecture and the Bauhaus*, tr. P. Morton Shand (1965 ed.). The basic statement.

———, *Scope of Total Architecture* (1962 ed.). A collection of shorter pieces.

Grote, Ludwig, *Der Blaue Reiter: München und die Kunst des 20. Jahrhunderts* (1949).

———, *Die Maler am Bauhaus* (1950).

———, ed., *Oskar Kokoschka*, essays, catalogue of the 1950 exhibition in Munich (1950). Good, like all of Grote's work.

Haftmann, Werner, *Emil Nolde* (1958; tr. Norbert Gutermann, 1959).

———, *The Mind and Work of Paul Klee* (1954).

———, *Painting in the Twentieth Century*, 2 vols. (2nd ed., 1965).

Hamilton, George Heard, *Painting and Sculpture in Europe, 1880–1940* (1967). A splendid volume in the Pelican History of Art; bulky but remarkable for its compression.

Heise, Carl Georg, *Persönliche Erinnerungen an Aby Warburg* (1947). Personal and moving reminiscences.

Hess, Hans, *Lyonel Feininger* (1961). The standard work, with *œuvre* catalogue. The book on Feininger's graphics is still a desideratum.

Kandinsky, Wassily, and Franz Marc, *Der Blaue Reiter* (1912; documentary ed. Klaus Lankheit, 1965). A document of critical importance.

———, *Über das geistige in der Kunst* (1912).

———, *Punkt und Linie zu Fläche: Beitrag zur Analyse der malerischen Elemente* (1926). Bauhaus-book No. 9.

Klee, Paul, *Pedagogical Sketchbook* (1925; tr. Sibyl Moholy-Nagy, 1953). Bauhaus-book No. 2; an important statement.

Kuhn, Charles L., *German Expressionism and Abstract Art: The Harvard Collections* (1957), with an introductory essay by Jakob Rosenberg; a splendidly informative catalogue.

————, *Supplement* (1967). Brings the Harvard catalogue up to date.

Kultermann, Udo, *Geschichte der Kunstgeschichte: Der Weg einer Wissenschaft* (1966). Though excessively popular, it contains useful chapters on the Expressionist period and the Warburg group.

McCoy, Esther, *Richard Neutra* (1960). Monograph on an important architect who left Germany in 1923.

Moholy-Nagy, Laszlo, *Malerei, Fotografie, Film* (2nd ed., 1927).

————, *The New Vision: From Material to Architecture* (1929; tr. Daphne M. Hoffmann, 1938).

Moholy-Nagy, Sibyl, *Moholy-Nagy, a Biography* (1950).

Myers, Bernard S., *The German Expressionists: A Generation in Revolt* (1963; concise ed., 1966). A splendid survey covering the movements and individual artists; with an excellent bibliography.

Panofsky, Erwin, "A. Warburg," *Repertorium für Kunstwissenschaft*, LI (1930), 1–4. A brief, perceptive obituary.

Pevsner, Nikolaus, *Pioneers of Modern Design, from William Morris to Walter Gropius* (3rd ed., 1960). A magnificently lucid analysis of the movement that led to the Bauhaus. Indispensable.

Redlich, H. F., *Alban Berg, the Man and His Music* (1957). Valuable biography of an important modern composer. (See also below under Reich.)

Reich, Willi, *Alban Berg: Leben und Werk* (1963).

Reifenberg, Benno, "Max Beckmann" (1921), in *Blick auf Beckmann: Dokumente und Vorträge* (1962), 101–109.

Reti, Rudolph, *Tonality in Modern Music* (1958). A composer looks at modern music, particularly the Germans—Schönberg, Berg, and Webern.

Richter, Hans, *Dada: Art and Anti-Art* (1965). A comprehensive account. (See also below under Rubin.)

Roh, Franz, *Nach-Expressionismus* (1925). A vigorous "obituary," calling for *"neue Sachlichkeit."*

Röthel, Hans K., and J. Cassou, *Vasily Kandinsky, 1866–1944, A Retrospective Exhibition* (1962). Splendid catalogue of the great retrospective at the Guggenheim Museum in New York.

Russell, John, *Max Ernst* (1967). A comprehensive, well-illustrated monograph.

Saxl, Fritz, "Die Bibliothek Warburg und ihr Ziel," *Vorträge der Bibliothek Warburg, 1921–1922*, ed. Fritz Saxl (1923), 1–10. Inaugural lecture by the Warburg Institute's first director.

————, "Ernst Cassirer," in *The Philosophy of Ernst Cassirer,* ed. Paul Arthur Schilpp (1949), 47–51. An important reminiscence of one of the Warburg Institute's most distinguished associates.

Scheffler, Karl, *Max Liebermann* (new ed., 1953). Biography of Germany's most popular painter; a vigorous Impressionist in an Expressionist age.

Selz, Peter, *Emil Nolde* (1963). Short but candid monograph and catalogue of a traveling exhibition of 1963.

————, *German Expressionist Painting* (1957). Good general account.

————, *Max Beckmann* (1964). An excellent catalogue and monograph.

Taylor, Joshua C., *Futurism* (1961). Good catalogue of a traveling exhibition of this important prewar movement.

Verkauf, Willy, Marcel Janco, and Hans Bolliger, eds., *Dada: Monographie einer Bewegung* (1958). Lavishly illustrated.

Warburg, Aby, *Gesammelte Schriften,* 2 vols. (1932). The seminal writings of a pioneering art historian and tormented human being.

Whittick, Arnold, *Erich Mendelsohn* (1940). Useful account.

Wingler, Hans M., ed., *Das Bauhaus, 1919–1933: Weimar, Dessau, Berlin* (1962). An enormous, thoroughly annotated and superbly illustrated collection of documents on the Bauhaus in all its aspects. Essential.

Worte zur Beisetzung von Professor Dr. Aby M. Warburg (n.d., end of 1929?).

Wuttke, Dieter, "Aby Warburg und seine Bibliothek," *Arcadia,* I, 3 (1966), 319–333. Informative article with excellent bibliography.

IV. LITERATURE

This section includes collected works, individual works, biographies and monographs of poets, novelists, and playwrights. Book on the theatre in general are also included.

Allemann, Beda, *Hölderlin und Heidegger* (2nd ed., 1954). Difficult study of an affinity.

Barlach, Ernst, *Das dichterische Werk,* 3 vols., ed. Klaus Lazarowicz and Friedrich Dross (1956–1959).

Benjamin, Walter, *Schriften,* 2 vols., ed. Theodor W. Adorno, Gretel Adorno, and Friedrich Podszus (1955). Collected writings by the brilliant social and literary critic who committed suicide in September 1940 on the Spanish frontier, on the verge of safety, hounded to death by Spanish officials. (There is a useful one-volume collection of his selected writings, *Illuminationen,* ed. Siegfried Unseld [1961].)

Beissner, Friedrich, *Hölderlin Heute: Der lange Weg des Dichters zu seinem Ruhm* (1963). Lecture by a foremost Hölderlin scholar.

Benn, Gottfried, *Gesammelte Werke*, 4 vols., ed. Dieter Wellershoff (1958–1961).

Bithell, Jethro, *Modern German Literature, 1880–1938* (2nd ed., 1946). Opinionated but dependable survey.

Boehringer, Robert, *Mein Bild von Stefan George* (1951). Two related volumes bound together; the second a picture gallery (much of it hilarious), the first a biographical record referring to the second.

Brecht, Bertolt, *Gesammelte Werke*, 8 vols., ed. Elizabeth Hauptmann (1967). Much the best edition so far.

———: *Bertolt Brechts Dreigroschenbuch* (1960). Contains the play, the film script, and other valuable documents.

Broch, Hermann, *Gesammelte Werke*, 10 vols. (1952–1961).

———, *The Death of Vergil*, tr. Jean Starr Untermeyer (1945). His major novel.

Büchner, Georg, *Sämtliche Werke*, ed. Hans Jürgen Meinerts (1963). One of several accessible editions.

Butler, E. M., *The Tyranny of Greece over Germany* (1935). An overstated but forceful argument that the German mind was seduced by a mythical Greek antiquity.

Cassirer, Ernst, *Idee und Gestalt* (2nd ed., 1924). Five civilized essays on German literature, including essays on Hölderlin and Kleist.

David, Claude, *Von Richard Wagner zu Bertolt Brecht: Eine Geschichte der neueren deutschen Literatur* (1959; German tr., Hermann Stiehl, 1964). Judicious history by a distinguished French scholar.

Dilthey, Wilhelm, "Hölderlin," in *Das Erlebnis und die Dichtung* (1957 ed.), 221–291. Though first written in 1867, this pathbreaking essay was rewritten for the first edition of this collective volume (1905).

Döblin, Alfred, *Die drei Sprünge des Wang-lun, Chinesischer Roman* (1915).

———, *Berlin Alexanderplatz: Die Geschichte von Franz Biberkopf* (1929). The two most remarkable novels by a first-rate Expressionist writer; the latter is particularly noteworthy.

Emrich, Wilhelm, *Franz Kafka* (2nd ed., 1960). Among the best studies. (See also below under Politzer and Sokel.)

Esslin, Martin, *Brecht: The Man and his Work* (1959). Comprehensive study of Brecht's life and writings.

Fairley, Barker, *A Study of Goethe* (1947). A brilliant essay, particularly relevant here since it analyzes Goethe's struggle for objectivity, which he came to equate with mental health.

Fallada, Hans, *Little Man, What Now?* (1932; tr. Eric Sutton, 1933). The typical depression novel; immensely popular in its day and still widely read.

Feuchtwanger, Lion, *Erfolg: Drei Jahre Geschichte einer Provinz,* 2 vols. (1930). Feuchtwanger's most popular novel; a *roman à clef* about Bavaria during the early 1920s, including a barely disguised Bertolt Brecht.

Garten, H. F., *Gerhart Hauptmann* (1954).

———, *Modern German Drama* (1959). Serious and helpful.

George, Stefan, *Gesamtausgabe der Werke,* 18 vols. (1927–1934). There is also a handy 2-volume selection, ed. Robert Boehringer (1958).

Gerhard, Melitta, *Stefan George, Dichtung und Kündung* (1962).

Goering, Reinhard, *Prosa, Dramen, Verse,* ed. Dieter Hoffmann (1961). Handy selections from the right-wing Expressionist who had one hit, *Seeschlacht,* in 1917.

Grimm, Hans, *Volk ohne Raum* (1926). The famous *völkische* novel.

Gundolf, Friedrich, *Shakespeare und der deutsche Geist* (1911).

———, *Stefan George* (1920).

———, *Heinrich von Kleist* (1922). Probably the most important works by this favorite George disciple.

Günther, Herbert, *Joachim Ringelnatz in Selbstzeugnissen und Bilddokumenten* (1964). Illustrated biography of a popular humoristic poet.

Haas, Willy, *Bert Brecht* (1958). Short, impressionistic.

Hasenclever, Walter, *Gedichte, Dramen, Prosa,* ed. Kurt Pinthus (1963). A generous selection from the works of this Expressionist writer.

Hatfield, Henry, *Thomas Mann* (rev. ed., 1962). Lucid, brief, dependable.

———, *Aesthetic Paganism in German Literature from Winckelmann to the Death of Goethe* (1964). Sensible; corrects E. M. Butler's overstatements on Hölderlin and others.

Hauptmann, Gerhart, *Sämtliche Werke* (Centenar Ausgabe) in prcgress, (ed. H.-E. Hass, 1962———).

Heerikhuizen, F. W. van, *Rainer Maria Rilke: His Life and Work* (1946; tr. Fernand G. Renier and Anne Cliff, 1951). Sensible biography amid a mass of extravagant writing.

Heller, Erich, *The Ironic German: A Study of Thomas Mann* (1958). A stylish study.

———, *The Disinherited Mind: Essays in Modern German Literature and Thought* (2nd ed., 1959). Stimulating collection.

Herald, Heinz, *Max Reinhardt* (1953).

Hering, Gerhard F., "Nachwort" to Zuckmayer, *Meisterdramen* (1966), 583–590. An instructive brief essay.

Hesse, Hermann, *Gesammelte Schriften,* 7 vols. (1957).

———, *Demian* (1919; tr. Michael Roloff and Michael Lebeck, 1965).

———, *Steppenwolf* (1927; tr. Basil Creighton, rev. Joseph Mileck and Horst Frenz, 1963).

———, *Magister Ludi* (1943; tr. Mervyn Savill, 1949). Hesse's three most popular novels in English.

Hofmannsthal, Hugo von, *Gesammelte Werke,* in progress, 15 vols. so far, ed. Herbert Steiner (1945 ———).

———, "Das Schrifttum als geistiger Raum der Nation," in *Die Berührung der Sphären* (1931), 422–442, a convenient collection of Hofmannsthal's prose.

Hölderlin, Friedrich, *Werke,* ed. Fritz Usinger (n. d.). One of many editions; this one has a good selection and useful introduction.

Holthusen, Hans Egon, *Rainer Maria Rilke: A Study of his Later Poetry* (tr. J. P. Stern, 1952).

———, *Rainer Maria Rilke in Selbstzeugnissen und Bilddokumenten* (1958). Both admiring but still rational.

Horvath, Ödön von, *Stücke,* ed. Traugott Krischke (1961).

Johann, Ernst, *Georg Büchner in Selbstzeugnissen und Bilddokumenten* (1958).

Kafka, Franz, *The Trial* (publ. 1925 by Max Brod; tr. Willa and Edwin Muir, 1937).

———, *The Castle* (publ. 1926, same ed.; same tr., 1930).

———, *Amerika* (publ. 1927, same ed.; tr. Edwin Muir, 1946).

———, *Hochzeitsvorbereitungen auf dem Lande und andere Prosa aus dem Nachlass,* ed. Max Brod (1953). Includes the letter to his father.

Kaiser, Georg, *Stücke, Erzählungen, Aufsätze, Gedichte,* ed. Walther Huder (1966). A good one-volume selection from Kaiser's vast and important production. (See also below under Kenworthy.)

Karasek, Hellmuth, *Carl Sternheim* (1965). A short, well-illustrated study of the witty playwright.

Kästner, Erich, *Kästner für Erwachsene,* ed. Rudolf Walter Leonhardt (1966). As the title makes clear, this selection omits the books for children—*Emil und die Detektive, Der 35. Mai,* and so on—that made him world-famous; it contains selections of poetry, autobiography, and his novel *Fabian: Die Geschichte eines Moralisten* (1931).

Kenworthy, B. J., *Georg Kaiser* (1957). Useful study in English.

Kesting, Marianne, *Bertolt Brecht in Selbstzeugnissen und Bilddokumenten* (1959).

Killy, Walther, *Deutscher Kitsch: Ein Versuch mit Beispielen* (1962). A fascinating collection of awful German literature, with an interesting interpretative introduction.

Kraus, Karl, *Ausgewählte Werke,* in progress, ed. Heinrich Fischer (1952 ———).

Kutscher, Artur, *Frank Wedekind: Sein Leben und Seine Werke,* 3 vols. (1922–1931). The standard biography of the great rebel of the German theatre.

Landmann, Georg Peter, ed., *Der George-Kreis* (1965). An intelligent and comprehensive anthology.

Lasker-Schüler, Else, *Sämtliche Gedichte,* ed. Friedhelm Kemp (1966).

Mann, Heinrich, *Little Superman* (1918; tr. Ernest Boyd, 1945).

———, *Small Town Tyrant* (1905, tr. in 1944). The novel on which the celebrated film, *The Blue Angel,* is based.

———, *Novellen* (1963). A collection of his shorter novels—or long stories. This list of three titles offers only a small selection from a large and extremely varied output.

Mann, Klaus, *Mephisto: Roman einer Karriere* (1936). A wicked novel; thinly disguised account of the meteoric career of Mann's erstwhile brother-in-law, Gustav Gründgens, actor and producer.

Mann, Thomas, *Gesammelte Werke,* ed. Hans Bürgin, 12 vols. (1960). Still the best edition, including four volumes of essays and speeches.

———, *Buddenbrooks* (1901; tr. H. T. Lowe-Porter, 1924).

———, *The Magic Mountain* (1924; same tr., 1927).

———, *Joseph and His Brothers,* 4 vols. (1933–1943; same tr., 1933–1944).

———, *Stories of Three Decades* (same tr., 1936).

———, *Essays of Three Decades* (same tr., 1947). (These English titles are only a sampling; practically all his work has been translated into English.)

Müllenmeister, Horst, *Leopold Jessner: Geschichte eines Regiestils* (1956). Useful German thesis; much more needs to be done.

Muschg, Walter, *Die Zerstörung der deutschen Literatur* (3rd, much enlarged ed., 1958). Bracing essays by a mortal enemy of cant and the German penchant to turn literary criticism into obscure metaphysics.

———, *Von Trakl zu Brecht: Dichter des Expressionismus* (1961). Vigorous, often brilliant studies.

Musil, Robert, *The Man Without Qualities* (first "complete" version reconstructed by A. Frisé, 1952; tr. Eithne Wilkins and Ernst Kaiser, 3 vols., 1953–1960).

Pinthus, Kurt, ed., *Menschheitsdämmerung: Ein Dokument des Expres-*

sionismus (1920; 2nd, improved ed., 1959). The first edition was an important gathering of documents; the second is even more valuable.

Piscator, Erwin, *Das politische Theater* (1929; ed. Felix Gasbarra, 1962). The manifesto of the radical theatre in Berlin in the late twenties.

Politzer, Heinz, *Franz Kafka: Parable and Paradox* (1962). Excellent.

Raabe, Paul, ed., *Expressionismus: Aufzeichnungen und Erinnerungen der Zeitgenossen* (1965). A comprehensive anthology of eyewitness accounts.

——, and H. L. Greve, eds., *Expressionismus: Literatur und Kunst, 1910–1923* (1960). Highly informative, well-documented catalogue of an important exposition at the Schiller National Museum at Marbach.

Remarque, Erich Maria, *All Quiet on the Western Front* (1929; tr. A. W. Wheen, 1929). The famous antiwar novel, *Im Westen nichts Neues*.

——, *The Road Back* (1931; tr. A. W. Wheen, 1931). The rather less famous sequel.

Riess, Curt, *Gustav Gründgens: Eine Biographie* (1965). Admiring and apologetic, but not uninformative life of a leading actor and producer. (See also above under Mann, Klaus.)

Rilke, Rainer Maria, *Sämtliche Werke*, ed. Ernst Zinn and Ruth Sieber-Rilke, 6 vols. (1955–1966). There is also a useful three-volume edition, containing a large selection, by the Insel Verlag (1966).

Roth, Joseph, *Romane, Erzählungen, Aufsätze* (1964). A generous selection from a novelist who drank himself to death in Paris exile.

Rühle, Günther, *Theater für die Republik, 1917–1933, im Spiegel der Kritik* (1967). A convenient, copious anthology of reviews of the Weimar theatre, with full annotations and an excellent introduction.

Salin, Edgar, *Um Stefan George: Erinnerung und Zeugnis* (2nd ed., 1954). Among the George disciples' work, perhaps the most informative. (See also above under Boehringer, and below under Wolters.)

——, *Hölderlin im George-Kreis* (1950).

Schick, Paul, *Karl Kraus in Selbstzeugnissen und Bilddokumenten* (1965).

Schmalenbach, Fritz, "The Term 'Neue Sachlichkeit,' " *Art Bulletin*, XXII, 3 (September 1940), 161–165. Analyzes an important name.

Schnitzler, Arthur, *Die erzählenden Schriften*, 2 vols. (1961).

——, *Die dramatischen Werke*, 2 vols. (1962). A convenient set of four volumes.

Schonauer, Franz, *Stefan George in Selbstzeugnissen und Bilddokumenten* (1960). Fairly straightforward account with some remarkable photographs.

Schröter, Klaus, *Heinrich Mann in Selbstzeugnissen und Bilddokumenten* (1967).

Schumacher, Ernst, *Die dramatischen Versuche Bertolt Brechts, 1918–1933* (1955). Though orthodox in its Marxism and hence often tedious, full of facts.

Sertorius, Lilli, *Der Wandel des deutschen Hölderlinbildes* (1928). Short dissertation demonstrating radical shift in Germans' view of Hölderlin.

Sembdner, Helmut, ed., *Heinrich von Kleists Nachruhm* (1967). A fascinating, well-organized and annotated anthology documenting the varying posthumous fortunes of a great German literary figure.

Sinn und Form, Special Issue, Bertolt Brecht (1949).

——, Second Special Issue, Bertolt Brecht (1957). Both, especially the second of these issues, are filled with important information outweighing their East German predictability.

Sokel, Walter H., *The Writer in Extremis: Expressionism in Twentieth-Century German Literature* (1959). A rewarding attempt to comprehend the essence of Expressionist German literature in economical compass.

——, *Franz Kafka: Tragik und Ironie* (1964).

Sontheimer, Kurt, *Thomas Mann und die Deutschen* (1961). A persuasive (but not wholly persuasive) defense of Thomas Mann's political opinions.

Steffen, Hans, ed., *Der deutsche Expressionismus: Formen und Gestalten* (1965). A set of essays, mainly on Expressionist poets, but on Expressionism in the other arts as well; generally satisfactory.

Sternheim, Carl, *Das Gesamtwerk,* ed. Wilhelm Emrich, 8 vols. (1963–1968). The collected works of that brilliant, untranslatable satirist.

Strich, Fritz, *Deutsche Klassik und Romantik* (1922).

Tank, Kurt Lothar, *Gerhart Hauptmann in Selbstzeugnissen und Bilddokumenten* (1959).

Toller, Ernst, *Prosa, Briefe, Dramen, Gedichte,* Preface by Kurt Hiller (1961). An ample selection, prefaced by some fighting words in Toller's defense.

Torberg, Friedrich, *Der Schüler Gerber* (1929). Novel about a student's suicide; typical of a genre.

Tucholsky, Kurt, *Gesammelte Werke,* ed. Mary Gerold-Tucholsky and Fritz J. Raddatz, 3 vols. (1960). Though not absolutely complete, the lacunae are indicated.

Viëtor, Karl, *Georg Büchner: Politik, Dichtung, Wissenschaft* (1949). Compact appreciation by a veteran Germanist.

Wassermann, Jakob, *Der Fall Maurizius* (1928). Perhaps still the best-known novel of a writer whose reputation was extremely high during the Republic, but is not now.

Wedekind, Frank, *Prosa, Dramen, Verse,* ed. Hansgeorg Maier, 2 vols. (1964). A convenient and rather full edition.

Weigand, Hermann J., *Thomas Mann's Novel 'Der Zauberberg'* (1933). An impressive analysis.

Weisstein, Ulrich, *Heinrich Mann: Eine historisch-kritische Einführung in sein dichterisches Werk* (1962). Short but useful.

Werfel, Franz, *Nicht der Mörder, der Ermordete ist Schuldig* (1920).

——, *Verdi* (1924; tr. Helen Jessiman, 1925). A milestone, for Werfel.

——, *The Forty Days of Musa Dagh* (1933; tr. Geoffrey Dunlop, 1934).

——, *Erzählungen aus zwei Welten,* ed. A. D. Klarmann, 3 vols. (1951–1954).

——, *Die Dramen,* ed. A. D. Klarmann, 2 vols. (1959).

Willett, John, *The Theatre of Bert Brecht: A Study from Eight Aspects* (1959). A good analysis.

Wolters, Friedrich, *Stefan George und die Blätter für die Kunst* (1930). Remains important.

Zuckmayer, Carl, *Meisterdramen* (1966). Contains his best-known work, but omits the early Expressionist plays.

Zweig, Arnold, *The Case of Sergeant Grischa* (1927; tr. Eric Sutton, 1928).

Zweig, Stefan, "Abschied von Rilke," (1926) in *Begegnungen mit Menschen, Büchern, Städten* (1956 ed.), 59–73.

——, "Hölderlin," in *Baumeister der Welt* (1951), 159–246.

——, "Heinrich von Kleist," in *ibid.,* 247–301.

V. THE FILM AND THE PUBLISHING INDUSTRIES

Publishers' autobiographies, like those of Piper and Wolff, are also extremely useful here.

Arnheim, Rudolf, *Film als Kunst* (1932). Translated in 1933 by L. M. Sieveking and Ian F. D. Morrow, but long unobtainable; substantial portions of this theoretical book are now reprinted in *Film as Art* (1966).

Balázs, Béla, *Der Film: Werden und Wesen einer neuen Kunst* (1961). Collected essays, many from the 1920s, by a Marxist who was a knowledgeable and intelligent critic.

"Ein Jahrhundert *Frankfurter Zeitung,* begründet von Leopold Sonnemann," *Die Gegenwart,* XI (October 29, 1956), special number. A generous, fascinating survey (though more could be done) of the best newspaper in Weimar Germany.

Erman, Hans, *August Scherl* (1954). Biography of the powerful Berlin newspaper publisher who sold his business to Hugenberg.

Griffith, Richard, *Marlene Dietrich, Image and Legend* (1959). A well-illustrated pamphlet.

Grothe, Wolfgang, "*Die neue Rundschau* des Verlages S. Fischer," *Börsenblatt für den deutschen Buchhandel,* Frankfurter Ausgabe, XVII (December 14, 1961). An interesting survey of a literate monthly for which the best writers were glad to write.

Hintermeier, Mara, and Fritz J. Raddatz, eds., *Rowohlt Almanach, 1908–1962* (1962). A splendidly bulky survey of a major publisher's list with some remarkable authors.

Kiaulehn, Walther, *Mein Freund der Verleger: Ernst Rowohlt und seine Zeit* (1967). An affectionate account; excellent addition to the *Rowohlt Almanac.*

Kracauer, Siegfried, *From Caligari to Hitler: A Psychological History of the German Film* (1947). An indispensable book, even if its thesis may be a little overextended. I am deeply in its debt.

Kurtz, Rudolf, *Expressionismus und Film* (1926). A pioneering essay.

Mendelssohn, Peter De, *Zeitungsstadt Berlin: Menschen und Mächte in der Geschichte der deutschen Presse* (1959). An exasperating book; full of details and excellent illustrations, but one-sided, often uncritical and superficial.

Osborn, Max, ed., *50 Jahre Ullstein, 1877–1927* (1927). Official.

Rotha, Paul, *The Film Till Now* (rev. ed., 1967). Comprehensive survey by a pioneer.

Schlawe, Fritz, *Literarische Zeitschriften,* Part II, *1910–1933* (1962). Comprehensive factual survey; very useful. The same is badly needed for the newspapers.

Ullstein, Hermann, *The Rise and Fall of the House of Ullstein* (1943). Full of irrelevancies and only occasionally informative.

Weinberg, Herman G., *Joseph von Sternberg: A Critical Study* (1967).

/ INDEX